Cultural Matters

Lessons Learned From
Field Studies of Several Leading
School Reform Strategies

UNDERSTANDING EDUCATION AND POLICY
William T. Pink and George W. Noblit
Series Editors

Cultural Matters

Lessons Learned From Field Studies of Several Leading School Reform Strategies

edited by

William T. Pink
Marquette University

George W. Noblit
University of North Carolina at Chapel Hill

HAMPTON PRESS, INC.
CRESSKILL, NEW JERSEY

Printed in the United States of America

Library of Congress Cataloging-in-Publication-Data

Cultural matters : lessons learned from field studies of several leading school reform
    strategies / edited by William T. Pink, George W. Noblit
        p. cm. -- (Understanding education and policy)
    Includes bibliographic references and index.
    ISBN 1-57273-477-9 (cl) -- ISBN 1-57273-478-7 (pbk.)
        1. Educational sociology--United States--Case studies. 2. Educational change--
    United States--Case studies. 3. Popular culture--United States. I. Pink, William T.
    II. Noblit, George W. III. Series

    LC191.4.C83 2003
    371.2'00973
                                                                    2003040705

Hampton Press, Inc.
23 Broadway
Cresskill, NJ 07626

Contents

Series Preface

Books in this series, Understanding Education and Policy, examine various perspectives to better understand the aims, practices, substances, and contexts of schooling, and the meaning of these analyses for educational policy. Our primary intent is to redirect the language used, the voices included, and the range of issues addressed in the current debates concerning schools and policy. In so doing, books in this series explore the varied conceptions and experiences that surface when analysis includes racial, class, gender, ethnicity, sexual orientation, and other salient differences. As a result, books in this series span the social sciences (anthropology, history, philosophy, psychology, sociology, cultural studies, etc.) and research paradigms.

Books in the series will be grounded in the contextualized lives of the major actors in school (students, teachers, administrators, parents, policymakers, etc.) and address major theoretical and methodological issues. The challenge our authors have taken upon themselves is to fully explore life-in-schools, through the multiple lenses of various actors and within the contexts in which these actors and education are situated. The range of empirically sound and theoretically sophisticated works that have been included in this series contribute to a fundamental and necessary rethinking of content, process, and context for school reform. They underscore the reform that all too often disadvantages some for the benefit of others. The challenge we see in these books is that educational policy has a complexity that few are willing to engage. This in turn requires that studies of education and policy have a critical yet constructive stance.

In this book, *Cultural Matters*, we have examined how several of the leading schools reform strategies play out in living school cultures. The case studies in this book teach us much about how central school culture is to successful school reform and what different reform strategies demand of, and do to, school beliefs and practices. These studies are important for those who wish to consider which reform strategies are best for their school. They are also important for scholars who wish to better understand what school reform looks like "on the ground." This book is particularly important in the current context of federal policy as well. "No Child Left Behind" as a piece of federal legislation ignores school culture entirely and seems to undercut the past 20 years of school reform endeavors. The case studies in *Cultural Matters* remind us how difficult school change is and reinscribes that culture does matter in school improvement.

About the Authors

Amee Adkins is an assistant professor in the Department of Education Administration and Foundations at Illinois State University, where she teaches courses in social foundations of education. Her professional interests include critical multiculturalism, education reform, and equity issues.

Kathyrn Borman is professor of Anthropology and Associate Director of the David C. Anchin Center at the University of South Florida (USF). She received her doctorate in the Sociology of Education from the University of Minnesota in 1976 and was Professor of Education and Sociology at the University of Cincinnati for several years before joining the faculty at USF. Dr. Borman has extensive experience in educational reform and evaluation studies and has written several books on these and other related topics. She is Principal Investigator of the NSF study, *Assessing the Impact of the National Science Foundation's Urban Systematic Initiative*, a project designed to investigate factors leading to improved student achievement and reduced gaps in student attainment. She is also the current editor of *Review of Educational Research*, and the Director of the Spencer Foundation-supported Consortium of Education Research in Florida (CERF)

H. Dickson (Dick) Corbett is an independent educational researcher. He spends his time studying school reform, with a particular emphasis on interviewing students (K-12) about their experiences in such situations. He also conducts evaluations of innovative programs and practices. Currently his work includes examining teachers' assumptions about urban students as learners and the effects of those assumptions on instruction and student performance; following a cohort of urban middle-schoolers through three years of a major city's reform efforts; studying the infusion of arts instruction into core academic subjects in rural and urban schools participating as pilot sites in a state's reform initiative; and conducting case studies of urban elementary science and math reform. He has published his research in books for Teachers College Press, Ablex, and the State University of New York Press, and has written articles for journals such as *Educational Researcher, Phi Delta Kappan, Educational Leadership, Curriculum Inquiry, The Urban Review,* and *Educational Policy.* He also edits a book series on restructuring and school change with Betty Lou Whitford for the State University Press.

Christine Finnan is assistant professor of education at the University/College of Charleston in Charleston, SC. She also directs the South Carolina Accelerated Schools Project. She is trained as a cultural anthropologist, with degrees from Stanford University, University of Texas at Austin, and the University of California at Berkeley. She is co-author with Julie Swanson of *Accelerating the Learning of All Students: Cultivating Culture Change in Schools, Classrooms and Individuals.* She has written articles and book chapters on school culture change.

Michael Gunzenhauser is assistant professor of Educational Studies at Oklahoma State University, where he teaches social foundations and qualitative research methodology. While a graduate student at the University of North Carolina at Chapel Hill, he participated in the evaluation of North Carolina A+ Schools Program. His areas of interest are philosophy of education, research methodology and critical social theory.

Michael E. Jennings is an assistant professor in the Department of Educational Policy and Policy Studies at the University of Texas in San Antonio. He received his BA from Hampton University and his MA and PhD from the University of North Carolina at Chapel Hill. His primary field of focus is the Social Foundations of Education and his research centers around three connected areas: cultural and racial diversity, critical pedagogy, and educational biography/autoethnography. He is particularly interested in research that emphasizes the collection and analysis of narratives focusing on the experiences of people of color in the American educational system.

Carol Malloy is associate professor in the School of Education at the University of North Carolina at Chapel Hill. Her research interest is in the culture of learning in schools. As a mathematics educator, she is interested in the influence of culture on the cognitive development of African-American students as it relates to mathematics learning, and the teacher/student interactions that lead to mathematics understanding.

Monica B. McKinney is an assistant professor in the Education Department at Meredith College. Her research interests lie in the areas of qualitative research methods, school reform, and classroom/school spaces.

George W. Noblit is a professor and Chair of the Graduate Studies Division in the School of Education at the University of North Carolina at Chapel Hill. He specializes in critical race studies, the sociology of knowledge, anthropology of education, and qualitative research methods. His 1996 book, *The Social Construction of Virtue: The Moral Life of Schools* (SUNY Press), was selected for a Critic's Choice Award of the American Educational Studies Association, and he has also published a set of studies covering his career, *Particularities: Collected Essays on Ethnography and Education* (Peter Lang, 1999). He won the Dina Feitelson Outstanding Research Award from the International Reading Association in 2000. Dr. Noblit is the editor of *The High School Journal* and co-editor of *The Urban Review*. He edits this book series, Understanding Education and Policy for Hampton Press. He is the immediate past president of the American Educational Studies Association.

William T. Pink is professor and Director of Doctoral Programs in Educational Leadership and Policy in the School of Education at Marquette University. He has published widely in the areas of delinquency, sociology of education, school culture and educational reform. He is the editor of *Educational Foundations*, the co-editor of *The Urban Review*, and edits this book series, Understanding Education and Policy for Hampton Press. His most recent book is *Continuity and Contradiction: The Futures of the Sociology of Education* (Hampton Press, 1995), co-edited with George Noblit.

Julie D. Swanson is assistant professor of education at the University/College of Charleston in Charleston, SC. With a background in gifted education in public education, she has combined research and practice through her work with the application of gifted education in schools serving primarily low-income students. She is co-author with Christine Finnan of *Accelerating the Learning of All Students: Cultivating Culture Change in Schools, Classrooms, and Individuals*. Her current interests include teacher change and use of innovative practice with all students.

Bruce Wilson is an independent educational researcher interested in studying issues of school reform. His most recent research attempts to bring the student voice to a more prominent position. Recent publications include *Listening to Urban Kids: School Reform and the Teachers They Want* (SUNY Press, 2001), co-authored with Dick Corbett, and *Effort and Excellence: Urban Classrooms and Schools that Demand (And Get) Both From Their Students* (Teachers College Press), co-authored with Dick Corbett and Belinda Williams.

1

Culture Matters in School Reform

George W. Noblit
University of North Carolina at Chapel Hill

William T. Pink
Marquette University

Our society is committed to reforming its schools. Politicians of all parties pledge to improve education. Parents also see the need for improvement and push for reform. What is lost in all this seeming agreement is that school reform means different things to different people. Some wish to make schools more efficient, whereas some want more equitable schools. Some want schools to produce higher academic achievement, whereas some want better citizens. Some want to improve the lot of the poor, whereas some want to improve the gifted. The list of disparate meanings is seemingly endless. Whatever people value somehow seems to find expression in the rhetoric of school reform. Some rhetorics, however, win political favor and become more powerful than others. As we argue next, the rhetoric of excellence has been enjoying a strong run. At the current time in both the political and educational arenas, the emphasis is on accountability. Accountability is based on the argument that schools and educators have become irresponsible and misguided in their practices. Thus, it is argued that the most effective way to bring schools back into line and ensure responsible behavior is to hold schools more publicly accountable. In this formulation, however, *accountability* is defined exceedingly narrowly: focused almost exclusively on increasing test scores on rather basic skills. On its surface, this seems reasonable (although it begs important questions about what knowledge and skills are missing from such a truncated view of student achievement). Yet as we argue, school reform can never be judged from its surface. School reform is deep with history and politics.

Accountability policy, as we refer to it, has deep meanings as well. It has altered school reform. Just a few years ago, for example, the excellence agenda of school reform, which has spawned accountability policy, understood school reform to require systemic change (Elmore, 1996). That is, changing schools was understood to be both difficult and complex. Schools, it was argued, had to be both restructured and recultured for reform to take hold (Whitaker & Moses, 1994). However, we argue that politicians have given up on systemic school reform, in large part, because they quickly discovered that it was a complex undertaking that could not be achieved from their legislative seat: Wishing it would not make it happen. Instead, they are supplanting their failed legislative efforts at systemic reform with accountability policy. They no longer seem concerned with the improvement of schools or the full development of children. Instead, they are going for gains in test scores. It seems not to matter to them that high-stakes testing is known to pervert teaching, or that the tests in use are of the worse kind to improve either instruction or learning (Corbett & Wilson, 1991). Even worse, it seems not to matter that even if accountability policy is successful, it means nothing for the economy we now have. Accountability policy is the ultimate expression of the factory model of schooling (Callahan, 1965). The problem is that we have exported the factory economy, and the new economy requires not the distinctive specialization of the manufacturing world, but the connective specialization of the knowledge-based economic order (Young, 1998).

We, together with the authors of the other chapters in this book, are writing to call attention to the fact that our political and educational leaders are abdicating reform as they rush to embrace accountability policy. We must understand that accountability policy, and the high-stakes testing programs it has spawned, is already failing (Hoff, 2000). For example, we know that high-stakes testing programs, where successful, have predictable patterns of initial gains that plateau after a few years primarily because these gains are manufactured by the narrowed focus of the testing program. Such programs do not result in improved instruction or more engaging curriculum materials. We suggest that even for such narrowly focused programs to have continual gains, it would he necessary to invest in improving schools and instruction. In short, what will be needed is what has been needed all along—namely, the systemic reform of schools.

SCHOOL CULTURE AND SYSTEMIC REFORM

Systemic reform involves altering the fundamental beliefs, organizational processes, and structures and practices of education—or as Whitaker and Moses (1994) put it: "School restructuring is nothing less than gut-level cultural change" (p. 144). Changing culture has emerged as both a difficult and complex undertaking, however, and this is why we believe school districts and states are abdicating systemic reform and embracing accountability policy. The political pressure at the state and local levels for "quick and dirty" results means that few wish to deal with the complexity and investments in time and personnel required to achieve cultural change at the school level. In part, the conceptual messiness of systemic reform is generated because culture is both the explicit policies, practices, and perspectives that any participant in a school can articulate, together with the implicit, taken-for-granted assumptions that undergird the explicit, but are not easily articulated. Understanding the interconnectedness between the ways things work at the school level and the taken-for-granted values and beliefs at the level of the broader culture is what is frequently missing when school reforms are constructed. Culture, of course, is also highly political (Wells & Serna, 1996). On one hand, change creates uncertainty; because identities and status are attached to the usual ways of doing things, uncertainty is both psychologically and socially disruptive. On the other hand, efforts to change a school's culture are often explicit political acts with real winners and losers. Indeed, we see the recent reform era as a competition about who will control schools. Each newly appointed school superintendent, for example, has used school reform as a means to exercise control over the school organization, budget, and personnel.

Although we are emphasizing culture at the school level in this book, all of our chapters document how important the external environment is to the school, especially in the development of culture (Noblit, Malloy, & Malloy, 2001). Schools are structured in many ways by their environments: parents, communities, school districts, state and federal educational policies, and societal values. Moreover, as we discuss later, the history of school reform shows that the environment is in conflict over what schooling should be about. This means that the messy work of changing school culture and engaging in systemic reform requires altering the environment of schools even as we work to change the actions and beliefs within schools. Pink and Hyde (1992), for example, have argued that professional development for teachers and administrators, designed to interrogate taken-for-granted assumptions about student learning and pedagogy, should be the centerpiece for recreating school cultures. Pink (1994, 1999), drawing on fieldwork in elementary schools, has demonstrated the importance of troubling teacher beliefs as a prelude to crafting systemic changes to both the culture of the school and practices. Moving beyond pockets of success in school reform has perplexed reform experts and led to a deeper examination of what this might take. Elmore (1996) argued that getting to scale with systemic reform across a school district and/or state requires: (a) strong external normative structures for practice, (b) organizational structures that intensify intrinsic motivation to change, (c) intentional processes to reproduce successes, and (d) structures to promote learning new practices and incentive systems to support such learning. New American schools have an even longer list of things they see as necessary for systemic reform, including school-level autonomy and decision making, professional development, standards of achievement, assessment systems, assistance and support services, technology, public engagement, reallocation of resources, and more (Kearns & Anderson, 1996). This work persuasively argues that systemic reform on a broad scale requires that school districts and states support changing school cultures, together with the external environment to those cultures in significant ways. Sadly, however, this responsibility is precisely what we see policymakers abdicating in their zeal to embrace accountability policy. Because the pursuit of accountability policy has already demonstrated its ineffectiveness as a school reform strategy, this book is dedicated to informing the development of a conceptual framework for fostering fundamental cultural change at the individual school level.

In this book, we explore the position that systemic reform requires addressing the culture of individual schools, and that various reform efforts address school culture in different ways. We want to emphasize that our goal is not evaluative. We do not compare reforms or try to calculate which reform is best. In fact, this way of thinking belies what we know about school culture. We want to state emphatically that there is no one best reform: We think that it is long past time to call a halt to the *silver bullet* approach to school reform. Rather, we want to emphatically state that the key to success is the match between the strategy in use and the setting. In short, everything depends on the interaction of a specific reform approach with the culture of a particular school. In the following chapters, reforms and their interactions in particular schools and school cultures are explored through fieldwork. These chapters clearly illustrate that when accountability policy has run its course, we need to reengage systemic reform. Such dramatic change requires schools to be both restructured and recultured. We can learn from the cases in this book what it takes to mount and sustain a systemic reform initiative at the school level. Thus, we offer this book to parents, school principals, teachers, and others as a window into how to think about reforming their schools even as they must comply with the demands of accountability policy.

In the remainder of this chapter, we try to give a perspective on the depth of understanding that we think our readers require to weather accountability policy. We do this in two ways. First, because school reform has a long history, it helps to understand both how we got to where we are and what else is possible. Without an understanding of the history of reform, it is easy to miss the deeper meanings of the current rhetorics of school reform. Second, accountability policy also has a depth not well understood. This involves both the history of school governance as well as the recent emergence of the marketplace metaphor that has become a new factor, especially in the reform of urban schools. We explore these two arenas because we see this as the new context in which systemic reform needs to be wrought.

A (SHORT) HISTORY OF SCHOOL REFORM[1]

Educational reform is often seen as a recent phenomenon, responding to the particular issues of the past 25 years or so. It is often argued that school reform began with *A Nation at Risk* (National Commission on Excellence in Education, 1983). However, this is not the case. School reform has a long and convoluted history (Noblit & Dempsey, 1996). Indeed, historians of education (Cuban, 1988; Kent, 1987; Tyack, Lowe, & Hansot 1980) have recounted the recycling of reform in this century, including a variety of waves in our current reform era. Cuban (1990) sees "the inevitable return of school reforms" (p. 3) as due not to the failings of schools or reform initiatives, but to "conflicts over values" (p. 7). He argued that reforms recycle because value shifts in the larger society lead the schools to accommodate or adjust their practices rather than undertake fundamental change. This happens, he argued, because the implementation of school reforms is limited by the same value conflicts that stimulate the reform cycles. In a similar vein, Kent (1987) saw the issues of the 1980s (the concerns for standards and accountability) as recycling the issues of the 1950s. He reasoned that, "the familiar demand pattern for reform, namely, a short burst of intense action followed by longer periods of inaction and neglect" (p. 148) is unable to resolve fundamental value conflicts. In short, this recycling pattern helps perpetuate value conflicts by periodically creating a perceived education crisis in education. For example, Cuban (1988) saw the fundamental value conflict, or crisis, as being excellence versus equity.

An examination of the last 100 years shows a pattern to our recycling of reform. The Committee of Ten report in 1893 (NEA), the reforms of the late 1950s, and the reforms of the 1980s (which continue until today) express the value of excellence. By contrast, the Cardinal Principles in 1918 (Commission on the Reorganization of Secondary Education), progressivism in the 1920s through the 1940s, and new curricula and programs of the 1960s and 1970s express the value of equity. These sets of reforms are not pure in their adherence to any single value. The value conflict is so ingrained in our society that any reform contains elements of both values. We argue that it is because each reform contains some of the elements of its contrary that initiating reform around one value inevitably sows the seeds of its own capitulation to the other.

This suggests that our society is conservative about education, in that it conserves the existence of an essential value conflict. These values and their opposition become reified, taken-for-granted assumptions that unconsciously shape how we think and act regarding education. Consequently, we have become little more than pawns of this value conflict. We play out one idea, then the other—viewing each reform as unique and new, not cognizant of their lineage, legacy, and historical pairing. Unknowingly, we re-create the value conflict in each generation, each reform, and each educational crisis. The bottom line is that we do not reform education; we merely recycle our educational reforms.

---

[1]This has been adapted from Noblit and Dempsey (1996).

There were two distinct waves to the 1980s reform efforts (Zeichner, 1991) that reveal how the expression of one value about education is soon tempered by another. It is important that we understand how each wave of reform is an artifact, revealing our basic value conflict. *A Nation at Risk* (National Commission on Excellence in Education, 1983) prompted a series of top-down initiatives that are now looking far less promising than they did in the early 1980s. *A Nation at Risk* justified a call for excellence by declaring that education had failed the nation, undercutting our economic competitiveness by "an unthinking, unilateral educational disarmament" (p. 1). The problem was portrayed as a retreat from standards concerning content, expectations, time, teaching, and leadership. Eight solutions were offered: (a) an increase in the number of courses required for graduation, (b) more rigorous standards and higher expectations for students, (c) more time devoted to instruction in the basic coursework, (d) higher standards for entering teaching, (e) rigorous evaluation of existing teachers, (f) a career ladder for teachers, (g) educational leadership that develops schools, and (h) community support and state and local responsibility for implementing the proposed reforms. In this conceptualization, we see the value of excellence rhetorically defined as a return to the (supposedly) high academic standards of the past, while re-creating the educational and economic dominance of the United States as a world power.

Just a few years later, the Carnegie report, *A Nation Prepared: Teachers for the Twenty-First Century* (1986), signaled a partial swing of the pendulum away from excellence. It warned that the early reforms have undercut the fundamental requirement of equitable education—notably, a teacher's ability to adapt instruction to the specific needs of the student. The proposal was only a partial step away from *A Nation at Risk*, balancing a call for rigorous national standards for teaching and teacher preparation with restructuring schools to allow for more teacher autonomy in deciding how to teach. Even this balance was somewhat one sided. Teacher autonomy concerned only site-level autonomy—primarily the means of instruction. Teachers were still to be held accountable for raising student achievement by delivering a standardized curriculum. Just as the American public readily agreed with *A Nation at Risk*, it also assented to *A Nation Prepared*. While the reforms of the 1980s led to increased centralization and standardization, the reforms of the 1990s seemed to begin the swing to a decentralization of education (once again) supposedly to allow education to be more responsive to the ways in which children actually learn.

Even as we write, this move has now been effectively countered by yet another articulation of excellence. This current manifestation portrays schools as markets for reform, particularly reforms geared to reasserting accountability. For example, the development of charter schools illustrates how schools can compete for students. In any case, it is safe to project that both kinds of reform will continue for the foreseeable future. They will continue to vie for the public's attention and support; they also will continue to alternate between these seemingly contradictory logics, not because the public is duplicitous, uninformed, or comprised only of blind followers of educational leaders, nor because the reforms are inherently inadequate or technically deficient on either side. Reform will recycle for two reasons, the first and foremost being that the American mind is *closed*. Bloom (1987) argued that the American mind is closed because we have failed to inculcate Western values in our youth. For us, however, the American mind is *closed* because Western culture has been inculcated quite effectively into the American mind. We argue that this socialization has been so effective that most Americans simply play out their culture without thinking. Again, we are unknowingly pawns of our culture and its most deep-seated, taken-for-granted assumptions and beliefs about education (Bowers, 1984).

Cuban's (1988) notion of ingrained value conflict highlights a second key reason that we are unable to reform schools. Simply put, educational reforms are framed in the language of technical rationality (Collins, 1982; Mannheim, 1936). As a consequence, the primary strategy for reforming schools is to reconfigure the personnel, restructure the school organization, redesign curricula, train teachers in new pedagogy, set new achievement standards, and monitor compliance. Education, however, is not ultimately about these things as important as they are: Reforms recycle, then, because we repeatedly misspecify the essential nature of education. Schooling is fundamentally a value-driven, not a technical, enterprise. As social institutions, schools express our values more than achieve goals. Reforms based in instrumental rationality ignore both the value conflict and its essential message that schools are less about instructing facts and more about constituting culture. Until we understand what this means, reform will remain a captive of our fundamental value conflict. Let us be clear about this: Schooling and school reform is about values. Sadly, what many fail to understand is that the instrumental rhetoric that surrounds schooling and school reform hides from us the values being promoted. We have tried to show the historical antecedents of reform initiatives, but for us the key is to see how reforms impact the culture of the school in which they are implemented.

This book is a collection of field studies conducted on several notable school reform models. Our intent is to provide an up-close, on-the-ground view of the implementation and impact of key reform models including Accelerated Schools, A+ Schools, Comer's School Development Program, Charter Schools, Disney's Celebration School, Talent Development, and Success for All. The authors systematically investigate how each reform model works in a particularistic school culture, and what values are promoted and expressed as a result of this implementation.

We should note that we are fully aware that a key finding emerging from these field studies—namely, that the effectiveness of reform models rise and fall on the fit between the demands of the model and the culture of the school in which it is implemented—means that this book will not be well received by many. In particular, we are fully aware that it will not be well received by those who see the improvement of schools to be a direct result of the efficient implementation of the single most effective reform model. Thus, we want to emphasize that the calls for accountability through statewide standards, the imposition of teacher and administrative "best practice," and high-stakes testing are not supported by the studies in this book. In many respects, then, this book is much like a fish swimming up river that is carrying a message that is both unpopular and complicated by knowledge of real life in schools when doing school reform. Yet swim up river we must—not because it is fun and rewarding, but because the message must be received. The message is that accountability policy does not effectively reform schools even if it does alter the governance structures of schooling.

ACCOUNTABILITY POLICY AND CHANGING SCHOOL GOVERNANCE[2]

We are currently in a time where the thinking of the majority of policymakers in the educational arena is driven by ideas about standards and efficiency. The prevailing policy ideas for creating more effective schools are no exception. At all levels—from the federal to local school district—there are repeated calls for greater standardization and accountability over what schools can teach and how they should teach it. Two brief examples illustrate this trend.

In campaigns for the 2000 presidential election, both Bush and Gore emphasized the need to hold schools more accountable primarily through the frequent use of standardized tests. Although this might be a popular idea politically, there was almost no conversation about the inevitable result of narrowing the curriculum to things tested and the inevitable deskilling of teachers in the rush to secure teacher-proof, packaged curriculum materials. Moreover, the proposed penalty for failing to reach the proposed test standards was that schools would be placed into academic receivership and either lose funding or be taken over by a team who "knew how to do schooling right." As the data in this book demonstrate so dramatically, the fundamental problem with this efficiency model is that it seriously misunderstands the culture of schools and what it takes at the school level to implement a reform that improves the lives and learning of students.

The emphasis on efficiency and accountability has also led to recent changes in the role of school districts in sponsoring systemic school reform. It has been argued that the school was the primary site for school reform, and the role of school districts was to identify the need for reform and assist schools in doing systemic change. As the focus on accountability has gained momentum, it is clear that school districts are now playing a new role. In Chicago, for example, Mayor Daley made his dissatisfaction with stagnant reading scores public by announcing that schools not reading at grade level would be required to select a new reading program from five (unidentified) programs approved by the Board. Somewhat lost in the resultant heated debate, which centered around

---

[2]Thanks to Dr. James Vietch for an earlier draft of this section.

the recentralizing of decision making back to the Board of Education (Chicago, you may recall, is still in the midst of a wide-sweeping governance reform experiment that devolved decision making from a Board of Education appointed by the Mayor to Local School Councils elected at individual schools), is the message that failing schools must adopt a preapproved reading program. The five programs, although unspecified, all involved elements of a standardized curriculum and direct instruction. Moreover, the manner in which the mayor presented his plan indicated that schools would have no choice but to comply.

What Mayor Daley, Gore, and Bush all proposed actually reflects how systemic reform is being abdicated in large urban districts across the country (Noblit, Malloy, & Malloy, 2000). Moreover, accountability policy is changing the district sponsorship of reform efforts. In fact, accountability policy is changing the role of school districts in the governance of schools. To demonstrate this, we give a brief history of educational governance focused on the role of school districts. We discuss the development of American school districts across historical periods and explore what factors have contributed to the development of current school district structures, roles, and behaviors. We also note that the new marketplace metaphor of school reform, which situates reform within school districts, has dramatic implications for the future of school reform. Such an analysis, we argue, may well enable us to better understand why things are the way they are.

The responsibility of Colonial American School Boards (c. 1600-1776) generally involved supervision of a single school. These Boards would do many things: locate a school site, hire a teacher, visit the school, adopt textbooks, set school rules, and communicate with townspeople. Consequently, local decisions for each school might differ from other, even nearby, schools. The prevailing wisdom was that the local nature of the School Board facilitated the people's business in a manner that inspired confidence in a time of one room schoolhouses (New York Regents, 2000). This model of localism has served as a blueprint for American education. In many ways it remains intact today (Swanson & King, 1997).

In the Early National Period (c. 1776-1840), major social, economic, and political themes emerged that would continue to affect the United States through the next century and a half. Urbanization, industrialization, and immigration contributed to urban poverty, crime, and a widening gap between rich and poor (Cremin, 1957). As part of fashioning an identity for the new nation, education was made a function of the states, although local school boards and districts generally continued to oversee schools and "resented all constraints placed on them" (Swanson & King, 1997, p. 53). In the early part of the 1800s, for example, Horace Mann and others believed that education should be available to and equal for all (Cremin, 1957). Mann and his supporters were instrumental in the creation of the first State Board of Education in Massachusetts in 1837, with Mann as its secretary. A year later, Connecticut followed suit, naming Henry Barnard as its secretary. Cremin (1957) noted that the reformers' ideas influenced the educational systems of both Massachusetts and the nation. The reformers' calls for increased teacher salaries, improved teacher training, abolition of corporal punishment, and nonsectarian education were an important part of moving education from the private to public sphere. States introduced formal programs of financial aid to school districts in this period. Although the authority of the State Board of Education was limited, reformers fostered the principle that school issues were state issues. This framed and centralized elements of educational policy in ways not done previously. Nevertheless, Cubberley (1947) explained that the local school district remained:

> well-suited to the primitive needs and conditions of our early national life. Among a sparse and hard-working rural population, between whom intercourse was limited and intercommunication difficult, and with whom the support of the schools was as yet an unsettled question, local control answered a very real need. The simplicity and democracy of the system was one of its chief merits. (p. 212)

The Common School Period (c.1840-1880) encompassed a period of great instability in America. Economic growth exploded, but not without repeated economic depressions and enduring poverty. Political upheaval, the Civil War, regional differences, industrialization's role in child labor and juvenile delinquency, together with a tide of immigration, combined to produce both conflict and change in the nation. Urbanization continued seemingly unabated. In 1820, only one American city had a population in excess of 100,000, but by 1860 there were nine (DeYoung, 1989). Through all this, many Americans continued to support a system of public elementary schools accessible to all. They saw these common schools as essential to the preservation of the nation's stability and growth. Common school proponents argued that such schools were an essential part of national development. It was argued that public schools could promote a republican form of government, ensure equality of opportunity, command respect from other nations, Americanize immigrant children, teach respect, reduce crime, and promote economic prosperity. The common school model called for taxation of citizens and compelled school attendance by children. To some parents and political conservatives, however, this activity represented nothing short of state intrusion into private affairs. Industrialists who depended on child labor resisted the common school movement as did those who resented being taxed to educate others' children. Many immigrants suspected that the movement would compromise their cultural heritage by Americanizing their children, whereas still others objected to the lay nature of education. Throughout this time period, both pre- and post-Civil War, large numbers of White southerners opposed the education of African Americans.

These various objections aside, schools increasingly assumed responsibilities to address a host of emerging social problems. States began to adopt compulsory attendance laws, beginning in Massachusetts in 1852. Federal legislation gradually and successfully began to end child labor abuse. Together, these would serve to increase the number of years that children spent in school, increase enrollment, and place pressures on schools unprepared for these results (Tyack, 1974). Common schools came to be broadly supported by the 1850s, especially in the north and midwest. Growing industrialization further promoted an interest in vocational education to meet the needs of the economy for more narrowly focused skills, and the Morrill Act's land grants provided a focus on the development of vocations that had not characterized education up to this point. The goal of education was increasingly seen as preparing immigrants to assume jobs in the new industrial order. Along with the challenges of educating immigrants came pressures for increased administrative centralization. The field of educational administration evolved in mid-century following the development of principal teachers. School administration to that time had generally been seen as part of the teaching role. Some believed that the importance of educational administration meant that teachers should not be left to manage it. Increasingly, it was felt that leadership needed to be centralized. The term *Superintendent of Schools* grew out of the terminology of the times (e.g., Superintendent of the Railroad and [Industrial] Plant Superintendent; Campbell Fleming, Newell, & Bennion, 1987) and preserved a hierarchical relationship with teachers and schools. This was followed, in 1867, by the first federal Department of Education, which existed at the subcabinet level (Gutek, 1988).

To be sure, widespread political corruption was undercutting democratic government, and School Boards were often involved in graft and cronyism (Cronin, 1973): issues of political significance that would continue into the 20th century. The politics of education were now fully engaged and, while schools were rhetorically for all students, inequities in education became more severe (Swanson & King, 1997). Yet in 1880, public schools enrolled over 65% of children ages 5 to 17, and elementary school attendance was approaching that of a common experience for every American child. Over the following several decades, the model became an American norm—one that served as the foundation for the modern American public school system.

Broad social, economic, and political transformations coalesced to influence educational decision making in the Common School Period. Although the dominant school reform in the period was increased control at the state authority level, Swanson and King (1997) noted: "Even at the state level (in the eighteenth and nineteenth centuries), the dispersion of population, the primitive means of communication, and the general lack of resources made state control of education impractical" (p. 53). Individual school districts continued to represent the primary form of school supervision, and Cubberley's observations about the Early National Period continued to ring true. Nonetheless, the *principle* of state authority was increasingly well established during this period of time.

In the Progressive Period (c. 1880-1920), the pace of industrialization served to heighten the economic, social, and political transformations begun in earlier years. The face of education, too, continued to change. The governance of education built on the principle of state authority. Pressure from powerful groups to standardize education, calls for increased efficiency in school district operations, and popular movements to stem political abuse would all combine to translate the principle of state control into an increasingly institutionalized practice.

Throughout the late 1800s and early 1900s, public schools were encouraged to expand and make more efficient both their curricula and their teachers' expertise beyond the teaching of classics (Callahan, 1965). In the schools, this resulted in differentiation of students, graded classrooms, testing for student placement, continued implementation of compulsory attendance laws, and distinct courses with specified course content. The expansion of the high school to serve all children was driven by pronouncements in 1892 by the National Education Association's Committee of Ten. Led by Charles Eliot, the President of Harvard University, this initiative was an early instance of education being expressed as a national interest.

Several factors contributed to the development of a firmer practical grip by states on school governance—a grip that would extend beyond the Progressive Period and into the beginnings of the Modern Era (c. 1920-pre sent). First, common school reformers coalesced with a new group of administrative progressives, these being the first educators formally trained in new schools of education. These groups collectively articulated education as a systematic, methodical activity. They would have an intense impact on 20th-century education (Tyack & Cuban, 1995). Educators also adopted an emphasis on the systematization and standardization that was sweeping the country during industrial expansion. Friedrich Taylor's work from 1900 to 1915, which concerned itself with the efficiency of factories producing more with less cost, effort, and material, was increasingly seen as appropriate to all organizations. Taylor's (1911) emphases were on scientific measurement, clear divisions of responsibility in the workplace, and a hierarchical, bureaucratic structure. The predominant societal view of schools was that they were essentially workplaces, with learning now perceived in terms of productivity. Hierarchy and bureaucracy, now seen as scientific, would revolutionize industry. Cubberley and other early-century historians believed that schools could be managed like factories. In this analogy, teachers are factory workers, whereas students are the raw materials (Cronin, 1973; Mirel, 1990). Thus, as American business principles were applied to education, students were transformed into products. Hence, any children whom the process could not turn into a successful product were encouraged to "drop out" of the production line. School concerns with deportment, diet, hygiene (which included the control of emotions), and cleanliness were added at this time. Schools became perceived as a social mechanism for changing the behaviors of immigrant children, as well as those who had moved from farm villages to crowded urban areas.

Educational leaders of the time also wished to enjoy high status, and the country's business orientation contributed to their attempts to simulate business strategies in school. At the district level, the incipient bureaucratic form that already existed (Katz, 1975) became both more elaborate and standardized. Separate departments were created for personnel, curriculum, accounting, and other functions. The previous emphasis on educational administration as a separate field of study resulted in the first training program for administrators early in the century at Teachers College of Columbia University. To accomplish all of this, state education codes were strengthened to promote standardization in education. These codes also specified the role of districts as ensuring compliance with state codes and even specified the structure of district bureaucracies. District administrators adopted newly developed school surveys (checklists of characteristics that schools should have) and implemented the recommendations these surveys implied (Tyack, 1974). These surveys became so popular that they gradually homogenized the structure of school districts and the specific functions assigned to individual departments within the districts.

As the 19th century drew to a close, the practice of each school having its own school board had become cumbersome. A move to reduce costs and increase efficiency led states and counties to consolidate school boards (Fuller, 1982) on the assumption that educational quality would improve. As might be expected, the result was a drastic decline in the number of school boards, together with a firmer institutionalization of those that remained (New York Regents, 2000). Consolidation of rural school districts also significantly reduced lay school trusteeship.

Popular discontent created a strong demand to end local political abuse. Earlier efforts at consolidation of schools in growing urban areas had been structured along multiple school districts with individual ward school boards (Rogers, 1973), where ward bosses often succeeded in maintaining a stranglehold on local functions including schools. In response, educational leaders initiated conversations with business and professional elites to transform urban school politics. Tyack and Cuban (1995) noted that

> School governance would be more efficient and expert if it were shielded from lay control. There was something they [the administrative progressives] wanted less of—the influence of School Boards, whose members they sometimes accused of being corrupt or ignorant meddlers. (p. 18)

The reformers succeeded. School boards would henceforth delegate decisions to the Superintendent and departmental specialists. In 1890, the average number of central school board members in cities of more than 100,000 inhabitants was 21; by 1920 it was 7. Most cities eliminated ward boards entirely. Additionally, the number of educated, wealthy members on school boards increased, more nearly reflecting the composition of corporate boards of directors. Urban school systems increasingly adopted this model, which soon developed into the standard for urban school governance (Cubberley, 1916; Tyack & Cuban, 1995). Tyack and Cuban noted the link between standardization and the resulting state bureaucracy:

> State legislatures increasingly standardized schools across the nation
> according to the model of a modern school proposed by the policy elite.
> State departments of education increased enormously during the twentieth
> century. In 1890 there was, on average, one staff member in state depart-
> ments for education for every 100,000 pupils; in 1974 there was one for
> about every 2,000. (p. 20)

In the Modern Period (c. 1920-present), centralization of schooling continued, and the federal government began to play an increasing role in the design,
functions, and structures of state boards of education. At the federal level, the
role of the Bureau of Education came to be seen as, at the minimum, educating
state legislators about what a modern school should be. In fact, in 1919:

> The Bureau . . . laid out a whole program of state legislation designed to
> standardize schooling to match the program of "reorganization" (their ver-
> sion of systemic reform) favored by the administrative progressives, treat-
> ing such topics as school consolidation, increased school financing, physi-
> cal education, improved school construction, state certification of teachers,
> and standard textbooks and curriculum. A comparison of that plan with a
> summary of "state legal standards for the provision of education" in 1978
> shows that most of the recommendations of 1919 were put into practice in
> the following six decades. (Tyack & Cuban, 1995, p. 19)

In fact, the pace was quite rapid in many states: "Thirty-four state departments
of education managed to 'standardize' more than 40,000 schools by 1925 in
accordance with legislation, regulations of the state board, or rulings of the state
Superintendents" (Tyack & Cuban, 1995, p. 20).

The federal role in education was expanded in 1929 under the Interior
Department's Federal Security Agency (Callahan, 1965; Gutek, 1988) as a result
of pressure applied on Congress. At the same time the number of local school districts continued its decline—dropping from 127,531 in 1932 to 16,960 in 1973.
Between 1930 and 1980, the number of one-room schools dropped from 130,000
to less than 1,000. As the number of small-town Superintendents and rural supervisors of teachers rose steadily, these administrators took over some of the functions formerly performed by lay trustees (Cubberley, 1914; McElhenny, 1947;
Tyack & Cuban, 1947), continuing the trend toward administrative specialization.
Tyack (1974) argued that the resulting depoliticization reduced accountability to
any identifiable constituency. This depoliticization and lack of accountability
would later lead to pressures for decentralization (Murphy & Beck, 1995).

In the 30 years between 1950 and 1980, equity became a major challenge to schools, both in terms of civil rights and school financing formulae
(Swanson & King, 1997). The cold war and the 1957 launching of Sputnik by
the Soviet Union brought schools under scrutiny and began a press for excellence that was delayed somewhat by federal court actions dismantling segrega-

tion. Court-induced desegregation orders, beginning with *Brown v. Topeka* in 1954, established that the fundamental source of equality for marginalized groups was the U.S. Constitution, which required an aggressive federal posture to promote inclusion of these groups in the educational process. The Great Society of Lyndon Johnson's presidency sponsored compensatory education programs that addressed disadvantaged students. Affirmative action initiatives mushroomed, with school districts becoming responsible for the administration and compliance with these categorical programs. This resulted in further expansion of state education codes and the bureaucracies that administered them (Driver, Thorp, & Kuo, 1997).

While increasing centralization was seen as necessary because school systems had been reluctant to desegregate, centralization was not able to effectively respond to the challenges at the school and district level to effectively educate those who had formerly been excluded. Swanson and King (1997) argued that one result of new inclusion was that:

> the task of educating all students grew harder and the results more ambiguous. When all populations were included, educational costs increased dramatically and average achievement scores dropped, giving the perception of declining standards and less efficiency. (p. 55)

While making desegregated schools work well was difficult, we now know that such conclusions as these were partial truths that enabled a crisis to be manufactured by those more concerned with excellence than equity (Berliner & Biddle, 1997).

The publication of *A Nation at Risk* (National Commission on Excellence in Education, 1983) was a key move in manufacturing that crisis. Its publication built on the federal presence in education that desegregation had promoted and reestablished the call for excellence that school desegregation was thought to have displaced. Characterizing American schools as a rising tide of mediocrity led to strident calls for educational reforms that have characterized the past 20 years. The first wave of reform involved state centralization, whereas the second wave borrowed from a new participatory decision-making approach utilized in business organizations. Borrowing heavily from the Japanese and Deming's Total Quality Management work, for example (Carlson, 1996), this approach devolves bottom-line responsibility for organizational success to individuals or groups in the business setting. In schools, this became site-based management. With current accountability policy, the second wave has all but collapsed into the first wave.

In the late 1980s, choice proponents proposed that an open, marketplace competition would energize schools. Coalitions formed to promote and oppose choice and each lobbied at the state and national levels, with almost universal resistance on the part of school boards and school administrators (Bolman & Deal, 1997). The choice debate continues today and now includes both public schools choosing a vision or mission, as well as efforts to create publicly funded alternatives to the existing public school systems. Yet as we discuss later, it is somewhat ironic that accountability policy has actually reduced choice in the reform of traditional public schools.

School governance, then, has changed dramatically since the origins of public education in the United States. Schools were originally extremely local institutions serving particular communities in different, but perceived as appropriate, ways. Over time, the potential for the schools to serve state and national interests led to schools being standardized and consolidated. As the potential for schools to serve economic interests became apparent, centralization took on specific ideological content. The factory model for schools was an explicit way to link schools to the needs of a national industrial economy. The current reform era continues these historical movements. In 1983, *The Nation at Risk* report was explicit in linking education to failures in the economic sector. Although the economy improved independent of changes in education, the logic continued to play out. What is clear now is that the current reform era is about changing the dominant economic metaphor that is to structure schooling (Murphy, 1999). Taylor's scientific management is being replaced with a marketplace metaphor. School choice perhaps shows most clearly how this plays out. Vouchers, independent, and charter schools are argued to be the most effective ways to change public schools by forcing them all to compete. In this model, each school, analogous to a business, is seen as functioning in a marketplace in which they and all other schools compete for students, resources, and, ultimately, power. We should note that this marketplace metaphor is more pervasive than the school choice controversy indicates. Indeed, there is mounting evidence that the marketplace metaphor pervades school reform. As the New American Schools initiative has argued, school reform can be understood as a market, where various designs can compete for funds, thus enhancing the total market share of school reform initiatives from public expenditures. We would point out, however, that this is a market for *public* funds, implying that citizens' tax dollars are not just for services to underwrite reform initiatives. Moreover, as we argue later, this new metaphor, like the one that preceded it, also promotes the increased centralization of education. The metaphor cannot become pervasive if schools serve the particularistic desires of the parents of children they serve. A shift in the dominant metaphor requires centralization, and accountability policy is an apt vehicle for this centralization. With high-stakes testing, for example, schools (and the public) are forced into an uninterrogated market mentality, which maintains the rhetorical illusion that schools are free to organize however they think best to meet the state standards.

The reform era in general, and the recent emergence of the marketplace metaphor in particular, have had a dramatic effect not only on schools, but also on school districts. School districts historically developed to maximize compliance and control functions via standardization and uniformity of policy and procedures. The first wave in the recent reform era asked school districts to emphasize one primary role—namely, the enforcer of state initiatives. The second wave asked districts to facilitate local schools reforming themselves, something with which schools or districts had little experience. This second wave constituted a significant challenge to any school district. Glickman (1993) explained the school district's dilemma of autonomy and control as ". . . to be able to support schools who have developed a . . . community ready to move ahead and to provide control and structure to those schools not yet ready for collective autonomy" (p. 1). This dilemma is a special case of the general question that reform has asked of the educational system of this country. As Elmore (1993) phrased it, reform has asked that we struggle with ". . . how much influence of what kind any given level of government should exert over what factors" (p. 51).

The second wave of the recent reform era was predicated on the realization that, even with increased centralization, it was exceedingly hard to improve schools. It was becoming more widely understood that for schools to change in significant ways there has to be both dramatic and deep alterations in school cultures and structures. In short, systemic reform was needed. However, the second wave emphasized that schools were local institutions and reform could not be centralized in any important ways. Perhaps more important, the second wave of reform is in direct contradiction to the rule-bound school district culture that developed over the last 200 years. This also threatened the deeper meaning of the recent reform era discussed before. Letting schools change in whatever ways they thought best is clearly not a guarantee that schools will adopt a new metaphor. Accountability policy, then, has functioned to undercut the second wave of school reform and push the marketplace metaphor into the foreground.

We are only now beginning to understand the deeper meanings of accountability policy. Although many have been concerned about the deleterious effects of high-stakes testing, we think it is important to consider how accountability policy is changing school governance as part of the larger shift in the dominant metaphor of schooling

Currently, school board and school district functions remain strikingly similar, *in form*, to those exercised in colonial times. Major responsibilities still include policymaking (setting the rules); selection of the Superintendent (schoolmaster); goal setting and appraisal (visitation); instruction (books and teachers); financial resources (buildings and services); students (eligible pupils); communication with the public (the community); advocacy for children (pupil support from the people); and adjudication and investigation (ensuring that school rules are followed). Thus, the American tradition of holding schooling as a local endeavor is, in many respects, confirmed. We argue, however, that it is in the *nature* of school governance that continuing tensions among federal, state, and local government remain. These tensions are played out in current school reform efforts.

ACCOUNTABILITY POLICY AND THE CHANGING ROLE OF SCHOOL DISTRICTS IN REFORM

One way to uncover the deeper meaning of accountability policy is to examine the recent shift in the role of school districts in systemic educational reform. As recently as 1998, Noblit, Malloy, and Malloy (2001) found that large urban schools were interested in systemic school reform even if their standard operating procedures and accountability systems impeded the cause. By 2000 however, Noblit, Malloy, and Malloy found that accountability policy had led to school districts abandoning or, perhaps more strongly, abdicating systemic reform. School districts are not alone in this abdication. The state, in many ways, was the first to abdicate in the name of accountability. Districts and schools, in turn, were found to be playing out the state's logic. We argue that the marketplace metaphor undergirds what Noblit, Malloy, and Malloy (2000) called "shopping-mall school reform" (p. 195). The marketplace metaphor is pervasive; if current thinking about the organization of schools and districts is correct, then this metaphor will dominate models of educational reform for some time to come.

In the districts Noblit, Malloy, and Malloy (2000) studied, there was a point in history when the central office gave sufficient guidance, provided funding, and protected the schools as they reformed. The districts wished the schools to engage in systemic reform and alter their cultures and structures. Today, there are only vestiges of this left. In each of four large urban districts studied, state accountability initiatives have undercut supports for systemic reform. High-stakes testing, as Corbett and Wilson (1991) have argued, has led to a perversion of reform. Indeed, as noted earlier, the definition of *reform* has undergone a shift from systemic efforts to improve schools to focused efforts for short-term achievement gains. While the district role continued to provide guidance on the importance of reform and funds for initiatives, both guidance and funds were being increasingly directed to a narrow range of activities thought to quickly alter test scores. Moreover, previous protections to allow for systemic reforms to mature over time were waning.

School districts have two powerful contexts that are altering their role in school reform. First, states have moved to high-stakes testing as the primary form of accountability policy. The press, then, is for short-term test gains, which, in turn, school districts transmit onto schools. As a consequence of this focus on standardization at the state level, districts have found it in their interest to leave schools responsible for achievement. Thus, school districts need a new organizational chart, in which they are not between the state and schools (Model A), but exist to the side in a supportive or service role (Model B). Figure 1.1 is a graphical representation of this idea.

The second important context for school districts in the implementation of systemic reform is the ubiquity of change. School districts are always subject

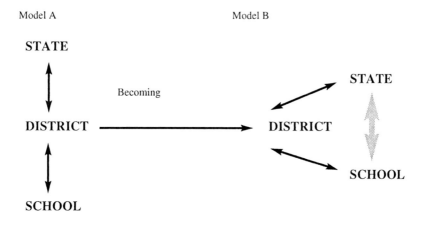

FIG. 1.1. Competing models for state, district, and school relationships.

to changes in state policy. Although districts historically were created to transmit state policy to schools, the current reform era has reinforced that role repeatedly, first as standards and second as accountability. However, districts do not always have stable leadership. For example, in each of the districts that Noblit, Malloy, and Malloy studied, Superintendents are temporary. The national average tenure for Superintendents is short—less than 3 years (Downey, 1998)—underscoring the ubiquity of leadership change for school districts. New Superintendents traditionally try to "put their stamp" on the district by promulgating new programs. This revolving door typically threatens staff commitments to any long-term programs of systemic reform. Such commitments are not necessarily terminated, but come to be pushed aside in the more immediate pursuit of programs that yield short-term and headline-grabbing achievement gains.

The salience of these two contexts, state-driven accountability policy and the ubiquity of change, played out in the way school improvement is now handled in the districts studied by Noblit, Malloy, and Malloy (2000). These districts, they argued, were engaging in shopping-mall reform. Schools in achievement trouble are encouraged to consider various short-term achievement program partners and purchase a reform. This new approach to school reform makes schools into consumers of prepackaged programs. Although there are problems with the factory metaphor for schools, it at least promoted the view that schools were producers. The products of schools, if unfortunately seen as students, entered the workforce or citizenry. If the products of schools were seen as knowledge, morality, or capabilities, then these were to be employed in the service of the economy, nation, public welfare, or even the people. However, schools as consumers are seen primarily as expenders of public funds. The school reform industry then accumulates this capital and uses it to increase its market share, garnering even more public funds. Our concern here is that shopping-mall reform takes the form of corporate welfare. Public funds underwrite a reform industry rather than serve the needs of children. We see the recent changes of New American Schools as further evidence of this trend (Hare, 1999).

Further, those with administrative training and roles see their jobs as developing organizational and management schemes that satisfy the reporting and compliance requirements of the school board, state, and federal government. District personnel are consumed with fulfilling the policy transmission role for which school districts were originally created. Following Meyer and Rowan (1978), the central office is about legitimation, whereas the schools are about educating children. Thus, in this model, instruction is relegated to the schools. Accountability policy functions to exacerbate this, in that it is in the interest of the central office to keep schools responsible for student achievement. Shopping-mall reform gives almost exclusive responsibility to the schools and the reform organizations for wise decisions on how to appropriately develop children. Again this allows the district office to confine its responsibility to funding the school's reform choice. Expertise in reform is not needed in the central office because they only need to function as a broker and fiscal agent. Similarly, technical expertise in curriculum and instruction also becomes the responsibility of the schools and reform agencies, not the districts, in this arrangement.

In each of the districts studied by Noblit, Malloy, and Malloy (2000), there was a history of supporting school change, improvement, and/or reform. This history means that there is or was considerable central office experience in helping schools change. The history of school reform in this country, however, indicates that such experience has not been accumulated into an articulate body of knowledge of school reform. People learned and became committed to specific approaches. When the state or district changed its priorities, central office personnel learned the requirements of the new initiative and, in turn, helped the schools learn the requirements of this initiative. Clearly, individuals may have seen similarities or differences among different approaches, but there was little reason to articulate these when each new legislative session or Superintendent was promoting specific new reforms. A secondary outcome of this leadership and change cycle was that few reforms were in place long enough for us to understand what worked or did not and why.

There is now even less reason to articulate an understanding or knowledge of school improvement and change at the district level. In the four urban districts that were studied, *local control* is being defined not as district responsibility, but as a school responsibility. In shopping-mall reform, the school selects a reform as part of constructing an explanation for student achievement and is then expected to meet their projected achievement gains in as little as 1 year. The district does not need to have any competence in school improvement beyond that of a commercial distributor of products. Clearly, there is also pressure on the districts as a reform distributor to broker just those reform packages marketed as producing short-term achievement gains. In this model, the shopping-mall reform school district provides the venue for quick reform vendors, as well as the public funds for schools to purchase from these vendors.

In each of the districts studied before, accountability policy is the state policy currently being transmitted. Because the states involved have also chosen high-stakes testing as the primary accountability mechanism, the key capacity evidenced in these districts is to convey to the schools that they are to be held responsible for student achievement gains. This demonstrates that the school board and Superintendent are acting more as agents of the state, rather than as the leaders of a local organization of public schools. Furthermore, each of the districts studied offers evidence that legitimization of education by the central office has failed to some extent. The schools were assumed to be problematic until they could prove otherwise. It is ironic that the districts are counting on accountability policy to help legitimate the schools even when many of the accountability systems employed by the states and districts has some form of a sliding scale. That is, increased achievement is the yardstick of success, but these same gains then come back as a baseline for even more achievement in the subsequent years. As Hoff (2000) argued, the current high-stakes testing systems that states and districts are employing will ultimately fail because of their press for escalating short-term gains. At some point, and we would argue much sooner than later, the failure to achieve systemic reform of education will result in stalled achievement growth. This means that state accountability policy will likely further undermine the current shaky legitimacy of public education.

Although we have articulated our concerns with the marketplace metaphor in educational reform, we want to emphasize that we understand it may well be the dominant metaphor for education for the foreseeable future. Clearly, however, it is a metaphor that school reform must address. As Murphy (1999) wrote:

> consumer-based control and accountability are simply a third act in the play known as school governance, an act that follows the professionally controlled governance structures that have dominated education for the past 75 years in the same way that professional control displaced the more democratically based models of school governance that characterized education in its formative years in the United States. (p. 405)

It is important to recognize that the emergence of the marketplace metaphor is not based in any assessment of its appropriateness in education. Rather, it is the case that many institutions are organized more externally than internally. Education in the United States is simply falling in line (Meyer & Rowan, 1978). As Rowan and Miskel (1999) concluded:

> If moving to a strong state-controlled educational system seems difficult to achieve in the American polity, perhaps a move towards deregulation and market controls makes more sense. . . . Market reforms have strong ideological appeal in liberal states around the world, in part because the ideological basis of liberal policies gives strong endorsement to the "private" enactment of "public" interest. (p. 71)

We remain unconvinced, however, that the marketplace metaphor is appropriate for education. We agree with Kertl (1996) that this shift in the organizing metaphor of schools is likely to "simply substitute a new set of difficult problems for old ones" (p. 513).

The use of the marketplace metaphor in educational policy has its origins in two places. First, Miron (1996) made a convincing argument that in the early 1980s there emerged an "entrepreneurial coalition" (p. 3) in urban areas that succeeded in "equating the social problems of the city with urban schooling" (p. 3). This coalition also sought to "advance the values of free enterprise through public education in the cities" and "gave rise to the reemergence of the state government as 'education regulator'" (p. 65). Miron's research makes it clear that "district superintendents do respond to the discourses of business" (p. 185). Because school reform emerged from the efforts of an entrepreneurial coalition, it is also easy to see this line of thinking fostering a new national consensus that sees education as a "tool of free enterprise" (Miron, 1996, p.185). In this analysis, the marketplace metaphor for education grew from a conscious and political construction driven by interests of business. School reform became but one move in a complex process to get education to advance the values of free enterprise and suppress other values that education has traditionally served—notably, equity.

Second, it has been argued that the emergence of the marketplace metaphor is embedded in increasing dissatisfaction with the prevailing model of government established in the Great Depression. This model placed government in the role of mediating the (unstable and inequitable) effects of the economy on the citizenry. Once a model becomes dominant, as Hood (1994) noted:

> dissatisfaction builds up over time. Unwanted side-effects [are] more clearly perceived. . . . At the same time, the shortcomings of the alternative orientation—the market in this case—are forgotten, because they have not been recently experienced. Pressure then starts to build for the policy orientation to go over on the other track. (p. 15)

Thus, the shift to the marketplace metaphor is not only the conscious assertion by business of its values, but a result of historical patterns. The recent success of the economy seems more promising than the public's long experience with a model of government established to mediate the potentially disastrous effects of the economy on the public. As Murphy (1999) argued, the shift toward the marketplace metaphor is based in at least two beliefs: (a) the structure of the public sector is flawed, and (b) decisions made in the public sector are less trustworthy than decisions made in the free marketplace. These beliefs underpin the perception that the marketplace is a more natural regulator than what is perceived to be an overly interventionist government.

Murphy (1999) pointed out that the concerns expressed earlier about reform becoming a form of corporate welfare are warranted. In part this is because our economy is increasingly becoming more of a service economy, which in turn means that "governmental services are a lucrative new market" (Darr, 1991, p. 9) for the private sector. Education is such a lucrative market because it is very large, has insufficient capital within it, has had little private sector penetration, and has relatively low startup costs. It should come as no surprise that the packaging and marketing of educational reform programs has become an attractive way to penetrate the market while shifting funds from the salaries of public employees to corporations (Rowan & Miskel, 1999).

The marketplace metaphor reveals that public schools are institutions that are structured in important ways by the increasing involvement of business leaders in school reform, as well as by a wider societal shift in its views of government. By actively promoting the view that government is both too inefficient and interventionist, corporations have been able to expand into the public sector, offering services historically provided by government agencies.

AFTER ACCOUNTABILITY AND SHOPPING MALL REFORM

We are convinced that accountability policy is failing and that understanding the deeper meanings of this failure make it even less palatable to the public. However, we want this book to do more than document the problematic nature of accountability policy and shopping-mall reform. In the chapters that follow, we argue that there is a productive way to think about systemic reform even if schools cannot he subjected to a one-size-fits-all view of reform. In short, our message is one of promise and hope, rather than despair. The field studies in this book demonstrate that engaging in a hunt for the single best practice model of school reform is naive at best and potentially dangerous for both students and teachers. The studies indicate that reform cannot be mandated through legislation or teacher-proofed. Consequently, a reform can never be fully achieved if this means replicating a single or even a small set of models across a range of schools. The idea of replication is simply not viable in schools because everything that happens in schools is adapted by the culture of that school. No two schools can ever do exactly the same thing; even if they could, they would not reap exactly the same results.

The field studies in this book are important because they illustrate that thinking about all schools as the same can lead to both faulty assumptions about how to fix schools, as well as what schools can achieve when they are mandated to adopt new school reform initiatives. By contrast, these studies demonstrate the importance of nurturing the resources, skills, and aspirations of the *local* school community in adapting a reform model to the culture of the school. Thus, these studies demand that we rethink how to go about reforming the nations' schools to better teach all students.

The field studies reported in this book also represent an important shift away from the conventional empirical-analytic research paradigm, grounded in positivism, that characterizes so much research on reform. Traditional empirical analytic research has employed such conventions as random sampling, statistical treatments of large-scale data sets, and the generation of normative statements that can be generalized across multiple contexts. Such paradigmatic thinking formulated (and answered) such questions as, "How effective is a reform model in raising student achievement as measured by norm-referenced tests?" or "Which of three implemented reform models is best at raising student achievement as measured by these same tests?" It is this paradigmatic thinking that has supported the long search for the single best reform model. However, this same research paradigm proved less than effective when different kinds of questions were posed (e.g., "What do students learn in a classroom using cooperative learning?" "In what ways is the thinking of teachers changed when classrooms are organized in more democratic ways?" "How can schools take advantage of reform to improve in ways they wish?") and when researchers' interests moved beyond the simple measurement of student achievement through standardized test scores. As the empirical-analytic paradigm generated a literature that recounted the failure of reform to improve schools (Adkins, 1997), it became clear that the situatedness of school reform required a more interpretive understanding. The interpretive paradigm required researchers to acknowledge that reality was socially constructed rather than given, that settings or contexts were constantly changing and could not be treated as the same even when they shared many similarities, and that the concept of generalizability was simply indefensible. Thus, fieldwork conducted within the interpretive paradigm focuses on generating detailed "emic" perspectives of the major actors within a specific contextualized setting. The goal then becomes to understand the *concrete particulars*— patterns of both regular and irregular behaviors and actions, rather than simply assessing a set of narrow outcomes. Most important, interpretive fieldwork generates a detailed case study that reveals a setting in action.

The studies in this book employ an interpretive paradigm and seek to help the reader understand how a particular reform works in a particular setting. Again, however, the intent is not to suggest that each case study is an evaluation of the effectiveness of a particular reform model. Taken together, these studies reveal the limitation of trying to identify the single best school reform model because each model has both strengths and weaknesses when viewed within the setting in which they were implemented. Put directly, these studies highlight the impossibility of discovering a silver bullet resolution to reform. Rather, the policy implication here is that more effort and resources should be given to schools as they implement reforms that connect with their culture, rather than giving the money to school reform vendors.

THE ORGANIZATION OF THIS BOOK

Our initial interest was to collect a series of field studies conducted on the popular major reform models. We were particularly interested in collecting work from researchers with little vested interest in the models. We were successful doing this, and we think you will find the studies better for such independence. The authors were asked to describe the models in ideal terms before they presented their case study data and analysis. They were also asked to remove details about their methodology from the main text and place it in an extended footnote. Finally, they were asked to make some comments about the policy implications of their findings. They were not asked to follow a formulaic frame work for presenting their cases. We were most interested to see what they would discover from an analysis of their case data without regard to any questions we might pose for them. To this end, we wanted and received stand-alone studies of these key reform models. We think each of these case studies contributes to a fuller understanding of how to reform schools, and we undergird our critique of the abdication of systemic reform currently in process.

Christine Finnan and Julie Dingle Swanson (chap. 2) have an ongoing research agenda with Accelerated Schools, a reform strategy begun by Henry Levin. Levin concluded that the premise of most prior efforts to improve the learning of poor children—that students had to master basic skills before they could learn more advanced knowledge and skills—was bogus. He reasoned that this premise meant that these students could never catch up to higher performing students. Thus, he proposed teaching these students as if they were gifted and talented students while placing the decision making about these students in the hands of the people closest to them. Many schools have found this strategy attractive and productive. Finnan and Dingle Swanson examine how Accelerated Schools worked at Rutledge School, a school serving African-American students, with all the hallmarks of a failing inner-city school. Accelerated Schools helped Rutledge change itself and led to remarkable improvements in achievement and student discipline. The Accelerated Schools strategy became the school's vehicle to revitalize itself. With the supportive efforts of the new principal, beliefs about students changed, as did the teaching practices thought to be appropriate for the students. The parents and community came to believe in the strategy and reveled in what was now possible. Most important, Accelerated Schools allowed the Rutledge educators to govern the change process themselves, as well as make the changes they felt were necessary. The result was a more unified set of beliefs and practices, tailored by the school community that functioned to integrate the reform approach with the school's culture.

Amee Adkins and Michael Gunzenhauser (chap. 3) have been studying A+ Schools, an arts-enhanced school reform strategy, over the last 6 years. A+ Schools were created as the initial project of the new Thomas Kenan Institute for the Arts. The program focused on expanding arts offerings and arts-integrated instruction in a set of North Carolina schools. Based on the ideas of Howard Gardner, A+ Schools used the arts to redefine both what intelligence is and how students demonstrate intelligence. The A+ strategy included extensive staff development in arts instruction (visual art, music, dance, and drama) and arts integration as well as the encouragement to adapt A+ to the local school culture and community. West Hollow School, the case Adkins and Gunzenhauser present here, is somewhat unusual. It is a K-12 mountain school with a culture quite unlike the other A+ schools. Yet West Hollow School found that A+ could be adapted successfully to their community and culture. The community was concerned that students who were successful in school left the community for higher education. These students were unlikely to return as they pursued economic opportunities in other geographic areas that their advanced education afforded them. A+ allowed the school to support an indigenous economy in mountain crafts and folklife, which the community saw as an attempt to help keep the children in the community. The school became successful in the state's high-stakes accountability system as well. A+ also had the added value of allowing the school to understand how to reform itself. Building on what it learned within the A+ network, West Hollow School was able to appropriate A+ for funding by the Annenberg Foundation for place-based education. A+ was the way the school adapted to its community and changed its culture to take advantage of school reform.

George Noblit and Michael Jennings (chap. 4) studied a large urban K-8 school populated by Chinese and African-American students. These communities were segregated both by neighborhood as well as within the school. The Chinese students stayed in the bilingual program, and the African-American students were in the regular classrooms. The school had problems with achievement and relations with both communities until a new principal was hired. This principal proved to be adept in school board politics. She was able to get a new building funded and held the school together while it was being built. The principal also saw that even with her power, she needed a mechanism to address the problems with achievement and foster community involvement. Although she had been able to end the segregation within the school's instructional programs, achievement still lagged as high-stakes accountability was being implemented in the state and district. James Comer's School Development Program (SDP) was already in the district, and Gregory School was invited to join the program. The SDP's governance mechanisms and decision-making principles enabled the school to involve all its constituencies and address the instructional program. It also tempered the power of a principal, who could easily have become an oligarch. Gregory School not only improved the achievement of its students, but it altered the school's historic response to change. The SDP became the vehicle for Gregory School to take charge of change and escape the fate so often ascribed to poor, minority, and inner-city schools. The new culture at Gregory was able to make significant changes, restructuring the school to better serve the children and community.

Monica McKinney's chapter (chap. 5) is an analysis of Success for All (SFA) in a rural, economically depressed community. The county school district was concerned with the low performance of their students, and had researched a number of reform strategies touted to raise literacy rates in the elementary schools. SFA was the program selected. Based on the assumption that all children can learn, SFA provided a comprehensive reading program that focuses the school on intensive and extension instruction. Marshall County shared SFA's belief that direct instruction was the best approach. SFA offered the schools a program of small ability groups that were taught for 90 minutes per day, with group placements being regularly reassessed and new groups formed. Howard Elementary School was convinced that it needed a comprehensive literacy program, and that it needed one that would provide the necessary training, materials, and processes for literacy to become the focus of the school. The school implemented SFA with considerable vigor and began to see results rather quickly. With SFA, the school restructured its reading instruction and saw that the beliefs embedded in SFA were viable. Yet the comprehensiveness of SFA also fit the district's historic tendency to buy a program only to move onto another program in a few years. Whereas instruction and beliefs about students changed, the staff did not learn how to change their own culture.

Carol Malloy (chap. 6) studied charter schools as part of evaluating North Carolina's Charter School initiative. Because charter schools are free to choose their mission, Malloy decided to compare two rather different schools to understand how choice and school culture affect one another. Her emphasis is pointedly on the education of African Americans in these disparate school cultures. School choice, of course, is a key element of the new marketplace metaphor for education and demonstrates that some reformers are pointedly against our current system of public education. The charter schools Malloy studied—Global Middle School and Liberty Academy—have different visions of appropriate schooling. Global Middle is intent on preparing students for the new global economy and believes that discovery learning not only is an effective pedagogy, but also the best preparation for life-long learning in a changing and uncertain world. By contrast Liberty Academy is especially focused on effective instruction for African-American students, which it defines as didactic basic skill instruction. The cultures of the schools also reflect the relative wealth of the students and sponsors of the schools. Global Middle has impressive resources, whereas Liberty struggles to have adequate facilities and resources. As Malloy demonstrates, the differences in the cultures extend to almost all areas of the schools. Yet there is a disturbing similarity. Neither school adequately serves African-American students. Global Middle, even as it prepares students for a diverse and changing world, assumes all students understand and are facile with the school's culture, which is not true of its African-American students. Liberty fits the culture of its African-American students better, but reproduces the dominance of White society by preparing students to fit the existing structure. Malloy reminds us of the complexity of school culture, which school reform packages frequently ignore.

Bruce Wilson and Dick Corbett (chap. 7) have been studying Talent Development for a number of years. Talent Development is a middle-grades program designed by researchers at Johns Hopkins University and the Center for Research on the Education of Students Placed at Risk. Wilson and Corbett focused on one school—Northern Middle School—but report data from other schools to show the significance of students' views in understanding how Talent Development affected school culture. Talent Development worked with Northern Middle to alter its organization so that students had more opportunities to develop relationships with teachers and to enhance the school's curricula and instruction. This chapter also highlights how some reforms are embedded in other reform initiatives. All the schools studied were part of Philadelphia's wider "Children Achieving" initiative, which has all the hallmarks of high-stakes accountability discussed earlier. Northern Middle saw Talent Development as its way to respond to "Children Achieving," and in doing so was able to deliver more challenging classroom instruction and a supportive school environment. This in turn led to better student test outcomes than the comparison schools. Wilson and Corbett demonstrate that talking to students is a powerful way to understand significant school change. They also underscore our argument that accountability policy needs to invest in systemic school reform. By itself, accountability policy only creates compliance, whereas true school reform needs creative action.

Kathryn Borman's chapter (chap. 8) ends our volume by describing an extreme case of corporate involvement in schooling: Disney's Celebration School. If schools are to embody the new metaphor of the market, then it is important to understand just how a market-driven school design alters what is usually offered to parents and students. In this case, the lesson is sobering. Although the popular image is that consumers drive market-based economic systems, Disney's Celebration School reveals that corporations decide what is available to the consumer. Borman also underlines how different the cultures of business and the public sector are. The former does its work behind closed doors, exercising considerable control over the possibilities, whereas the latter conducts its business in full view of all constituencies, making negotiation and compromise the rules of the day. Thus, it may be that the market metaphor now being embraced in educational reform will be altered by the institution of public schooling. Indeed, Borman's chapter reminds us how deeply schools are embedded in our culture and how the public may work to limit the possibilities for reform to fit their ideas about what is appropriate education. Educators and corporations may find the evidence convincing that discovery learning, project-based curricula, authentic assessment, and student involvement are the best practices in education, but parents may see their own experiences with schooling as better guides to true best practices. Celebration School may be the best school corporate involvement can design, but a clear lesson for reform is that innovation that is not systemic and does not involve all the constituencies will likely be reined in over time. School and community culture, then, are strongly interdependent.

EMERGING QUESTIONS

We have resisted the temptation to develop a concluding chapter for the book—a chapter where we would tell the reader what everything means. We have resisted for two important reasons. First, we believe that it is conceptually wrong-headed to proceed to construct generalizable normative statements from case study data collected by different researchers across a range of reforms. Second, and perhaps more important, we believe that the reader must construct the meaning in any and all of these cases. In short, the power of the message in these cases about the implementation of particular school reforms is in their ability to first trouble and subsequently inform the readers' understanding of implementing reform in the context of their own school culture. Thus, we invite the reader to read these cases with a critical eye, asking, "What are the implications of this case for the reform of my school in my district and community?"

We do, of course, bring our own perspectives and bias to a reading of these cases. Consequently, we want to end this chapter with a set of questions that readers may wish to consider as they think about the various reform models investigated in this book:

- How does the local school context help determine which reform model is selected at the site?
- What are the roles played by the wider contexts in each case (e.g., parents, community, district office, state department, etc.)?
- What is the tension between adoption versus adaption of the reform model at the local school site, and how is this tension resolved?
- What cultural adjustments within the school are key to the successful implementation of a reform model, and how does the reform model facilitate or inhibit these adjustments?
- What is similar and dissimilar about the successful implementation of reforms across the models?
- What changes in the local school culture are most important in what contexts?
- What is the role of leadership, both in and outside of the school, in the implementation of the reforms?
- How is equity and excellence advanced by each reform?
- What are the implications of these cases for initiating and sustaining a reform model in the school(s) in which you have a stake?

REFERENCES

Adkins, A. (1997). *The colonial vestiges of education reform.* Unpublished doctoral dissertation, University of North Carolina, Chapel Hill.

Berliner, D. C., & Biddle, B. J. (1997). *The manufactured crisis: Myths, fraud, and the attack on America's public schools.* White Plains, NY: Longman.

Bolman, L. G., & Deal, T. E. (1997). *Reframing organizations: Artistry, choice, and leadership* (2nd ed.). San Francisco: Jossey-Bass.

Bloom, A. (1987). *The closing of the American mind.* New York: Simon & Schuster.

Bowers, C. (1984). *The promise of theory.* New York: Teachers College Press.

Callahan, R. E. (1965). *An introduction to education in American society.* New York: Knopf.

Campbell, R. F., Fleming, T., Newell, L. J., & Bennion, J. W. (1987). *A history of thought and practice in educational administration.* New York: Teachers College Press.

Carnegie Forum on Education and the Economy. (1986). *A nation prepared: Teachers for the twenty-first century.* New York: The Carnegie Commission.

Carlson, R.V. (1996). *Reframing and reform: Perspectives on organization, leadership and school change.* While Plains, NY: Longman.

Collins, R. (1982). *Sociological insight: An introduction to non-obvious sociology.* New York: Oxford University Press.

Commission on the Reorganization of Secondary Education. (1918). *Cardinal principles of secondary education.* Washington, DC: U.S. Government Printing Office.

Corbett, H. D., & Wilson, B. L. (1991). *Testing, reform, and rebellion.* Norwood, NJ: Ablex.

Cremin, L. A. (1957). *The republic and the school: Horace Mann on the education of free men.* New York: Teachers College Press.

Cronin, J. M. (1973). *The control of urban schools: Perspective on the power of educational reformers.* New York: The Free Press.

Cuban, L. (1988). Why do some reforms persist? *Educational Administration Quarterly, 24*(3), 137-150.

Cuban, L. (1990). Reforming again, again, and again. *Educational Researcher, 9,* 3-12.

Cubberley, E. P. (1914). *Rural life and education: A study of the rural-school problem.* Boston: Houghton-Mifflin.

Cubberley, E. P. (1916). *Public school administration: A statement of the fundamental principles underlying the organization and administration of public education.* Boston: Houghton-Mifflin.

Cubberley, E. P. (1947). *Public education in the United States.* Cambridge, MA: Riverside Press.

Darr, T.B. (1991). Privatization may be good for your government. In R.L. Kemp (Ed.), *Privatization* (pp. 60-68). Jefferson, NC: McFarland.

DeYoung, A. J. (1989). *Economics and American education: A historical and critical overview of the impact of economic theories of schooling in the United States.* New York: Longman.

Downey, C. (1998). Is it time for us to be accountable too? *The AASA Professor, 22*(1), 1-4.

Driver, C. E., Thorp, V., & Kuo, V. (1997). *Sustaining school restructuring by reforming school districts.* Chicago: American Educational Research Association.

Elmore, R. (1993). *The development and implementation of large-scale curriculum reforms.* Paper prepared for the American Association for the Advancement of Science, Harvard Graduate School of Education, Center for Policy Research in Education, Cambridge, MA.

Elmore, R. (1996). Getting to scale with good educational practice. *Harvard Educational Review, 66*(1), 1-26.

Fuller, W. E. (1982). *The old country school: The story of rural education in the middle west.* Chicago: University of Chicago Press.

Glickman, C. (1993). School district policies supporting school renewal. In L. Avila (Ed.), *Integration or fragmentation: The impact of site-based decisionmaking* (pp. 1-17). Austin: Texas Association for Supervision and Curriculum Development.

Gutek, G. (1988). *Education and schooling in America* (2nd ed.). Englewood Cliffs, NJ: Prentice-Hall.

Hare, A. C. (1999). *Exploring the effectiveness of nonprofit organizations encouraging education reform. A case study.* Unpublished doctoral dissertation, University of North Carolina, Chapel Hill.

Hoff, D. (2000, January 26). Testing's ups and down predictable. *Education Week*, pp. 1, 12-13.

Hood, C. (1994). *Explaining economic policy reversals.* Buckingham, England: Open University Press.

Katz, M. (1975). *Class, bureaucracy, and schools: The illusion of educational change in America* (2nd ed.). New York: Praeger.

Kearns, D. T., & Anderson, J. L. (1996). Sharing the vision: Creating new American schools. In S. Stringfield, S. Ross, & L. Smith (Eds.), *Bold plans for school restructuring* (pp. 9-23). Mahwah, NJ: Erlbaum.

Kent, J.D. (1987). A not too distant past. *The Educational Forum, 51*(2), 123-135.

Kertl, D. F. (1988). Government by proxy and the public service. *International Review of Administrative Sciences, 54*(4), 501-515.

Mannheim, K. (1936). *Ideology and utopia.* New York: Harcourt, Brace.

McElhenny, W.B. (1947) Where do we stand on school district reorganization? *Journal of the Kansas Law Association, 16*, 245-251.

Meyer, J.W., & Rowan, B. (1978) The structure of educational organizations. In

M.W. Meyer, J. H. Freeman, M. T. Hannan, J. W. Meyer, W. G. Ouchi, J. Pfeffer, & W. R. Scott (Eds.), *Environments and organizations* (pp. 78-109). San Francisco: Jossey-Bass.

Mirel, J. (1990) What history can teach us about school decentralization. *Network News and Views*, 9(8), 40-47.

Miron, L. (1996) *The social construction of urban schooling.* Cresskill, NJ: Hampton Press.

Murphy, J. (1999) New consumerism: Evolving market dynamics in the institutional dimension of schooling. In J. Murphy & K. S. Lewis (Eds.), *Handbook of research on educational administration* (pp. 405-419). San Francisco: Jossey-Bass.

Murphy, J., & Beck, L. (1995) *School-based management as school reform.* Thousand Oaks, CA: Corwin.

National Commission on Excellence in Education. (1983) *A nation at risk: The imperative for educational reform.* Washington, DC: U.S. Government Printing Office.

New York Regents. (2000). State education history. May 15, 2000 (http://unix2.nysed.gov/edocs/education/sedhist.htm#chal).

Noblit, G. W., & Dempsey V.O. (1996) *The social construction of virtue: The moral life of schools.* Albany: State University of New York Press.

Noblit, G. W., Malloy, C. E., & Malloy, W. W. (2000). *District context and Comer schools: How school districts manage school reform.* A report submitted to the Rockefeller Foundation.

Noblit, G. W., Malloy, W. W., Malloy, C. E. (Eds.). (2001). *The kids got smarter: Case studies of successful Comer schools.* Cresskill, NJ: Hampton Press.

Pink, W. T. (1994, April) *Competing views of change: Reforming school culture.* Paper presented at the meeting of the American Educational Research Association, New Orleans, LA.

Pink, W. T. (1999) Critical dialogue and the transformation of schools and schooling: Urban and suburban sister schools. In F. Yeo & B. Kanpol (Eds.), *From nihilism to possibility: Democratic transformations for inner city education.* Cresskill, NJ: Hampton Press.

Pink, W. T., & Hyde, A. A. (Eds.). (1992). *Effective staff development for school change.* Norwood, NJ: Ablex.

Rogers, D. (1973). Foreword. In J. M. Cronin (Ed.), *The control of urban schools: Perspectives on the power of educational reformers* (pp. xiii-xx). New York: The Free Press.

Rowan, B., & Miskel, C. (1999). Institutional theory and the study of educational organizations. In J. Murphy & K. S. Lewis (Eds.), *Handbook of research on educational administration* (pp. 359-384). San Francisco: Jossey-Bass.

Swanson, A. D., & King, R. A. (1997). *School finance: Its economics and politics* (2nd ed.). New York: Longman.

Taylor, F.W. (1911). *The principles of scientific management.* New York: Harper & Row.

Tyack, D. (1974). *The one best system: A history of American urban education.* Cambridge, MA: Harvard University Press.

Tyack, D., & Cuban, L. (1995). *Tinkering toward utopia: A century of public school reform.* Cambridge, MA: Harvard University Press.

Tyack, D., Lowe, R., & Hansot, E. (1980). *Public schools in hard times: The great depression and recent years.* Cambridge, MA: Harvard University Press.

Wells, A. S., & Serna, I. (1996). The politics of culture: Understanding local political resistance to detracking in racially mixed schools. *Harvard Educational Review, 66*(1), 93- 118.

Whitaker, K. S., & Moses, M. C. (1994). *The restructuring handbook.* Boston: Allyn & Bacon.

Young, M. F. D. (1998). *The curriculum of the future.* Philadelphia: Falmer.

Zeichner, K. M. (1991). Contradictions and tensions in the professionalization of teaching and the democratization of schools. *Teachers College Record, 92*, 363-379.

2

Changing School Culture: Rutledge Elementary[1] as an Accelerated School

Christine Finnan
Julie Dingle Swanson
University/College of Charleston

The Accelerated Schools Project is committed to providing challenging, relevant, and engaging educational experiences for all students through involvement of teachers, staff, and parents in the school's decision-making process. Accelerated schools share the philosophy that all children should experience the enriched, demanding curriculum and instruction usually reserved only for students identified as gifted and talented. Although the idea of setting high standards for all students is not unusual today, it was not common practice in the mid-1980s when the Accelerated Schools Project began.

Dr. Henry Levin, then a professor of education and economics at Stanford University, was concerned that the press for increased rigor brought about by reports such as "A Nation at Risk" (National Commission on Excellence in Education, 1983) ignored the effects of poverty and the substandard condition of many schools serving poor and minority students. Through a series of research projects, Dr. Levin found that the number of economically disadvantaged students had risen since 1970; children from low-income backgrounds entered school without many of the developmental skills and behaviors expected by teachers, and they fell increasingly behind as they progressed

---

[1]The school's name has been changed.

through school. This history of failure led to chronic unemployment, involvement in criminal activity, and dependence on welfare (Levin, 1985, 1986).

This research made Dr. Levin curious about possible solutions. In examining the literature and visiting schools across the country, he found that the problem did not rest in the teachers or students. Rather, it rested in the belief shared by most educators that students have to master basic skills before they can move on to more advanced ones. Efforts to remediate students, he found, slowed their progress, leaving them several years behind students who did not need remedial help. Those students fell so far behind that it became literally impossible to ever catch up. The only bright spots Dr. Levin found in his visits were the small, isolated classrooms dedicated to enrichment for students identified as gifted. His question became, "What would happen if all students were educated as if they were gifted and talented?" From this premise and a commitment to placing decision making in the hands of the people closest to students came the Accelerated Schools Project (Levin, 1996).

Since 1986, when the Accelerated Schools Project began with two pilot schools, it has grown to serve over 1,000 schools in the United States and a growing number of schools in other countries. The National Center for the Accelerated Schools Project, now located at the University of Connecticut, coordinates the work of 11 satellite centers located in colleges and universities, state department of education offices, and school district offices nationwide. The satellite centers provide training and follow-up support to schools in their geographic area and ensure that state and local issues are addressed. In addition to satellite center support, the Accelerated Schools Project requires that each school has a trained coach who provides school-level assistance as the project is implemented. The following provides a brief description of the Accelerated Schools Project philosophy, the concept of powerful learning, the governance structure, and the decision-making process.

ACCELERATED SCHOOLS PROJECT—PHILOSOPHY

The Accelerated Schools Project is based on John Dewey's belief that the schools we want for our own children should be the schools we want for all children (Dewey, 1990). To accomplish this, accelerated schools embrace three principles: unity of purpose, empowerment coupled with responsibility, and building on strengths. Unity of purpose *refers to the commitment of parents, teachers, students, and administrators to meet a shared vision. Unity of purpose occurs when all parties are involved in setting the school's vision and determining the best strategies to achieve the vision.* Empowerment coupled with responsibility *refers to the school community members' need to make important educational decisions and take responsibility for their outcome. By making decisions jointly and taking responsibility for them, the "circle of blame" that exists in so many schools disappears.* Building on strengths *refers to shifting from a focus on students' weaknesses and what is wrong to identifying and building on strengths and what is already working well. This principle applies to finding the strengths of students, parents, teachers, staff, administrators, and the community. Accelerated schools find that they can build on strengths, but they cannot build on weaknesses. By building on strengths, school community members are apt to set higher goals for themselves and address weaknesses that prevent them from reaching these goals (Finnan, St. John, McCarthy, & Slovacek, 1996; Hopfenberg, Levin, & Associates, 1993).*

This guiding philosophy also includes a set of values, beliefs, and attitudes described in Table 2.1. The values, beliefs, and attitudes are at the core of how decisions are made, how children are taught, how the school interacts with the wider community, and how all school community members interact with each other.

TABLE 2.1
Values, Beliefs, and Attitudes Guiding the Accelerated Schools Project

Equity	All students can learn and have an equal right to high-quality education
Participation	Everyone participates in the accelerated school's transformation process, and all people's ideas count
Communication and collaboration	The entire community collaboratively works toward a shared purpose by meeting with, talking with, and learning from each other's experiences
Community spirit	A strong sense of community spirit arises because the school has built strong connections among its members in the service of the children
Reflection	Time is provided to reflect, to do research, to work together, to share ideas
Experimentation/discovery	Change involves taking informed risks and engaging in thoughtful experimentation
Trust	Trust is essential, and it is built when the school community comes to believe in each other, support one another. and focus on each other's strengths
Risk taking	All parties are encouraged to be entrepreneurial or informed risk-takers
School as center of expertise	The members of the school community recognize that they possess the vision and the talent they need o make their dreams a reality

Note. From Hopfenberg, Levin, & Associates (1993)

ACCELERATED SCHOOLS PROJECT—POWERFUL LEARNING

As described earlier, the Accelerated Schools Project is committed to providing powerful learning opportunities for all students. Powerful learning is based on an integration of curriculum, instruction, and educational context commonly seen in classes designed for the gifted and talented (Hopfenberg, Levin, & Associates, 1993). The strategies allow students to explore, think deeply, and relate their learning to prior knowledge. Powerful learning strategies are characterized as authentic, inclusive, continuous, learner centered, and interactive (Keller & Huebner, 1997). The Accelerated Schools Project does not package curriculum or instructional strategies for its schools. Rather it provides school communities with guidelines to assess educational practices, enabling each school to determine the fit among educational strategies, school culture, needs of students, and the concept of powerful learning. Part of the Accelerated Schools Project process is for schools and those closest to students to determine how best to build on students' strengths. Schools use the process to find their own way.

ACCELERATED SCHOOLS PROJECT— GOVERNANCE STRUCTURE

For shared decision making to truly work, a clearly defined governance structure must be in place that allows all key players in the school community to engage in consensus-based, collaborative inquiry. This structure allows key players to identify and work on critical issues that will move the school toward its vision. Accelerated schools adopt a governance structure that operates on three levels.

The basic work of the Accelerated Schools Project happens at the level of cadres. Cadres, the smallest unit (usually 5-20 people), are established to engage in inquiry related to key challenge areas identified by the whole school. Most schools have four to five cadres addressing issues such as reading/language arts, mathematics, science, social studies, student behavior/social skills, arts, and multiculturalism/language diversity. Cadres are made up of teachers, other school staff, parents, community members, and, in some cases, students. Cadres do not work in isolation from the rest of the school. Regular reports are made to the steering committee, and the school as a whole makes final decisions on all actions proposed by cadres (see Fig. 2.1).

The steering committee consisting of cadre representatives and the school principal (schools may choose to include other people on the steering committee) is another key component of the governance structure. The steering committee serves many purposes. It ensures that cadres' work will move the school toward its vision and that the cadres use the inquiry process. This check and balance prevents a school from jumping on the latest bandwagon by requir-

School as a Whole

Steering Committee

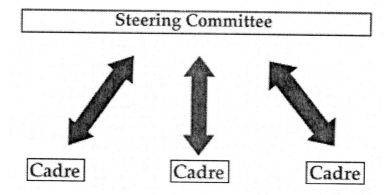

Cadre   Cadre   Cadre

FIG. 2.1. Accelerated Schools Project governance structure.

ing evidence and solid research to support any recommendations for decision making. It also serves as an information clearinghouse so that cadres do not work in isolation. The steering committee representative provides a conduit for information back and forth between cadre and steering. The steering committee screens outgoing information from cadres (e.g., surveys, letters, action plans) and deals with incoming information from outside the school, determining whether actions should be taken by the cadres, principal, or ad hoc committees.

The final level of the governance structure is the school as a whole. The school as a whole refers to everyone at the school site as well as representative parents and students. The school as a whole approves all major decisions on curriculum, instruction, and resource allocation that have implications for the entire school.

ACCELERATED SCHOOLS PROJECT—DECISION-MAKING PROCESS

Once schools join the Accelerated Schools Project, they engage in a decision-making process that is inclusive, research-based, and continuous. The process is inclusive because it attempts to include members from all parts of the school community: faculty, staff, parents, and children. The process is research-based because schools continuously engage in research, including collecting baseline "taking stock" data, conducting inquiry into the reasons for problems, researching appropriate solutions, and formally assessing the actions taken. The process is continuous because a school is never as good as it could be; all improvement is relative to the starting point (see Fig. 2.2 for a graphic representation of the process).

During the first year, each school community engages in a process of forging a shared vision that describes their dream school and sets standards for student achievement. In addition to creating a shared vision, they also engage in taking stock of their current situation, comparing the "here and now" with their vision of what they as a community want to be. Once taking stock is completed, they set priorities to determine the most pressing school needs. The priority areas are subjected to examination by cadres through an inquiry process. The inquiry process involves developing and testing hypotheses that offer a range of explanations for why problem areas exist. Once hypotheses are tested, the cadre analyzes the results to determine the most likely cause of the problem. At this point, the cadre will begin to look for solutions that address the problem's underlying cause, are within the school's control, and will encourage powerful learning. Cadres develop action and evaluation plans approved by the school as a whole. These plans are implemented (either as a pilot or schoolwide), evaluated, and adjusted as needed. Once an action is underway, the cadre identifies additional challenge areas and uses the inquiry process to address them.

THE NATURAL HISTORY OF THE ACCELERATED SCHOOLS PROJECT AT RUTLEDGE ELEMENTARY

In fall 1991, when Rutledge Elementary School made the decision to become the first accelerated school in South Carolina, it had many features that characterize inner-city schools. Nearly all of the pre-K through fifth-grade students were African Americans who qualified for free- or reduced-price lunch. Most of the students lived in neighboring public housing or other low-income dwellings. Some students were driven to school, but most walked. The neglected, crumbling physical facility contributed to the inner-city school image. Built in the 1950s, the U-shaped, brick two story building suffered from a leaky roof, peeling paint, and foul-smelling bathrooms. Play areas were small dirt yards with minimal play equipment. Rutledge should have been the neighborhood school for some of the wealthiest families in Charleston, but these families all opted for private or magnet schools.

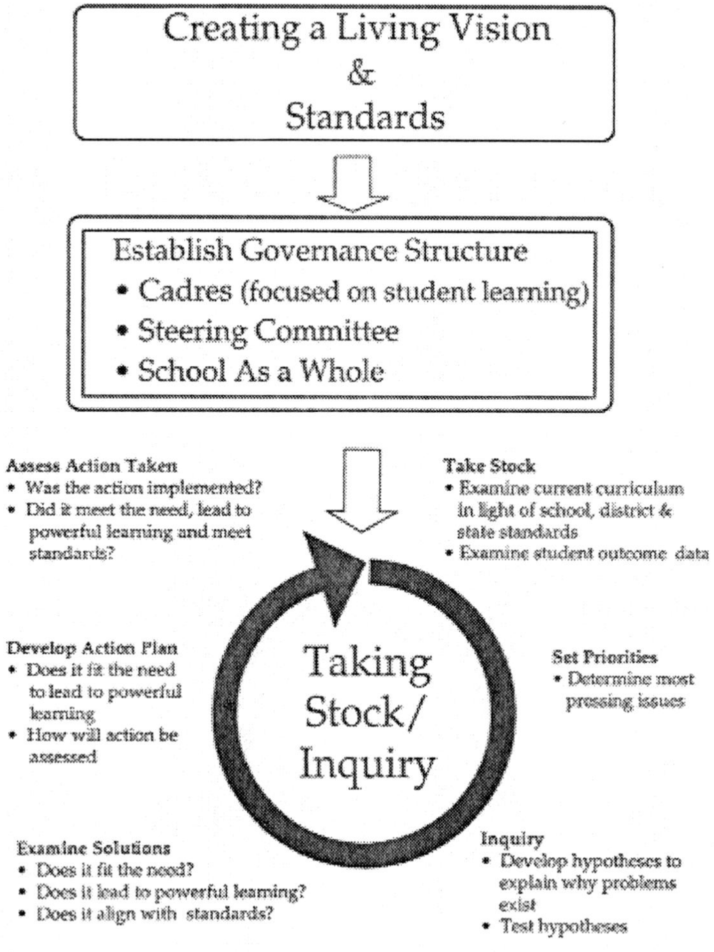

```
┌─────────────────────────────────────┐
│      Creating a Living Vision        │
│                &                     │
│            Standards                 │
└─────────────────────────────────────┘
```

```
┌─────────────────────────────────────┐
│   Establish Governance Structure     │
│   • Cadres (focused on student learning) │
│   • Steering Committee               │
│   • School As a Whole                │
└─────────────────────────────────────┘
```

Assess Action Taken
• Was the action implemented?
• Did it meet the need, lead to powerful learning and meet standards?

Take Stock
• Examine current curriculum in light of school, district & state standards
• Examine student outcome data

Develop Action Plan
• Does it fit the need to lead to powerful learning
• How will action be assessed

Taking Stock/ Inquiry

Set Priorities
• Determine most pressing issues

Examine Solutions
• Does it fit the need?
• Does it lead to powerful learning?
• Does it align with standards?

Inquiry
• Develop hypotheses to explain why problems exist
• Test hypotheses

FIG. 2.2. A graphic representation of the decision-making process.

The school was not seen by the White community as a great place to work or send children. Students brought attitudes and social interaction patterns appropriate to the streets with them to school. Fights were common, and many teachers felt they had to control with an iron fist. Faculty turnover was high, although many of the veteran teachers were strong, with a genuine commitment to working with inner-city children. The district had used Rutledge to experiment with new initiatives in the past with little lasting positive effect.

Despite these negative characteristics, there were reasons to believe Rutledge would be successful with the Accelerated Schools Project. A new principal had been hired over the summer, and her leadership style and commitment to children was a perfect fit with the Accelerated Schools Project philosophy. In addition, Rutledge had a strong core faculty. As described earlier, many veteran teachers remained at Rutledge because of their commitment to the children and the community. Although the facility was crumbling and the school's reputation in the White community was poor, the African-American community was proud of Rutledge, and families were happy to send their children there. A sense of pride pervaded it despite the many strikes against the school. In addition, Rutledge had the potential of taking advantage of many resources; it was two blocks from the College of Charleston and near the school district's central office and downtown government offices. The college, the school district, and the city all wanted to have a showcase school downtown.

How did Rutledge Elementary School become the first school in South Carolina to join the Accelerated Schools Project? During spring 1991, an informal partnership among the College of Charleston, the South Carolina State Department of Education, and Charleston County School District was formed to begin implementing the Accelerated Schools Project in South Carolina.[2] Representatives from the three institutions agreed that Rutledge Elementary would be an ideal pilot school because of its close proximity to the College of Charleston, its population, its reputation for being open to innovation, and its new, progressive principal. The principal of Rutledge recalls her initial reaction to the suggestion that Rutledge pilot the Accelerated Schools Project:

> I had just opened school as a brand new principal. In meeting with my faculty I promised them that we would spend the first year getting to know each other—that I would not impose anything new on them. A few days after school started, I received a packet of information about the Accelerated Schools Project from the Associate Superintendent; he said to call him as soon as I read it. I was furious. I didn't want the district telling me I had to do something when I had just promised my faculty that we would move slowly. I tried a little passive aggressive behavior and didn't call him, but after he left me several messages, I thought I should break down and at least read the stuff. I couldn't believe it. It was my philosophy! I kept reading and became very excited. I realized that this could be a real "win-win" situation. I could make the district happy by willingly participating, and I could have some support from the College to make something I wanted to do anyway happen. I took the idea to my faculty, had [the project director] come in and talk about the project, and after a long talk, we voted to join.

---

[2]From 1991 to 1993, the Accelerated Schools Project was supported by funds from The State Department of Education. Since 1993, the Accelerated Schools Project has been funded by the State of South Carolina through Education Improvement Act funds.

A few weeks after the faculty voted to join the project, all of the faculty, staff, and interested parents and community members were introduced to the Accelerated Schools philosophy, the concept of powerful learning, and the decision-making process. They began the process of developing the school's vision and taking stock of its current situation with a great deal of enthusiasm and excitement. School community members joined committees to take stock of the school's various aspects: curriculum and instruction, students, family and community involvement, and school history. Simultaneously, people began collecting ideas from all school community members for the vision. By January 1992, the vision was approved. It states:

> Our VISION for Rutledge Elementary School is boundless! All avenues to educate and enrich our children will be explored. We will provide quality academic and enriching experiences for all of our students. Our children will be effective communicators and learn to use appropriate social and decision making skills to develop their individual uniqueness as they perform to the best of their abilities and REACH BEYOND!

Four inquiry cadres were formed to investigate problems and identify solutions in the following areas: curriculum and instruction, family and community involvement, students, and facilities and resources. In the spring, the entire school marched to a public square in downtown Charleston to celebrate the vision for an accelerated Rutledge

The first year in a new effort is often exciting and energizing. Once the real work of implementation begins, some of that enthusiasm turns into determination and frustration. In the subsequent years, Rutledge has continued to make the Accelerated Schools Project philosophy its own, encourage powerful learning in classrooms, and consistently use the governance structure and decision-making process. As the data to be presented in this chapter illustrate, Rutledge's school culture and the Accelerated Schools Project philosophy are highly compatible, and that compatibility has been a strength for moving change forward in this school. The project implementation has not always been smooth; Rutledge does not represent a textbook case of project implementation. That is one of the reasons that Rutledge was selected to exemplify ASP as a school change model. Using a case that has had uneven implementation, being able to illustrate the highs and lows, what has strengthened and moved the effort for improvement forward, as well as obstacles that this specific school has faced will help the reader understand more deeply the complexities of school change.

Cadres, the steering committee, and the school as a whole have met regularly since 1991, and they continue to meet on a schedule set early in the process. Cadres and the steering committee meet twice a month, and the school as a whole meets once a month

Cadres have implemented action plans, and a sense of unity prevails in the school. Some cadres formed strong bonds among the members, whereas others experienced dissension. One cadre, the family and community involvement cadre, disbanded as members left to join other cadres. The curriculum and instruction cadre implemented several plans (e.g., an annual multicultural fair), but members were often frustrated by the enormity of their task and by dealing with conflicting agendas. For example, some teachers wanted to develop more school wide experiential events, such as a multicultural fair, whereas others found these events disruptive and too time-consuming. In other instances, the cadre spun its wheels as it considered implementing new ideas suggested by the district or the college, although these ideas did not result from the inquiry process. Further, although teachers felt free to experiment and take risks in their classrooms, a school-wide understanding of and commitment to powerful learning had not really emerged.

The uneven implementation of the Accelerated Schools process can be attributed to factors both external and internal to the school. The major external factors relate to district and state mandates. Rutledge, like most other schools attempting to initiate reform, finds it difficult to balance the demands of meeting district and state mandates, while trying to make informed, research-based decisions. After a positive first year as an accelerated school, the Rutledge faculty was told by school district officials at the beginning of the 1992-1993 school year that they needed to prepare for a visit from the regional accreditation body, Southern Association of Colleges and Schools (SACS). Although the SACS process and the Accelerated Schools process complement each other to a certain degree, considerable time was spent by cadres preparing sections of the SACS report that were unrelated to their Accelerated Schools work. Momentum was lost during this time in terms of using the inquiry process to make decisions. Instead of using inquiry to question and hypothesize, the staff was busy putting together a voluminous report for accreditation.

Another mandated planning process was required during the 1994 1995 school year. At this time, all schools and districts in South Carolina were required to complete a strategic planning process and a 5-year plan as a result of recent legislation—The Early Childhood Development and Academic Assistance Act of 1993 (Act 135). Five-year plans included the following components: beliefs, vision, mission, learner standards, needs assessment, performance goals, strategies, action plan, and evaluation. As with the SACS planning, the Act 135 planning complemented the Accelerated Schools Project process.[3] However, creating the plan took attention away from the cadres' focus and forced the school community to identity strategies and develop action plans without the benefit of careful inquiry. Teachers experienced 2 years of researching and putting together reports for external agencies. The intensity of that work was high and drained away some of the energies that may have been spent in moving the school forward in the Accelerated School Project.process.

---

[3]In South Carolina schools have incorporated learner standards from the Act 135 strategic planning process into the Accelerated Schools Project process because they encourage schools to focus on student learning.

In addition to these external factors, a number of internal factors also influenced implementation. First, the school community received intensive, direct coaching in the first year, but for a variety of reasons the coach became less involved in monitoring their progress in subsequent years.[4] Although the coach remains involved in the school, she was not able to maintain the initial level of involvement. Second, by being the first accelerated school in the state, Rutledge received considerable positive feedback from groups visiting the school. Although this praise was appreciated, it probably prevented them from reflecting on weaknesses, seeking help for problems, and keeping up with adaptations made by the South Carolina Accelerated School Satellite Center to the decision-making process, governance structure, and concept of powerful learning. Third, the Rutledge faculty, like most other faculties, found the inquiry process slow and unnatural. Teachers are accustomed to making quick decisions and are not familiar with the slow, messy process of researched-based inquiry. The demands for 5-year action plans required by both SACS and Act 135 did not help develop commitment to the inquiry process.

RUTLEDGE ELEMENTARY SCHOOL—1999

Rutledge is beginning its eighth year as an accelerated school, and the entire school community is proud of the changes that have occurred in that time. The physical facility is greatly improved because of the persistent efforts of the facilities cadre, the principal, and a group of parents. Student discipline is no longer an issue. The principal recently explained to a community organization that in the 8 years since she has been at Rutledge, students who were once eager to display their street smarts and fight at the drop of a hat now behave like little children. They giggle, engage in fantasy play, and dream of bright futures. Discipline is no longer an issue in the school, and reports of behavior outside of school are good. Teachers report that representatives from museums and parks frequented by school children find that Rutledge children are unusually well behaved. Children are treated with respect and affection; in turn, they treat the staff and faculty with warmth and respect.

Student achievement has improved since 1991 as indicated by a steady rise in standardized test scores.[5] Changes in standardized scores are presented in Table 2.2. In addition to students scoring higher on standardized tests, the number of students identified as gifted and talented has also increased over time. Parent involvement in the school has increased, and parents report that they feel

---

[4]Christine Finnan, one of the co-authors, was the original coach for Rutledge. As the project grew, her responsibilities made it difficult to continue to provide intensive coaching. In addition, faculty at Rutledge took pride in doing it their own way.

[5]In 1991 all schools in South Carolina took the Stanford 8. Beginning in 1995, schools administered the Metropolitan Achievement Test 7.

TABLE 2.2
Student Achievement as Measured by the Metropolitan
Achievement Test [MAT7]

Grade 1 MAT7	1995-1996	1996-1997	1997-1998
Reading	62	60	70
Math	57	54	60
3 R's	n/a	57	59
Grade 2 MAT7	1995-1996	1996-1997	1997-1998
Reading	37	41	54
Math	44	64	50
3 R's	n/a	57	50
Grade 3 MAT7	1995-1996	1996-1997	1997-1998
Reading	30	32	40
Math	59	61	65
3 R's	n/a	48	62
Grade 4 MAT7	1995-1996	1996-1997	1997-1998
Reading	24	39	27
Math	29	64	57
3 R's	29	47	48
Grade 5MAT7	1995 1996	1996-1997	1997-1998
Reading	13	11	27
Math	33	31	64
3 R's	23	22	46

welcome at Rutledge. During spring 1998, Charleston County School District sent out surveys to parents in all its schools asking for levels of satisfaction with academics, discipline, safety, cleanliness, parental involvement, school as inviting, communication, and involvement in decision making. When the 77 schools in the district were ranked, Rutledge was ranked Number 1 in parent satisfaction. Parents are very supportive of the faculty and the principal, although the principal and over half of the faculty are White. Parents are able to see past skin color to know that the principal and faculty truly care for their children.

Although Rutledge has made impressive gains in many areas, the school as a whole recognized that it needed to engage in a revitalization of its involvement in the Accelerated Schools Project. As part of this revitalization, it revisited the vision created in 1991, the Act 135 learner standards created in 1994, and has begun to take stock of where the school is now in relation to the vision and the learner standards[6]. This process began in spring 1998 and contin-

---

[6]In South Carolina all accelerated schools structure their taking stock to focus on where they are now with the vision and the learner standards.

ues. As a result, the school created new cadres: reading/language arts, math, science, social skills, and social studies. The cadres are currently taking stock and have been retrained in the inquiry process. They have indicated a desire to better understand powerful learning at both the classroom and school level and to make a connection between powerful learning and state content standards.

Rutledge is an example of a school where the philosophical fit between the Accelerated Schools Project and key actors, especially the principal, makes it a showcase accelerated school, although it does not exemplify use of the decision-making process or make special efforts to encourage school-wide powerful learning activities. The following data, drawn from two research studies,[7] illustrate how a school can exemplify the importance of a strong commitment to the Accelerated Schools Project philosophy. That they have not always followed the prescribed process perfectly should not detract from the effect that strength of conviction brings to a school.

---

[7]Data used in this case study came from two studies conducted at Rutledge Elementary School. The first study was conducted by Dr. Julie Swanson during the 1996-97 school year. This year-long study included two additional schools and had several sources of data: classroom observations; interviews at each school with the principal, selected teachers, and persons from the school community; and document review. Interviews were the primary data source with observations and document review serving as points of triangulation. Twenty-six persons were interviewed from all three schools; five of whom were from Rutledge. Interviews were taped; they were 60- to 90-minutes long; notes were made from the interviews and used along with the taped interviews. Classroom observations were conducted in two classrooms at Rutledge. Observations were conducted in the fall and the spring; during each period observations were conducted from 3 to 5 days for approximately 4 hours daily. Observer's comments were kept separated from fieldnotes. Documents reviewed included parent and teacher handbooks, ASP cadre reports, meeting agendas, and demographic and achievement profiles of the schools. Four features of the study design strengthened its trustworthiness (Lincoln & Guba, 1985). First, the use of multiple methods of data collection increases the likelihood of representing varied perspectives. The use of a variety of sample populations (teachers, parents, district, and community persons, principals) and the use of interviews, observations, and document review strengthens the study's credibility. Second, the audit trail of research (Lincoln & Guba, 1985) includes the researcher's journal, taped interviews, transcribed notes, fieldnotes, unitized data, the wallpaper approach (Maykut & Morehouse, 1994), and varied charts leading to inductive discoveries provides the reader with evidence to judge the study's trustworthiness. Finally, the use of a peer debriefer and member checks helped during and after the data analysis process and allowed the researcher to see potential bias and make that bias explicit as well as check for accuracy of description and interpretation (a more detailed description of the study can be found in Swanson, 1997).

The second study was conducted in Spring 1998 by Christine Finnan. Dr. Finnan has a long history of involvement with Rutledge, serving as the school's first coach and maintaining close contact with the school in a number of capacities. The study is part of a series of research projects on school culture. The research began in 1991 with an ethnographic study of the first year of implementation of the Accelerated Schools

INTEGRATING REFORM INTO SCHOOL CULTURE

The philosophy of the Accelerated Schools Project has been internalized into the school culture at Rutledge. Through the words and actions of the faculty and administration, through the behavior of children, and through the involvement of family members and the community, it is evident that the three principles and values described earlier are alive in Rutledge's school culture. Through previous research and a review of the literature on school culture, we have identified five aspects of school culture that determine both the effectiveness of schools and the ease with which a school will exemplify a reform model:

- the beliefs and assumptions about students held by adults,
- the beliefs and assumptions students hold for themselves and their peers,
- the beliefs and assumptions about adults (teachers, parents, administration) held by adult members of the school community,
- the educational practices that are considered acceptable by the school community, and
- the reaction of members of the school community to change.

These components are used to frame the discussion about Rutledge's progress in its efforts to reform education. The professional literature paints a negative picture of the school culture in most schools serving low-income and minority students. Studies document evidence of adults holding low expectations for

Project (Finnan 1992, 1996; Finnan & Hopfenberg 1997). This study inspired further literature review on school culture, resulting in the development of a set of components of school culture (Finnan & Levin, 2000; Finnan & Swanson, 2000). The study reported here represents an effort to examine the culture of a school engaged in a reform effort through the lens of the identified components of school culture.

The data were collected through semi-structured interviews with Rutledge teachers and the principal. Teachers were asked to volunteer to be interviewed. Interviews lasted approximately 40 minutes and were conducted during school hours. A substitute was provided to cover teachers' classes during the interviewing process. Twelve teachers and the principal volunteered to participate in the study. The pool of teachers represented five teachers who were at Rutledge before it joined the Accelerated Schools Project and seven who were hired more recently. They represent all grade levels (except kindergarten/pre-kindergarten), special education, and special areas. Their experience ranges from 24 years to 2 years as classroom teachers.

Teachers were asked broad questions about each of the five identified components of school culture. The responses were recorded both through written notes and tape recording. Once the interviews were completed, a list of responses by component was developed. This list was analyzed for consistency of response and divergent patterns. The validity of the analysis of data was checked by comparing the data to that collected previously by Dr. Swanson and by asking a sample of the interviewees to review a draft of this chapter.

low-income and minority students (Brophy & Good, 1970; Darling-Hammond, 1997; Ford, 1996; McQuillan, 1998; Oakes & Guiton, 1995; Smith, 1980). Other studies show that students, especially high school students, have developed low expectations for themselves and their peers (McDermott, 1997; McQuillan, 1998; Solomon, 1992). Teachers in schools serving low-income students are often treated as inferior to other teachers (Darling-Hammond, 1997; Metz, 1978; National Commission on Teaching and America's Future, 1996; Sizer, 1984); parents are seen as part of the problem (Fine, 1991); and principals are encouraged to be authoritarian and concerned only with control (Christensen, 1996; McQuillan, 1997). In addition, studies illustrate that the educational practices used in most schools serving low-income students focus on remediation and drill and practice (Knapp, 1995; Means, Chelemer, & Knapp, 1991; Oakes & Guiton, 1995). Because of a concern with control and order, teachers are discouraged from trying anything that might stimulate students (McCollum, 1994; McQuillan, 1998). Schools serving low-income and minority students are often told to change, but they are rarely given the opportunity to determine how they should change. Following wave after wave of externally imposed, failed change, teachers become resistant to change, adopting the attitude that "this too shall pass" (Cuban, 1990; Sarason, 1996).

Obviously, highly successful schools are at the opposite end of the continuum from the schools described before. Everyone in the school holds high expectations for students and for the adults associated with the school. Educational practices are exciting, relevant, and challenging, and change is welcome and planned for as much as possible by school community members. The question for this case study is, where is Rutledge Elementary School on this continuum of change? The following describes the school culture at Rutledge in the words of the faculty and administration, giving the reader a sense of where Rutledge Elementary School is in the change process.

The Beliefs and Assumptions About Students Held by Adults

Rutledge faculty is consistently described as having high expectations for all students and a belief that all students have strengths. The following are several descriptions provided by the faculty:

> We assume that all kids have the ability to learn, and they have the right to be treated equally.

> Most of the teachers treat kids like their own. They care for them.

> Everyone has extremely positive attitudes. They believe each student can excel, and they don't expect anything different.

> All people at Rutledge have the belief that every child can be successful. It is beyond just saying it. Every meeting has to do with the children and how to make them successful—even the facilities cadre; they worked to see how the building could be fixed to accelerate learning.

This positive belief in the students' capacity was not always a part of the school culture. Several veteran teachers described how this belief in all students has grown recently. One teacher said that before the current principal and the Accelerated Schools Project came, they had no focus. She said, "Each teacher was an island. Accelerated Schools gave us a focus and opened communication." Another teacher who has been at Rutledge over 20 years said, "There has been a change. The faculty didn't think kids could do well. They didn't put much effort in. At the same time, there were good teachers who pushed. . . . This faculty now all wants to see kids succeed and do well." The principal commented that the inclination to blame parents and children has essentially disappeared and been replaced by a belief in all children. She said, "All kids can learn. We went through a period where people said this but didn't believe it. Now more believe. They are looking for the key to unlock what is in the child. Now they are behaving as if they believe." Classroom observations support the notion that teachers hold the expectation that all students listen, respond, and do their work. A strong work ethic is evident in students; they consistently involve themselves in learning.

There is evidence in classroom observations of some inconsistencies in what teachers say they expect and the level of challenge offered students. In one of the classes observed, one student finished most assignments quickly and easily; the level of challenge of those assignments was too low for him. However, he was not given anything different or more challenging. In the other class, assignments were open-ended so that students could respond in a variety of ways. This approach to providing students of varied levels of achievement the opportunity to stretch fits with what teachers at the school say about their expectations of students.

Teachers who have taught in other schools find the culture at Rutledge unusual. One teacher said,

> I have never been in a school with such positive views of kids. That's why we are so successful with kids who have been behavior problems at other schools. I now have a boy who was asked to leave another school. We had a rough time, but in the other school he was out of class every day. Here he has only worked with the resource teacher ten days; he has only been sent home twice. There is an attitude that these [difficult] kids are going to be successful.

A striking example from classroom observations supports this positive and respectful attitude toward students and their differences. For example, a second grade classroom had a verbally gifted student, an autistic student, and two severely emotionally handicapped students. The teacher created a community where students helped and supported each others' learning through interaction among individuals and small groups. This classroom illustrates that young children can be accepting of others' differences and willing to help each other learn.

When asked why a culture of high expectations exists at Rutledge, the teachers credited the principal, the Accelerated Schools Project, and the collective beliefs of the faculty. Teachers describe the principal as a role model. One teacher commented, "Teachers see her attitude toward students, and they model after her. She is the driving force. She wants everyone to have a part, and with the Accelerated Schools Project, that actually happens. She wants a team that works together." Another teacher said that a lot of the attitude at Rutledge has to do with the principal, but also, "so many people believe the same and since so many believe, they bring people along. Fifteen years ago, kids would be held back in first grade. That would not happen today." The daily announcements in the school are thoughtful and respectful, reinforcing the value of respect that flows between students and teachers.

The Beliefs and Assumptions Students Hold for Themselves and Their Peers

The teachers reported that students hold high expectations for themselves and others. Some teachers stated that nearly all students hold high expectations for themselves. One teacher said, "They hold high expectations for themselves. We try to set them high but reachable goals. When they get frustrated, they work through it. They have a lot of pride and are very determined. It is really neat to see the light bulb go off." Another teacher added, "Kids can have high expectations if you teach them to. Kids go with the person who facilitates. If you have high interest in them, they will see it." The second-grade class described earlier exemplifies that high expectations exist among students. The students in that class were there to learn; observations provided evidence that those students expected to learn. In the observations of the fourth-grade class at the school, students held the expectation for themselves that their job was to do their work. As one of the teachers stated earlier, those students really followed the tone set by their teachers and worked up to the expectations held by those teachers.

Other teachers agreed that students hold high expectations, but they usually qualified this statement. Teachers indicated that they would like all students to hold high expectations for themselves, but they recognize that the community, family situation, peer pressure, and students' innate ability and inclination to work can limit the expectations students hold. For example, one teacher said,

> There are a range of expectations. They have an awareness of what's available. Some are highly motivated because of what is at home. Others have no vision. They go through the motions. Education is constantly helping

people know their potential and the beautiful things in the world. There are those who just want to play every day. We have to deal with them. It would be great to just take those who want to learn, but we can't leave the others behind.

Although there is evidence that students have high expectations for themselves, there is also evidence that the influences of home and poverty negatively impact influences on these expectations.

The Beliefs and Assumptions About Adults (Teachers, Parents, Administration) Held By Adult Members of the School Community

There is universal agreement among teachers interviewed that Rutledge has a strong, highly committed faculty that is interested in the children and taking responsibility for the school. Teachers repeatedly reported that they teach at Rutledge by choice. For example, one teacher said, "Lots of teachers taught at lots of schools, but they choose to come here. Teachers find this [setting] to be a challenge. They can really make a profound change in kids. No one is here because they have no other option." Another teacher added,

> People in the community ask, "Why do you stay there?" Overall, teachers are not looked at with lots of respect. I stay because I know I'm good. No one is here because it is a last resort. People are here because they love the kids. We have a faculty with diverse backgrounds and beliefs. The belief that all children can learn ties us together.

Another teacher echoed her statement,

> I taught in a private school in an inner city for seven years. People have the impression that only new teachers go to the inner city. Teachers in the inner city have to be highly creative; they need multiple plans. They need to create an atmosphere to create experiences for kids since the kids haven't had many experiences.

Although the teachers indicated that Rutledge's school culture encourages deep commitment to students, it allows for a diversity of approach. The principal was repeatedly praised for her willingness to support diversity in teaching. For example, "There is freedom to teach in a style you want. The administration backs you up and sends you to workshops that you and she find interesting." Another teacher described the principal by saying,

The expectations are high. She takes a professional view and wants us to maintain it. We have teachers with different styles which are all respected. She encourages teachers to expand their repertoire as long as it supports success. I know that the principal will back my decisions so I make more professional decisions.

Teachers also reported that the Accelerated Schools Project process contributes to a culture of professionalism among the faculty and forges trust and empowerment. For example, a veteran teacher said,

We expect to see more professionalism from each other than in other schools. As a group we are aware of how as individuals we contribute to the image of the faculty. The level of professionalism has risen in both conduct and education. The Accelerated Schools Project gives us the opportunity to make decisions. We have been given a passport; the gate opens and we have permission to look for new ways. Most teachers deep down feel they can reach all the students, but the system has us so hemmed in that even though we feel that way, we don't always act. Accelerated School opens it; it makes us sassy.

As indicated, the principal contributes greatly to a culture of high expectations for the school community's adult members. Teachers repeatedly credit her with promoting and supporting their professional attitude and growth. As one teacher said, "She builds on strengths. For example, she wanted me to do more hands-on teaching. She said it in a non-threatening way, but she wants growth. She supports my efforts to grow. She doesn't insist or desire a cookie cutter teaching style. We are diverse and like it. We teach in the style we are comfortable with, but we keep the door open for new ideas." The principal described her philosophy: "My expectations for teachers is to do whatever you need to do for kids to learn. Be a problem solver, don't push the blame on others. . . . There was a feeling that we are pretty good and leave us alone. Rather than force them to be a certain kind of school, I encouraged individual change—teacher by teacher—rather than school wide."

The teachers' comments provide evidence that the adults who work in the school expect to grow, learn, and become better at what they do with students. Comments are positive and hopeful, indicating a level of trust among teachers at Rutledge that fosters a respect for and places a high value on differences. The comments also point to the expectation that, although the school is involved in a school-wide reform effort, change has to happen on an individual level.

Expectations from the faculty and staff for parental involvement are high and, at present, are not being met. Teachers reported that parents appear to feel welcome in the school, but they are not as actively involved as the teachers would like. As one teacher said, "The majority of parents are concerned about their kids' education. They bring them and pick them up. They talk to the teachers at that time. They are involved, but not to the point they need to be. They don't look at the school as a whole—only about their own child." The principal talked about some of the ways she had worked to involve parents more in the school community. She said, "Do not assume they [parents] don't care about their children. Once barriers [teachers hold] break down and there is a willingness [for teachers] to think about parents in a different way, the parents and children respond differently. That [response] begins a cycle that is mutually reinforcing."

The principal also pointed to the success that parents experienced when they lobbied for school building improvements. The school board heard their collective voice and has begun to act. This success of "working within the system" helped build the confidence of parents that they could indeed act as advocates for their children's education. The principal continued, "You have to help parents feel comfortable in the school. Teaching children is more than just what takes place in the classroom. If you don't have parent support, and you don't have the community support, you are impeding progress."

Observations before and after school confirm that parents frequently visit with teachers and parents and teachers interact comfortably with each other. Teachers meet parents positively and welcome them into the classroom. The two parents interviewed for one of these studies were involved in school governance and as volunteers. Both of them knew parents who were not as involved as they could be.

The Educational Practices That Are Considered Acceptable by the School Community

Eclectic is a term repeated frequently to describe the acceptable educational practices at Rutledge. One teacher said, "It is very eclectic. Each teacher has a style. In fourth grade each teacher is very different, but we borrow from each other. We formed the fourth grade style. We will try anything if it works for kids. We are flexible and try different things. Styles are mixing." The principal recognizes the need to allow for individual style, but recognizes underlying similarities.

> What is common? A respect for children, lots of work, student validation. The instructional practices are as varied as any teacher from the most traditional to the most creative. I allow them to be themselves and to be reflective about what is happening in the classroom. This way we have better instruction. You can't force them in a way they find artificial.

The Accelerated Schools Project provides a frame for making sure that that "all children learn at high levels." A traditional teacher at Rutledge described how the principal and Accelerated Schools had influenced her style of teaching as well as her philosophy of teaching:

> [Our principal] could have initiated some of these beliefs without Accelerated Schools—but Accelerated Schools gave us the framework . . . she [the principal] encouraged us to take risks and try new things. . . . When I came here, my desks were in rows, and I was pretty formal with the children. . . . I used to be a traditional teacher, some would still call me that. . . . I used to teach the textbook, and now I teach children. I am a lot more child-centered now. . . . That [change] has come through education and freedom to develop that.

Interviews with this teacher revealed that the principal gently nudged and encouraged her to experiment with different teaching strategies. The principal used positive examples of classroom instruction to clearly illustrate to teachers what she wanted them to be doing, rather than negative, "don't do this" examples.

Another teacher confirmed this freedom for each teacher to find her own style. She said, "[Our principal] allows each teacher to teach her own way. . . she doesn't confine you. . . . She puts a lot of opportunities before us, and we can take what we want. We have freedom and support."

Observations in classrooms, too, provide evidence of very different styles of teaching. One observed class was quite traditional, with the textbook as the source of knowledge and the teacher as the director of learning. Another classroom was the opposite, with student learning being shaped by students' experiences and the teacher using student knowledge as the starting point to build classroom learning. In one classroom, much of the time was spent on individual seatwork; the other classroom was lively and interactive, with students working in whole groups, small groups, pairs, and individually.

Much of the teaching as described by the teachers fits the Accelerated Schools Project definition of powerful learning. Teachers described a desire for teaching to be engaging, interactive, and learner-centered. The focus is on the child and finding ways for all children to learn. As one teacher said, "It goes back to powerful learning. In the classes that I most often visit, I see projects that grasp kids' interest; they are hands-on. Kids are actively involved. We try to think about developmentally appropriate activities." A veteran teacher reflected on changes in educational practices: "I've seen changes over the years. At the lower level, you see centers and hands-on activities. The biggest change I like is at the fourth and fifth grades. They used to expect the kids to sit and listen to lectures. Now they do more hands-on. They do things with teddy bears, manipulatives."

The Reaction of Members of the School Community to Change

A veteran teacher sums up the attitudes expressed by many Rutledge teachers toward change:

> Change just to change isn't necessary. I have seen so many things come and go. Every two to three years the county [school district] changes things.

> Some resist change, but once they see it as working, it is easier to do.
> Accelerated Schools allows us to make our own changes. We can decide to
> throw this out and try something new. We feel empowered to [make those
> changes we see fit].

Other teachers mentioned that change usually brings on fear and insecurity, but
that the Accelerated Schools process helps. For example, "Accelerated Schools
guides change. It is an organized way to reach consensus and goals." Another
teacher added,

> If people are unsure, insecure, they are more resistant to change.
> Accelerated Schools guides change. It isn't a quick fix. But there is no
> quick fix available. It involves attitudes, ideas, values that need to change.
> Freedom carries a lot of responsibility. You can't say yes to the "want to
> do" and ignore the "have to do." Because we are given so much freedom,
> so many choices, we have to make good choices.

The psychological climate at Rutledge makes the environment conducive to change. Teachers often spoke about feeling supported in trying out
new approaches, taking risks, and learning from what they were doing. The
encouragement and support provided by the principal was consistently heard in
interviews and seen in the observations. Rutledge's principal said:

> I try to have a leadership style that I would want as a classroom teacher. . . .
> [As a classroom teacher] I know that I wanted to have some control over
> some of the decisions that were made. I was the one when the rubber hit the
> road. I was the one next to the kid, so those decisions needed to be mine. . . .
> I wanted to make some decisions based on what I knew about my kids. So,
> I tried very hard to provide for the teacher an environment in which they
> can feel okay about making those kinds of decisions.

A teacher concurred, "I really feel like our opinions matter—that our ideas are
important and respected. That this is our school."

When the principal first took over at Rutledge, she allowed the teachers to make a "big mistake" that they then had to remedy without her help. The
principal tried to advise them as they were making the decision. However, the
teachers went ahead against the principal's recommendation. When teachers
realized their decision was in error, they had to "fix" what they had done.
Allowing teachers to make their own decision and live with the responsibility of
correcting the decision was empowering to teachers and helped establish trust.
The entire school community learned that empowerment coupled with responsibility was an ideal that the principal supported through her actions and not just
her words. The principal demonstrated an understanding that change involves
taking risks and making mistakes and that learning can result from mistakes.

Teachers' comments indicate a comfort level with the Accelerated Schools process; the process helps them change what they do.

CONCLUSION

As the data show, the Accelerated Schools Project philosophy is integrated into the school culture at Rutledge Elementary School. This is evident in the way teachers talk about their work and their children, in the way students interact with each other and with teachers, in the easy rapport exhibited by parents and teachers, in the student work that covers the halls, and the messages sent daily by the principal through memos, announcements, and on the daily news. This school is a thriving example of doing for all students what you would want for your own child. A unity of purpose exists, teachers understand that to be empowered to make decisions involves taking responsibility for these decisions, and efforts are made by everyone in the school community to identify and build on strengths.

It is clear from this research that it would be erroneous to claim that the Accelerated Schools Project created the school culture that now exists at Rutledge. It would be equally erroneous to conclude that the school culture at Rutledge caused the successful integration of the Accelerated Schools Project philosophy in the school. In fact, Rutledge exemplifies the symbiotic relationship that must exist for schools to successfully implement school reform models like the Accelerated Schools Project.

The Accelerated Schools Project is a complex mixture of a philosophy and a process. It is not a reform that can be implemented by following a standard script. Equally, school cultures are a complex mix of philosophies (beliefs, values, assumptions held by all members of the school community) and processes (processes for educating children, guiding interaction among and between adults, and for moving children through a larger system). When schools choose to join the Accelerated Schools Project, the symbiotic relationship between the reform and the school culture begins. Where the Accelerated Schools Project grows and develops, the symbiosis that develops between the project and the school culture nurtures and feeds the school. The roots of the Accelerated Schools Project and the school culture grow deep into the heart of the school and change occurs that benefits all children. This process reminds teachers and administrators why they chose to enter the teaching field; it gives them a sense of pride in their work and challenges them to continually strive to be more effective.

The irony in this case is that, by many measures, Rutledge would not be a showcase accelerated school. It has not implemented the inquiry process in a textbook manner, and powerful learning does not emanate from every classroom. Even the principal—the greatest booster for Rutledge—acknowledged that her school would probably not meet a set of foundational standards she is helping the

South Carolina Accelerated Schools Project develop. When assessments of effectiveness are determined solely through implementation checklists or rubrics, the complexity of implementation and the importance of the symbiosis between the reform's philosophy and the school's culture disappears.

As stated, this case points to the difficulty of implementing and evaluating complex school reform initiatives like the Accelerated Schools Project. This complexity exhibits itself in a number of ways.

First, the project seeks to change teacher practice, but it does not prescribe how to do so. The Accelerated Schools Project has not developed curricular materials or instructional handbooks. Teachers do not attend training sessions outlining a step-by-step process to change their teaching practices; they are not given an instructional manual and set of materials and told "do this." In fact, the concept of powerful learning is presented to teachers as a broad concept that is open to multiple interpretations. Broad as it is, most teachers realize that it describes an approach to teaching that is very different from standard practices. Some are frustrated that they are not given clear steps to implement powerful learning, whereas others welcome the opportunity to build their own set of strategies appropriate to their own teaching style and needs of their students. Obviously, it is difficult to evaluate the effectiveness of the Accelerated Schools Project in changing teacher behavior because uniformity in what they are expected to do does not exist. If all teachers were given a set of curricular materials and an instructional manual and taught how to use them, it would be easier to assess the materials' effectiveness. Given that teachers and school communities make their own determinations of what is powerful learning, standard evaluation methods are difficult to apply. As described, Rutledge Elementary has been successful in improving students' scores on standardized tests. This is a positive indication of the effectiveness of the teaching at Rutledge, but standardized tests are not always the best measure of student learning, especially of learning to think, apply, and reflect.

Second, the Accelerated Schools Project provides a decision-making process foreign to many schools. Most planning processes provide a vehicle for setting goals, conducting a needs assessment, and developing action plans. These processes are usually completed by a small group of teachers, administrators, and possibly parents in a short period of time (often in a few months). Strategic planning typically results in a checklist mentality, in which the school community members outline a diverse set of actions that they think might help their school. These actions are often the type that are easily checked off a list. The school community often meets all its goals, but does not make any lasting changes in the school culture or student achievement.

In contrast, the Accelerated Schools Project provides an ongoing planning and implementation process. Planning in an accelerated school involves allowing actions to build on prior actions. Setting actions to be taken 3 or 4 years in the future is counter to the ongoing research base of the Accelerated Schools Project. This process can be frustratingly slow, and it is foreign to those comfortable with more typical strategic planning. As this case study illustrates, the strength of this more intensive approach to planning can be diminished by demands from external agencies to engage in more traditional strategic planning (e.g., regional accreditation, state-mandated planning processes).

This case also illustrates the difficulty in assessing the effectiveness of using the Accelerated Schools Project process. Most members of the Rutledge community would admit that they have not always used the process in its pure form. The many reasons for this have already been described. That the Rutledge community decided that it needed to be retrained in the taking stock and inquiry process demonstrates its realization that it could be even more effective if it made better use of the process. The message here is not that schools can become accelerated schools without using the process, but that we need to understand why they fall away from using it and what we should do to encourage their continued use of it.

Third, the Accelerated Schools Project seeks to involve the whole school community (i.e., teachers, parents, administrators, students, other members of the wider community) in making changes. Involvement of everyone leads to deeper commitment to change, but it also makes decision making slower and more complex. No two communities are the same, and techniques to encourage involvement that work for one school community will not necessarily work for others. Each school needs to determine how to involve its members in this research-based process and how to accommodate people's diverse desires and needs (e.g., those who are impatient with the process and want instant action and those who are reluctant to take action until every aspect of an issue has been thoroughly researched). Evaluation of this aspect of involvement in the Accelerated Schools Project is also difficult because this is an area of great diversity. A head count of involvement does not paint a meaningful picture of what involvement of the whole school community really means.

Fourth, the Accelerated Schools Project builds on a philosophy that is easy to support verbally, but harder to support in action. The belief that all students benefit from challenging and engaging curriculum and instruction flies in the face of conventional wisdom. It is difficult to convince some teachers and parents that children who struggle with the basics, especially reading, often excel when offered a chance to apply higher order thinking skills. Additionally, it is easy to say that diversity of opinion should be sought, but it is more difficult when that same diversity appears to delay actions supported by the majority of actors. It is easy for school communities to fall back into old patterns, beliefs, and values related to student learning because they represent the conventional wisdom held in the wider community. That is why reforms like the Accelerated Schools Project do not take hold in schools that do not have a strong cohesive culture like that found at Rutledge. Short of conducting case studies of schools, it is difficult to assess commitment to a philosophy. As this case study illustrates, one does not gain a true understanding of the integration of a philosophy into the school culture without spending considerable time in the school and asking deep questions.

In summary, this case study of Rutledge Elementary School illustrates that, to make lasting change, a school community needs to work on cultivating the integration of the reform philosophy and school culture. If these do not mix, implementation of complex reform projects such as the Accelerated Schools Project will result in little more than surface changes. Those interested in encouraging all schools to become involved in comprehensive school reform initiatives need to recognize that both implementation and evaluation of these reforms is difficult and complex. These reforms have no user manual, and there is no one picture of what the ideal accelerated school looks like. Proponents of comprehensive school reform models must constantly strive to find a productive balance between foundational standards of the model and the specific needs, conditions, and dispositions of the school implementing the model.

REFERENCES

Brophy, J., & Good, T. (1970). Teachers' communication of differential expectations for children's classroom performance: Some behavioral data. *Journal of Educational Psychology, 61*, 365-374.

Christensen, C. (1996). Toward a new leadership paradigm: Behaviors of accelerated schools' principals. In C. Finnan, E. St. John, J. McCarthy, & S. Slovacek (Eds.), *Accelerated schools in action: Lessons from the field* (pp. 185-207). Thousand Oaks, CA: Corwin.

Cuban, L. (1990). Reforming again and again. *Educational Researcher, 19*, 3-13.

Darling-Hammond, L. (1997). *The right to learn: A blueprint for creating schools that work*. San Francisco: Jossey-Bass.

Dewey, J.(1990).*The school and society*. Chicago: University of Chicago Press.

Fine, M. (1991). *Framing dropouts: Notes on the politics of an urban public high school*. Albany: SUNY Press.

Finnan, C. (1992). *Becoming an accelerated middle school; Initiating school culture change*. Stanford, CA: Report to the Accelerated Schools Project.

Finnan, C. (1996). Making change your friend. In C. Finnan, E. St. John, J. McCarthy, & S. Slovacek (Eds.), *Accelerated schools in action: Lessons from the field* (pp. 104-123). Thousand Oaks, CA: Corwin.

Finnan, C., & Hopfenberg, W. S. (1997). Accomplishing school change: The journey of an accelerated middle school. *Journal for a Just and Caring Education, 3*(4), 480-493.

Finnan, C., & Levin, H. M. (2000). Changing school culture. In H. Altrichter & J. Elliott (Eds.), *Images of educational change* (pp. 87-98). Milton Keynes, UK: Open University Press.

Finnan, C., St. John, E., McCarthy, J., & Slovacek, S. (Eds.). (1996). Resources, 297-303. In C. Finnan, E. St. John, J. McCarthy, & S. Slovacek (Eds.), *Accelerated schools in action: Lessons from the field*. Thousand Oaks, CA: Corwin.

Finnan, C., & Swanson, J. D. (2000). *Accelerating the learning of all students: Cultivating culture change in schools, classrooms, and individuals.* Boulder, CO: Westview Press.

Ford, D. (1996). *Reversing underachievement among gifted black students.* New York: Teachers College Press.

Hopfenberg, W. S., Levin, H. M., & Associates. (1993). *Accelerated schools resource guide.* San Francisco: Jossey-Bass.

Keller, B., & Huebner, T. (1997, March). *Powerful learning in accelerated schools: Researching the opportunities for implementation as well as impediments of developing powerful learning school-wide.* Paper presented at the annual meeting of the American Educational Research Association, Chicago, IL.

Knapp, M. (1995). Introduction: The teaching challenge in high-poverty classrooms. In M. S. Knapp & Associates (Eds.), *Teaching for meaning in high-poverty classrooms* (pp. 1-11). New York: Teachers College Press.

Levin, H. M. (1985). *The educationally disadvantaged: A national crisis.* Philadelphia: Public/Private Ventures.

Levin, H. M. (1986). *Educational reform for disadvantaged students: An emerging crisis.* Washington, DC: National Education Association.

Levin, H. M. (1996). Accelerated schools: The background. In C. Finnan, E. St. John, J. McCarthy, & S. Slovacek (Eds.), *Accelerated schools in action: Lessons from the field* (pp. 2-23). Thousand Oaks, CA: Corwin.

Lincoln Y., & Guba, E. (1985). *Naturalistic inquiry.* Beverly Hills, CA: Sage.

Maykut P., & Morehouse, L. (1994). *Beginning qualitative research: A philosophic and practical guide.* London: Falmer Press.

McCollum, H. (1994). *School reform for youth at-risk: Analysis of six change models* (Vol. 1). Washington, DC: Policy Studies Associates.

McDermott, R. (1997). Achieving school failure 1972-1997. In G. D. Spindler (Ed.), *Education and cultural process* (3rd ed., pp. 82-118). Prospect Heights, IL: Waveland.

McQuillan, P. (1998). *Educational opportunity in an urban American high school.* Albany: State University of New York Press.

Means, B., Chelemer, C., & Knapp M. (1991). *Teaching advanced skills to at-risk youth.* San Francisco, CA: Jossey-Bass.

Metz, M. (1978). *Classrooms and corridors: The crisis of authority in desegregated secondary schools.* Berkeley: University of California Press.

National Commission on Excellence in Education. (1983). *A nation at risk: An imperative for educational reform.* Washington DC: U.S. Department of Education.

National Commission on Teaching and America's Future. (1996). *What matters most: Teaching and America's future.* New York: Author.

Oakes, J., & Guiton, G. (1995). Matchmaking: The dynamics of high school tracking decisions. *American Educational Research Journal, 32*(1) 3-34.

Sarason, S. (1996) *Revisiting "The culture of the school and the problem of change."* New York: Teachers College Press.

Sizer, T. (1984). *Horace's compromise.* Boston: Houghton Mifflin.

Smith, M. L. (1980) Meta-analysis of research on teacher expectations. *Evaluation in Education, 4*(1), 53-55.

Soloman, R. (1992). *Black resistance in high school: Forging a separatist culture.* Albany: State University of New York Press.

Swanson, J. (1997). *Factors which support and inhibit the use of gifted and talented teaching strategies with Title I students.* Charleston, SC: College of Charleston.

3

West Hollow School and the North Carolina A+ Schools Program: Integrating the Arts, Crafting a Local Agenda for Reform

Amee Adkins
Illinois State University

Michael Gunzenhauser
Oklahoma State University

Imagine a learning community that embodies Howard Gardner's (1983) theory of multiple intelligences, expressing it specifically by using the arts as a basis of instruction. Children in this learning community visit at least one arts classroom daily, and during the course of the week they receive instruction in drama, music, dance, and visual arts. They do not learn art for art's sake alone. Rather, the curriculum they experience integrates the arts and other subject areas within thematic units shared across grade levels and occasionally even school-wide. Classroom teachers and arts specialists collaborate together to design experiential, hands-on instructional activities to convey these thematic units.

The hallways and school calendar are replete with other artifacts of this approach to teaching and learning. Student products are displayed in classrooms, on hallway bulletin boards, and sometimes in special galleries near the main entrance of the school. The collections reveal considerable variation in the ways students have chosen to express what they have been learning. Some sets are based on using a particular medium, such as a collection of different rag weaves, tie-dye patterns, or percussion instruments. Others depict content areas, such as models of different lighthouses that coincide with a study of coastal heritage and mathematical scale or a class mural depicting a tropical seaside.

Of course, not all products are static displays. Some are performances and demonstrations by students that take place in class, before the student body, or as part of a public event. The school calendar notes that the fifth graders are hosting a PTO meeting during which they will present a play they wrote and choreographed about their study of ancient indigenous peoples of the Americas. Once a month at lunchtime in the local public library, classroom representatives come together for a community meeting to present an overview and examples of their most recent unit project. The children are poised and confident in front of an audience.

This arts-enhanced learning community plays frequent host to "artists in residence," who share their craft and skills with students. At times these events serve as anchor points for thematic units; at others they are positioned to introduce or culminate an area of study. For example, an elementary school hosts two visual artists who share a specialty in Japanese art forms: one, a potter demonstrates raku firing; another, a calligrapher helps third graders develop a Japanese-English dictionary. In the meantime, in their classrooms the students learn about Japan in social studies, read and write Japanese haiku in language arts, and in art they fire their own pots using different methods and learn the art of origami. Other engagements may not be as elaborate: Artists or performers come in for a single day to offer a series of class demonstrations or school assemblies.

If this sounds too good to be true, that is because it is an idealized depiction of a comprehensive reform model being implemented in the North Carolina A+ Schools Program. All of these activities are going on, just at different schools. In many ways, this depiction remains the ideal to which schools in the network aspire, as teachers and administrators continue to explore ways to deliver the model of integrated, arts-based instruction. In practice, schools have selected priorities from among the elements in the previous depiction. Some have chosen to emphasize the aspect of hands-on instructional techniques, while others have embraced the idea of integrating the curriculum across subject areas and the arts. Still others tapped into the opportunity to build stronger connections with the local community, using A+ as a way to bring local talents into schools and A+ performances as a way to draw community attention to their work. As of the 1999-2000 school year, there are 35 schools participating in the network of A+ Schools Network, and there are virtually 35 different versions of A+ in action. This variation seems fitting given that this particular comprehensive reform is premised on the value added to education based on general premises of the value of arts integration, thematic instruction, and exploring multiple forms of intelligence. The shorthand name for the program—"A+," which stands for "Arts Plus"—vaguely connotes excellence without necessarily making the arts central to its public image. The schools have adapted the premises of the program to their local contexts, interpreting the central ideas of the program and implementing change that respects various goals and localized constraints. Each school is a case study in educational reform.

This chapter presents a case study of one of the A+ schools, the West Hollow School[1], a preK-12 school in the rural Appalachian Mountains of North Carolina. West Hollow School is a vital part of a community that sees itself in a struggle for cultural and economic survival, and the school's participation in the A+ Schools Program is bounded by its ties to the community and its teachers' strengths and interests. West Hollow teachers have taken what they have learned from A+ training institutes about arts integration and thematic instruction and modified it to support their own goals for the school. Instead of following the A+ model directly, West Hollow has developed a hands-on orientation to curriculum integration using a broad definition of the arts to encourage wider participation by the faculty, students, and community in the process of integrating instruction. Hands-on instruction at West Hollow connects the A+ Program to other, complementary initiatives at the school to serve the larger goals of preserving the community and providing for an economic future.

This chapter describes how the West Hollow community learned to craft its own agenda for reform. West Hollow learned lessons from the A+ Program and pushed beyond the constraints of geographic isolation and limited local financial resources to explore a future with the assistance of outside funding sources that still allow the community to retain control of its own destiny. What follows is a comprehensive review of the possibilities originally imagined by the A+ Schools Program's sponsors, the North Carolina Thomas S. Kenan Institute for the Arts. Following that is a more sustained portrait of West Hollow, presented as one school's experiences with the A+ Program and an account of how the possibilities of A+ enabled West Hollow to craft its own agenda for local reform.

INSTRUCTIONAL CHANGES: INTEGRATED INSTRUCTION THROUGH THE ARTS FOR MULTIPLE INTELLIGENCES

When planning began in 1993, the Kenan Institute for the Arts envisioned the A+ Schools Program as an initiative based largely on the needs of local schools. What began as a small pilot project in two elementary schools in southeastern North Carolina developed into a larger pilot project of 25 additional schools statewide, clustered in four regions of the state. The schools selected to participate had sent representatives to planning meetings, during which educators and arts advocates helped the Kenan Institute develop the fundamental ideas of the program.

---

[1]All names have been changed.

As envisioned, The A+ Schools Program brings together Gardner's (1983, 1993) theory of multiple intelligences, thematic instruction, integrated curriculum, and an infusion of the arts to provide a new approach to teaching the standard curriculum, known in North Carolina as the Standard Course of Study. Two interests drive the program: increasing academic engagement and achievement, and promoting a wider general appreciation of the arts. Specifically, the program emerges from the belief that the arts appeal to multiple intelligences, therefore they are a way to provide opportunities for children to learn more effectively.

According to Gardner, intelligence is not a singular capacity. Instead, he argued that people have multiple domains of intelligence, including linguistic, logical-mathematical, musical, spatial, bodily-kinesthetic, interpersonal, intrapersonal (1983), and naturalistic (1993), although schools traditionally teach primarily through the first two. The theory of multiple intelligences contends that instruction adapted to the full range of intelligences will increase students' facility across the range of intelligences. The A+ Schools Program is rooted in this perspective of learning, but it emphasizes the arts, in particular, as an effective way to structure this adaptation.

Integrating instruction with an emphasis on the arts suggests multiple benefits for students in an A+ learning community. Even though students may see several teachers throughout the school day, their learning activities share common themes. The students have opportunities to transfer content, and the teachers are able to reinforce concepts and ideas. Integrating curriculum with instruction through thematic units lends itself to more holistic attention to the concepts that form the state curriculum. It also enables teachers to incorporate more experiential, hands-on activities, which appeal to a broader array of learning styles among students. Children frequently comment that they learn better when they "see it," or "do it," or "draw it." When these activities are arts-based, the students also experience an affective benefit: They create their own unique product as they learn new content. This raises an important distinction about an arts-enhanced learning community: Children engage in creative and expressive processes, not cookie-cutter, follow-the-directions "art" activities. Students not only see their work featured, but they also see how their classmates express what they are learning.

Performances provide students with other avenues for demonstrating what they have learned and give them valuable experience communicating before an audience. Public performances in particular draw parents and the community into school to see the kinds of learning activities taking place and allow them to appreciate the place of arts and multiple forms of intelligence in students' learning. Displays of student work in the school building, in local businesses, and at art shows are additional opportunities for students to perform, and they connect students more fully to the larger community. Early experiences with A+ have demonstrated increased student attendance, decreased discipline issues infractions, increased parental involvement (at least in the form of attendance at performances), and overall gains in student engagement with their learning activities.

PROFESSIONAL DEVELOPMENT: LEARNING TO TEACH THROUGH THE ARTS

Although some of the A+ Schools had begun implementing some aspects of the A+ program beforehand, most teachers in the A+ Schools were not prepared for this pedagogy of integrated, arts-enhanced, experiential education when the program began in the 1995-1996 school year. Many teachers had been exposed to thematic instruction and arts integration, yet most were trained in traditional teacher preparation programs that presumed disciplinary-based curricula, methods, and structures. Most of their professional experience has been spent teaching in isolation so that they have had sole responsibility for developing units and planning instruction. Furthermore, both their preparation and practice emphasized traditional assessment methods of highly structured written tests and assignments. Many were intuitively disposed to this more holistic and aesthetic view of teaching and learning, but nearly all needed knowledge and skills to implement it. Teachers need professional development on how to adapt the curriculum to themes, how to integrate the arts into daily instruction, and how to form structures for working together with arts teachers and other specialists.

Likewise, arts teachers in the A+ Schools were not in a regular habit of collaborating on instructional design. Arts teachers in more traditional settings are isolated by their area's status as "supplemental," especially when several schools share itinerant teachers, whereas arts specialists in this learning community had to learn to plan units with each other and with grade-level teachers. They needed to integrate their own instruction, as well as serve as resources for teachers integrating arts activities in the regular classroom.

Implementing the A+ Schools Program requires the intense need for rich professional development. One source is the typical after-school and inservice professional workshop format that targets particular needs within each school. Adequate funding and time are are not always available to schools to support their unique needs. The A+ Program sponsors annual, week-long Summer Institutes to address issues of more widespread concern among the A+ Schools. The first A+ Summer Institutes in 1995 provided intensive training in multiple intelligences, thematic instruction, and teaching through the arts, and they incorporated substantial time for curriculum development time during which teachers applied what they learned, shared, and expanded ideas. Subsequent Summer Institutes have been less lengthy, but have continued to bring teachers together with arts educators, practicing artists, and curriculum specialists. This has helped establish connections and reinforce the network of educators and resources that teachers may draw on during the school year.

Collaboration has been key to effective curriculum integration in A+ Schools. The Summer Institutes have provided some guided practice for teachers to collaborate as they developed their instructional plans, but for the most part the art of collaboration is learned in the midst of practice. At many schools, collaboration has been difficult to sustain without regularly scheduled opportunities for common planning. Most schools incorporate grade-level planning into their weekly schedules, allowing classroom teachers to communicate with each other and draw from a variety of resources to make the arts integral to student learning. Planning with arts specialists is more difficult and less likely to be structured. In schools that have effective communication in place, classroom teachers work closely with the arts specialists as they plan common thematic units and integrate their instruction. This cooperative planning facilitates mutual reinforcement of key concepts for students. Also, it allows arts specialists to serve as important resources for brainstorming and developing arts-based learning activities for the classroom. As classroom teachers become more skilled with arts integration, they, too, become resources for each other, swapping ideas for activities and insights for techniques.

Schools have also enhanced instruction by collaborating with community arts resources, hosting artists-in-residence, and tapping into performance circuits, such as Poetry Alive! and the Georgia Sea Island Singers. Often these activities are connected to unit themes. Working with local artisans, such as quilters, book makers, or dancers, can have the same advantage, but they offer the additional benefit of being available locally to collaborate in planning even when they might not be serving in residence. Additionally, most communities with an A+ School also have a local arts council, whose members are available to serve as advisory members in the day-to-day planning for A+ activities and events. To the extent that A+ Schools are located near postsecondary institutions, colleges and universities have offered arts and education faculty who can assist in planning and professional development. These resources have supplemented the quality of arts-based instruction in schools and have reinforced a sense of an arts-enhanced learning community that extends beyond the building walls. In many A+ Schools, collaboration has fostered a collective sense of purpose that invests the community in the school.

A+ ON SITE: WEST HOLLOW

West Hollow School sits along a two-lane road that winds through a narrow valley in the the Southern Appalachian Mountains. The school unites several small, rural communities in the western portion of Hollow County in a preK-12 school of about 425 students. For grades preK-8, there is typically one teacher per grade, with 18 to 28 students per grade, although one grade level is slightly larger and is split into two classes. Another K-8 school feeds into the high school, bringing the K-12 population to about 200 students. The attendance area reaches about 20 miles north and south, and 10 miles east and west, making for many long bus rides on narrow twisty mountain roads. The county is isolated from the rest of the state, several hundred miles from the state capital, closer in fact to six other states' capitals than its own.

Much like other rural areas in the South, poverty is evident throughout the community, with few service businesses or employment opportunities. A mining company and a hydroelectric operation once employed hundreds of workers, but they have cut back substantially on their employment in the past 25 years, and few new manufacturing industries have filled the void left in the labor market. In 1995, per capita income in Hollow County was less than $14,000—among the five lowest income figures among the state's 100 counties (Kinney, 1995). In the past, plant closings have led to decreases in school enrollment, but for the past 15 years enrollment has remained stable. More so than in the past, residents are commuting daily or weekly to cities for work, although the nearest city, Rockland, is about 75 miles away. "Kids live with mothers while dads go off during the week to work. They come back on weekends" (Teacher). Farming in the rolling hills of Hollow County is no longer profitable, although many residents supplement their income by raising small herds of cattle.

In the midst of commercial and economic flux, community leaders in West Hollow recognize the need to find alternatives. In 1996, the county began extending water and sewer lines toward West Hollow to encourage and prepare for potential growth. The community has seen a growing number of retirees moving into the area and anticipates an increased tourist market in the years ahead. "Tourism seems like the most promising industry for the area" (Administrator). At the same time, there is a recent rise in the number of professionals moving into Hollow County—a move made possible by the flexibility of telecommuting and one made attractive by the perceived simplicity of life in a rural area. "There is a range economically from poverty row to extremely affluent" (Administrator). As a result of these recent transitions, some in the community anticipate a change in culture should more outsiders move into the area.

West Hollow demonstrates a long history of a fragile economy that makes the community vulnerable to external forces. The newest trends represent yet another episode in that history, and once again the community's identity is at stake. The teachers and administrators at West Hollow School are keenly aware of this pattern of vulnerability. They perceive it in terms of the community, and many define part of their educational mission as preserving their local culture and heritage in a changing economy. One significant way to do that is to ensure that the students do not have to leave to be able to support themselves. As an administrator expressed it, "The community is losing its best and brightest due to a lack of employment. Creating employable skills is vital to the continued life of our community. Keeping our sons and daughters as members of our community is a primary goal." In fact, a large part of the story of West Hollow and the A+ Schools Program revolves around this mission.

West Hollow School also feels a more direct impact amidst economic pressures—namely, a push in the county to consolidate community schools into fewer, larger, and more comprehensive units. Talk of consolidation began in the early 1990s, and the school board held community meetings for each of the three high schools. More than 150 people turned out at West Hollow to oppose consolidation—about five times the number at each of the other two meetings. According to the school counselor, their resolve comes "because the school is their life, their community, and if you're talking about consolidation, you're talking about getting rid of the school. That would kill the community." At the time, the school board agreed to maintain all three high schools, but the threat of consolidation lingers in Hollow County. The principal and teachers believe the best way to maintain their school, and thus their community, is to find a useful niche and fill it extremely well.

For the time being at least, the small size and geographic seclusion of West Hollow and surrounding area contributes to a community of people who describe themselves variously as "close-knit," "conservative," and "proud." "Christianity is a strength. Most children are Christian, and there is a family atmosphere" (Teacher Assistant). The teachers are a stable force in the school, which boasts a low turn-over rate, and about one third of the staff at West Hollow grew up in the community. In fact, in 1 year, a teacher counted 17 family connections among staff and students. "We had a game the other night. . . . We probably had eight or nine hundred here, and that was on a Monday night" (Teacher). As the center of the community, West Hollow School has a role tied closely to the community's past and future.

MAKING IT FIT: ADAPTING A+ TO THE COMMUNITY

As the center of the community, West Hollow School has a role tied closely to the community's past and future. This is a weighty matter that figures constantly in educators' minds as they plan to educate West Hollow children. When they consider new opportunities or address emergent problems, they must count the impact not only on resources and learning, but on the community as well. Ideally they only undertake alternatives that enhance all three. Sometimes this means they avoid efforts that pose significant threats to any of them.

Because the school is remote in the contexts of both state and district relations, West Hollow staff have become accustomed to and adept at resisting mandates they think are not in the school's and community's best interests. Rallying parents in opposition to the consolidation initiative is a prominent example of this. Another example is West Hollow's response to the state's school accountability program, implemented during the 1996-1997 school year, the second year of the A+ Schools Program. Whereas West Hollow has embraced other state initiatives, the accountability program generated considerable anxiety and frustration. The program is known as the ABCs of Public Education, with ABC standing for accountability, basics, and local control. West Hollow teachers have resented the intrusion of legislative power and see it as a threat to local control. The controversy stems from the narrow definition of *effective education* implied by the standards movement.

Keeping pace with recent educational trends, North Carolina has adopted a standards and accountability model like others that took hold across the nation in the late 1990s. School effectiveness is tied to test scores on standardized tests in math, reading, and writing. The state board of education has prescribed performance scales to assess schools' progress. Schools that demonstrate expected growth over time are eligible for teacher bonuses. Schools that fail to meet growth standards are ineligible for bonuses; schools failing growth standards and that have 50% or more performing below grade level are declared *low performing* (note here that grade level is a figure based on prior averages). Of these schools, the lowest performing receive state-appointed assistance teams. Although the program tends to earn the state high marks from policy makers for measures such as improving teacher quality" (Jerald, 2000; Manzo, 2000), as some researchers have found, it has resulted in widespread teacher dissatisfaction and deemphasis on nontested areas:

> Although the state does not go so far as to eliminate the study of science, social studies, or the arts, the plan stipulates that "principals are free to focus additional instruction in other subject areas as they wish." The result is that science, social studies, and the arts are subjects that are pushed aside and taught only if there is extra time left in the schedule. (Jones et al., 1999, p. 200)

West Hollow students have generally scored above the state averages on standardized tests and have been able to dodge negative publicity associated with test score performance. In the 1996-1997 school year, when high schools were not included in the testing formula, West Hollow did not meet its growth standard. It avoided being named a low-performing school that year by having, by the state's account, nearly 70% of students testing above grade level. In subsequent years, the school has met the state's exemplary growth standard, which has qualified the school for teacher bonuses. In 1998-1999, West Hollow was one of 66% of the state's public schools that were named as exemplary (in a year in which only 16% of schools did not meet expected—or average— growth; North Carolina Dept. of Public Instruction, 2000). As suggested by the high number of schools that have performed exemplary feats in test score growth, West Hollow has taken a strategy common to many North Carolina schools. After 3 years of experience with the accountability program, educators at West Hollow have learned to attend to test score improvement while pursuing their own goals.

West Hollow does not reject all outside influences on its educational mission. At the same time, in assessing the educational and social needs of West Hollow, teachers have embraced several innovations based on their unique contribution to the school's mission. One peculiar adaptation, the conga band, demonstrates West Hollow's commitment to students' interests. Probably nowhere would one be more surprised to find a conga band, equipped with a storeroom full of pan drums, tropical print shirts, and palm branches than in a small union school in the Appalachian Mountains. Old-time string music or bluegrass may come to mind as possible specialties, but not Caribbean music. The band director abandoned the traditional marching band or orchestra mainly because the cost of instruments and uniforms proved prohibitive in economically stressed West Hollow, but also the student body is too small to support a full complement of instruments anyway. Forming a conga band was a unique opportunity because the music director knew someone who makes steel pan drums. He negotiated a feasible deal with the musician that enabled the school to gradually amass more than 20 steel drums. Moving to common percussion instruments, purchased at a discount and through school-based fundraising efforts, West Hollow is able to host a full and energetic band that not only performs at community and sporting events, but also successfully competes nationally.

Another initiative, Project REAL, accommodates student and community interests. Project REAL is funded by a grant from Levi-Strauss, a major textile presence in the region. REAL is an entrepreneurial program that provides high school students with business planning and managing experiences to develop the skills necessary to start their own businesses. The program is headed by a vocational arts teacher who gears it toward the noncollege-bound West Hollow students. Working with instructors from a nearby community college, local small business owners, and area trades people, he helps students determine products to manufacture or services to offer, develop business plans, create marketing materials, and implement their plans. Funds from Project REAL provide support for students 5 years beyond graduation, with an overall goal of incubating future small businesses in the local community. REAL offers a response to the area's fragile economy by cultivating home-grown, independent businesses to keep young people in the community and bolster the economic infrastructure.

DRAWN TO A+: WEST HOLLOW JOINS
THE A+ SCHOOLS PROGRAM

Much like its participation in Project REAL, West Hollow's participation in the A+ Schools Program demonstrates its willingness to join an outside initiative as long as it does not lose control. A district administrator first introduced the idea of participating in A+ to the principal and the secondary visual art teacher at West Hollow. The aspect that originally drew their attention was the program's grounding in Gardner's multiple intelligences theory, with which Laura Ellwood had become familiar. Furthermore, its promise of funding to support professional development in integrated arts instruction and its claim to enhance student achievement especially appealed to the principal, Ted Johnson. An important consideration was the degree of local discretion built into the program implementation. Ellwood and Johnson knew their faculty and community well enough to know that they would not stand for association with a highly prescriptive reform agenda, nor would they likely cooperate with an even moderately prescriptive program if it contradicted their collective sense of the students' best interests.

Both Ellwood and Johnson had several opportunities to meet with representatives from the Kenan Institute, and Kenan agents repeatedly described their vision of A+ as a grassroots reform. They said they provided a broadly stated vision for an arts-enhanced learning experience, but they fully expected schools to flesh out the practice of that vision for themselves. Their vision encompassed six components: "daily arts instruction; weekly arts (visual arts, music, drama, dance); curriculum integration; thematic planning; Gardner's theory of multiple intelligences; and community partnerships" (Corbett, Wilson, & Noblit, 1996, p. 4). Kenan staff assured school representatives that schools would be free to interpret the Kenan Institute's Vision to fit the individual school and equally free to implement the program in ways that made the best sense given local circumstances. West Hollow, just as any other schools that applied, weighed the opportunities embedded in the A+ Schools Program against the risk of micromanagement later in the process.

As it turned out, most of the schools that joined the A+ Schools Program were elementary schools. There were only a few middle schools, and West Hollow was the only school to include a high school unit. This, too, afforded them a unique measure of independence as they implemented the reform because they were somewhat on their own in learning how to alter and integrate the traditionally rigid disciplinary distinctions of secondary education.

As the implementation progressed, many of the A+ Schools experienced the normal tensions associated with change efforts. Some struggled to keep the vision of arts-enhanced instruction in focus. Others were frustrated by their struggles and wanted to look to the Kenan Institute for answers. Meanwhile, Kenan representatives worked through their own struggles to negotiate a balance between supporting implementation efforts, but not prescribing them. Other schools seemed satisfied with forging their own definition of "A+ in action" and were less concerned with fulfilling external expectations at least as far as A+ was concerned. They and others still had to contend with the statewide standards and accountability movement, as well as typical local pressures in terms of budgets, basics, and various politics.

West Hollow was not immune to these tensions. Indeed, West Hollow teachers reported feeling all of them, at least at various points. The following sections review their progress with implementing the ideas of A+, including their challenges, obstacles, and adaptations in the process of reform.

PROGRESS TO DATE

From Collaborative Planning to Cooperative Linkages

Throughout the A+ Schools Program, teachers faced the challenge of learning to collaborate with their colleagues and plan thematic units to integrate the subject area curricula. Some schools with three or four classes per grade found a solution where administrators arranged the weekly schedule of *specials* (arts and other special classes such as library, computer lab, and P.E.) so that at least once a week each grade level had common planning time. Specialists typically met together first thing in the morning or during lunch. Many schools also scheduled monthly or quarterly meetings with specialists and grade-level teams to enhance their unit plans with arts-based activities. Nearly all schools had a communication structure in place through which grade-level teachers informed arts specialists of their unit plans, although in some cases it was in the form of memos or bulletin boards.

Smaller schools like West Hollow, however, struggled to find ways to bring teachers together to integrate subject areas and the arts. With only one teacher per grade and often specialists onsite only part time, no amount of creative scheduling could bring them together consistently. Most of the specialists at West Hollow shared responsibility for serving elementary, middle, and high school programs, further tightening their time constraints. Under these circumstances, collaborative planning was incidental, rather than systematic. Likewise, the quality of integration depended greatly on whether a teacher was already disposed to find connections across the subjects, as opposed to resulting from organized professional growth and development.

These issues seemed frustrating from the perspective of implementing fully integrated units. However, a different vantage point sheds light on the opportunities the A+ program created for them. The principal noted at a faculty meeting, "A+ has been the greatest thing for opening up communication and working together. I really think we're doing a better job now because you know what your neighbor is doing and can help out." A teacher likewise noted the benefit of increased communication even if it did not amount to full-fledged collaboration:

> The difference I can see with what we're doing here and other schools I've worked in is the communication between the arts teachers and the classroom teachers. Ideally, it's that we get our planning done in a group setting. In reality, that very rarely happens. It's just either me sharing my unit plans with other teachers. Or the elementary art teacher comes and asks, "What are you doing? How can I help you out? Here's something that I need to do, do you have something that I can do that works in with that?"

Increased communication is certainly not the equivalent of collaborative planning, but it is nevertheless a benefit to participation in the program for the teachers at West Hollow.

Between small staff and block scheduling in the high school, teachers at West Hollow found it difficult to arrange time to plan together or even communicate with each other about their unit plans. A middle school teacher described her method of collaborating this way:

> The truth? I meet them in the hall! Just whenever I can get them. Just like yesterday, we were starting a new science [unit], and I wanted to get it in before Christmas, so I could start with animals. I met [the music teacher] in the hall. When did I get [the elementary art teacher]? Oh yeah, she was out here in the hall putting art work out in the wall. So really, it's just whenever. We do have a group once every six weeks. But really whenever I need it, I say, "Hey, I need some help on this."

Many of the classroom teachers agree that specialists are eager to accommodate their requests, even ones made while passing in the hallway. However, the limitations of this method are clear. It is difficult to keep track of spontaneous requests and follow up on them. It is also difficult to manage teaching plans when new suggestions and ideas keep popping up. In the absence of systematic collaborative planning, it illustrates how the burden of making connections can fall on the specialists' shoulders. Ideas may come from the classroom teachers, but in the prior example, the arts specialists are the ones to implement them.

These kinds of connections made at West Hollow are better described as links rather than collaboration. Increased communication among faculty have helped them recognize opportunities to connect their topics, but the constraints have often prevented them from planning tightly integrated units. Groups of teachers have linked their classroom instruction through activities, events, or visiting artists. These served as centerpieces that crossed several classes and provided a sense of a shared school experience across classes and grade levels.

As an example, West Hollow made curricular links around visits by two local craftspeople—an herbalist and a weaver. A science teacher in the high school unit had invited a Native-American herbalist from the community to talk about varieties of local plant life and their traditional uses as food, medicines, and dyes. During lunch one day, she mentioned this to Laura Ellwood, who teaches visual arts and an Appalachian Studies course. As they ate, Ellwood quickly suggested connections to other curricula, such as folklore in language arts classes and geography and history in the social studies curriculum. They identified teachers in those areas from the elementary, middle, and high school units and arranged a schedule of times during which the herbalist could meet with different classes. Through this informal lunch conversation, an elaborate set of opportunities emerged.

Several teachers coordinated units in conjunction with the herbalist's visit. Biology students worked through a unit on identifying and classifying plants. The chemistry class studied the chemical processes of rendering plant extracts. Another class, Appalachian Studies, focused on traditional methods of using plant extracts to dye yarn and decorate pottery, as well as the craft of quilting and the heritage of different patterns. When the herbalist met with the biology students, she led them outside to identify and gather various indigenous plants. They classified them according to their use as decorative, medicinal, and edible. The Appalachian Studies and chemistry classes met together with her and they prepared the plant samples to make several basic dyes. The students experimented with different combinations and then dyed samples of wool to see the result. Their samples were hung for display on a wall in the main entrance of the school.

Shortly after the herbalist's visit, Ellwood coordinated an extended visit from a local quilter, Julie Richards. Richards spent several days over a period of 3 weeks, working with middle and high school students. She met with a high school computing class to demonstrate graphic design for quilting patterns. Meanwhile, a math class overlapped with that activity by making paper quilts using repeated geometric patterns. The quilter spent most of her time on site working with small groups of students. She set up a spinning wheel and several looms in the school gallery, located off the main hall, so that students could take turns spinning yarn and weaving rugs. Using their scheduled time for art classes and any other free time they had during the day, middle and high school students visited the gallery in groups of three and four to make their rugs. By the end of Richards' visit, the students' rugs filled the gallery floor and walls and spilled out into the hallway.

The work with the herbalist and quilter created an integrated learning experience for many of the high school students. Likewise, Richards' activities provided a point of integration between the middle and high school students in their visual arts curriculum.

This example demonstrates how teachers at West Hollow—the secondary teachers especially—transformed the A+ notions of *collaboration* and *integration* into their own notions of *cooperation* and *links*. Their links tend to be sporadic, although not necessarily infrequent. That is, every year offered many instances of instruction linked through special events and it became a fairly regular part of school life at West Hollow. Still the links were generated by an occasion so that they did not lead to systematic changes in curriculum to daily instruction. This is a reversal of the ideal imagined by the Kenan Institute, where an occasion is attached to a set of planned integrated instruction perhaps as a culminating activity.

Nevertheless, this form became the most consistent and effective strategy for getting the high school teachers at West Hollow to work together. This pattern seemed to reflect the professional culture of secondary teachers. As one administrator explained,

> At the high school level they are much more discipline-oriented. . . . As students become older, maybe they can internalize the relationships among the disciplines themselves. Maybe they don't need the teachers to make the connections for them.

Teachers were more willing to step outside their subject areas of expertise if they had a working relationship with someone from a different subject area.

As such, most of the collaboration at West Hollow emerged from existing social networks among the teachers. Common planning time was scarce during the regular school day, leaving only informal times—such as passing in the halls, before and after school, and lunch—for impromptu discussions of their ideas. Lunch groups came to be the richest opportunity for identifying links across their classrooms. A core group of about five high school teachers, including the art, science, math, and home economics teachers, eat lunch together regularly in the home economics room and are sometimes joined by others. There they share casual conversation about current events, personal matters, and local gossip, and quite regularly their talk has turned to their work at school, including ideas for new units and opportunities to invite guests for special activities. Their conversations take off as they see new ways to bring their classrooms together or try new activities in their own classes.

The home economics lunch group formed the central social network that anchored West Hollow's A+ program efforts to cooperate on A+ activities, but each has ties to other social networks in the school by virtue of specialty area, friendship, and family relation. Through these secondary networks, opportunities for instructional links spread beyond the core group. Some of the richest connections involved links to the vocational program. For example, to complement classwork in her Appalachian Studies and visual arts classes, Ellwood invited a knife maker and basket weaver to demonstrate how they used traditional methods to create their pieces. The home economics teacher noted that her class could benefit from time with the basket weaver, and she also suggested that the vocational teacher would be interested in incorporating into his class the metal working aspect of the knife maker's process. The three teachers worked out the details of the visit, and the artisans set up their materials in the shop room. Ellwood arranged a schedule for various classes to visit their station and watch demonstrations of their crafts. For vocational students in particular, she scheduled longer periods with the knife maker, who helped them learn to use the forge and work the metal into rudimentary forms. In a conversation about the visit, Ellwood shared her objective for the vocational students—that the knife maker would awaken them to entrepreneurial artistic possibilities in the world of metal working. Meanwhile, for her visual arts students, both his knives and his wife's baskets illustrated the concept of functional art—items that served as tools but also conveyed creative interpretations.

A handful of teachers, however, were not connected to any of these networks. One interesting dynamic involved a group of male teachers who constituted their own social network through involvement with different athletic activities. They remained uninvolved in nearly all A+-related activities. These men did not necessarily oppose the A+ Schools Program, and they were willing to cooperate in some of the activities, but they were unlikely to initiate projects. Late in the second year of implementation, the core A+ network began looking for strategic opportunities to draw in the less involved faculty. In one instance, West Hollow scheduled an engagement with an outfit called "Poetry Alive!", which sends a team of actors to work with large groups in the auditorium and go into individual classrooms to perform selected poems. In this, they saw an opportunity to link with the male English teacher who agreed to have the "Poetry Alive!" actors come into his class for a workshop. Since then, he has used more activities in his class, such as skits and role-playing.

By virtue of its K-12 structure, West Hollow discovered many opportunities to connect the secondary students with the elementary classrooms around units in science, social studies, and math. They discovered this process in their second year of implementation when the school dedicated a teacher workday to reviewing the school-wide curriculum. Teachers learned to use the special events as vehicles for making connections across grade levels. The herbalist's visit, mentioned earlier, provided an opportunity to link the senior level biology course and the fourth-grade social studies curriculum. Ellwood facilitated this linkage through her knowledge of the learning standards for each grade level. High school students taught the fourth graders mini-lessons about identifying and classifying local plants and discussed their traditional uses as dyes and medicine. The fourth-grade teacher used this activity to link her class' work in science and social studies and the elementary art teacher had the fourth graders use the plants they had collected to make acrylic prints of leaf patterns on t-shirts.

All of the A+ Schools struggled with the goal of collaborative planning to integrate instruction, and from those struggles many different processes for collaboration and integration emerged. West Hollow School stood alone among the schools in terms of the challenges and obstacles it had to overcome to bring its teachers together to link their curricula. Relying on existing social networks among teachers has meant that planning takes place more often in casual and impromptu contexts. Cooperation is mostly limited to those who were already part of a network; outsiders tend not to be involved at least until some insiders draw them in through special events. Lacking the flexibility in terms of time and personnel, West Hollow found little opportunity to coordinate systematic planning for integration, so they learned to connect their instruction via links. Other schools in the A+ Schools Program have developed effective planning strategies, whereby teachers work together to integrate their curricula through thematic units. For them, A+ is about learning new ways to plan their instruction. For West Hollow, A+ is about using new opportunities in the midst of planning instruction.

Underlying these forms of collaboration is a significant aspect of leadership at West Hollow that has subtly encouraged collaboration, hands-on instruction, and the arts. This leadership has been crucial for West Hollow's adaptation of the A+ Schools Program. In most of the A+ Schools, the principal or an influential teacher has served as an A+ champion, defined as someone who, when the A+ Program began at her or his school, already understood the possibilities of the arts or integrated instruction. At most schools, this person (in some cases, there have been several A+ champions at one school) played a role in the school's application to participate in the A+Program. If the A+ champion were someone other than the principal, then this person typically became the A+ coordinator or served as an informal resource for teachers invested in the program.

In most cases, A+ became infused throughout a school when the principal either enforced a vision of A+ or facilitated teachers creating their own visions. At West Hollow, the principal's role reflected a combination of vision and facilitation—a leadership scenario that carried over from Johnson's tenure as principal to the principalship of Jane Franklin, who became principal at West Hollow in the middle of the third year of the A+ Schools Program. In his role as principal, Johnson cultivated multiple leaders among his faculty—most who have strong and lengthy ties with the community—and hired Franklin as an assistant principal, hoping that she would succeed him when he retired. Rather than forcing teachers to adopt A+, he encouraged the visions of others (notably Ellwood, the art teacher) who understood possibilities associated with the A+ Program that were not necessarily the same as those intended by the Kenan Institute. He also linked his concerns for the welfare of the community to their concerns for arts-enhanced instruction and successfully bridged a gendered divide between arts advocates and the nonplayers. This leadership style worked well in the relatively loose context established by the Kenan Institute.

ARTS-ENHANCED INSTRUCTION LEADS TO HANDS-ON, FOLK ART EMPHASIS

As it was originally envisioned, the A+ Schools Program was meant to affect the nature of instruction thoroughly. The arts were to become a primary means of instruction in the classroom instead of a supplementary activity in the school day. Multiple intelligences theory helped justify this approach because the arts are natural avenues for engaging students in the learning process. One teacher at West Hollow said,

> We're trying to tap into the experiential aspect, the total experience, to use the visual, for example. Some of our poorer performing students, we've found, do better when they include a visual component. This is the basis of A+, to tap those intelligences, because we realize that the students don't all

learn the same way. They don't all contribute the same way. They need to feel good about school, about the things they're trying to do.

The Kenan Institute emphasized a full complement of artistic forms, including visual art, musical, drama, and dance, as ways to teach curriculum concepts and skills. Through professional development activities and increased collaboration with arts faculty, classroom teachers would cultivate a new approach to teaching their curriculum.

West Hollow's experiences with arts-enhanced instruction revealed many of the same variations in response to the challenge of integrating the arts in their classrooms. These variations seemed to coincide with their willingness and perceived ability to adapt the arts to their classrooms. As with schools throughout the A+ Program, for most of the West Hollow teachers, teaching through the arts presented a learning curve that was longer for some than for others. When the learning curve was relatively modest, particularly for teachers who felt naturally disposed to using lots of activities and projects in their teaching, teachers incorporated more creative opportunities more frequently. When their learning processes were longer, however, teachers relied more heavily on the arts specialists for support, sometimes surrendering the task of arts integration to them entirely and sometimes turning to the specialists for ideas to use in their own classrooms. Others were more traditional teachers who were reluctant to use arts-based methods.

The matter of this learning curve was a complicated issue throughout the A+ Schools Program, but Ellwood developed a nuanced understanding of it in her role as the A+ Coordinator at West Hollow. For Ellwood, the issue was embedded in the ironic nature of A+ as a reform. In her assessment, the intent of the A+ Program was to promote more common, everyday use of the arts in classrooms so that children would learn more effectively and develop an appreciation of artistic forms. What prompted the reform was the typical absence of the arts in classrooms and a widespread lack of appreciation or familiarity with various art forms. The teachers who were being asked to implement the A+ reform were graduates of arts-deficient schools that generated the need for the program in the first place. In other words, part of the purpose of A+ was to make students more comfortable with the creative expression of their ideas using different artistic means, but the teachers who were supposed to lead the change were products of a traditional educational system that rendered the arts unfamiliar. Thus, one of the deepest challenges in implementing A+ was finding ways to help teachers overcome their own anxiety about art, expressed in the sense of sentiments "I can't do that" and "I'm not creative or artistic."

Ellwood and Johnson, in their respective roles as A+ coordinator and principal, sensed that art anxiety might lead teachers to say, "That's not for me," and leave it to the arts teachers to implement. In response, they agreed to downplay references to the arts when they talked about A+. They came to describe A+ as a hands-on program. As Ellwood explained, "We're less about integrated art, but more about hands-on. Making the curriculum more hands-on is more effective, and it doesn't limit the concept of what 'art' is." As an art teacher, she has a broader sense of art as creative expression and conveying perspective, but she recognized that for others there was a sense that art required training, expertise, and aesthetic sensibility. Rather than quibbling over definitions or trying to correct teachers' views, Ellwood opted to bypass the anxiety and avoid explicit references to art among those who seemed intimidated by the concept. Ellwood encourages their forays into hands-on activities, and when asked for suggestions for activities she subtly slips in some art. For example, when a teacher was looking for an activity for a unit on ancestry, Ellwood suggested, "Why don't you ask your students to design their own family quilt pattern?"

Redefining arts as hands-on helped teachers find ways to work with the A+ Program. When asked about A+-inspired activities, they could give plenty of examples that demonstrated Ellwood's goal of encouraging activities that allowed for student expression without necessarily emphasizing art. A science teacher described how she had students "act out the atoms. I asked them to stand up and act out what's happening. It only takes like 2 minutes, but it helps them understand." A history teacher thought of a hands-on activity to teach about the powers delegated by the Constitution: "Instead of just going over the dry list in the book, we got out butcher paper and newspapers and magazines and found visuals that express the powers, and they made collages in groups." Subsuming the arts under the moniker of *hands-on activities* seems to accomplish some of the A+ Program's goals in terms of teaching through creative expression and appealing to multiple intelligences theory; it circumvents some of the anxiety associated with the term *art*.

The same irony of art anxiety had consequences for public relations. Johnson learned that presenting this program to the public required careful language. A+ inspired a controversy among some congregations when it included dance as part of the school day. Among A+ Schools, West Hollow was not alone in this controversy, and many schools came to refer to dance as "creative movement," which seemed less objectionable. West Hollow did not completely abandon the arts emphasis. Instead, they chose to concentrate on traditional Appalachian folk arts and crafts. The visiting craftspeople represent the rich traditions of Appalachia. As examples of functional art, their specialties reinforced the way these crafts blended creativity with utility in Appalachian culture. Further, traditional arts and crafts were familiar forms to the students, teachers, and parents of West Hollow, and they conveyed a sense of cultural pride. Working to connect teaching through folk art reflected a purposeful reinforcement of the bond between school and community, rather than an attempt to reform it with values imported from beyond.

Learning to teach through the arts continues to challenge the A+ Schools Program. In addition to the Summer Institutes, an important way to develop this approach to teaching is through guided practice—the primary method at West Hollow. Ellwood and the elementary art teacher are central to this process because of a shared sense of the possibilities for working with the arts. Other teachers who are more adventurous or more confident also provide guidance by working with others to introduce more hands-on activities or connect their instruction to events associated with visiting artists. Approaching the implementation through guided practice, as well as shifting to a dual emphasis of art as hands-on and folk art, comprise West Hollow's strategy for incremental change. The idea is to bring teachers into the arts-enhanced model slowly, building from what is familiar to teachers so they become neither overwhelmed nor alienated.

BUILDING COMMUNITY TIES THROUGH A+

As the Kenan Institute envisioned the A+ model, they imagined a school-based reform that seeks fundamental changes in teaching and learning through the integration of the arts. Yet they also thought strategically about the nature of school-based reform, and they articulated an approach to change that was driven by the participating schools rather than external mandates. They developed their vision for the A+ Schools Program from the assumption that schools would have to learn to sustain the effort, which meant cultivating community support and learning to navigate local and state politics.

The Kenan Institute addressed the latter concern through the organization of an A+ Schools Network—a structure that could succeed the A+ Schools Program after the 4-year funding timetable ended. The Kenan Institute brought together administrators and teachers from A+ Schools to identify emerging issues and develop responses to them. The Network's initial activities revolved around the issue of assessment. Partly in response to the state's accountability plan, the ABCs of Public Education, teachers at A+ Schools were concerned that they did not have appropriate means for assessing student learning through the arts. The ABCs initiative exacerbated this concern. Many teachers felt frustration that while they were trying to implement a new approach to teaching and learning they would still be held accountable to the end-of-grade test results, which were based on very traditional measures of achievement. School representatives discussed the matter at several Network meetings. As a result, the Kenan Institute drafted a Goals 2000 grant proposal on behalf of the schools to explore alternative assessment methods more in keeping with arts-based instruction. The proposal was funded and has been renewed, with funds underwriting numerous committee meetings and conferences on the subject of assessment. The Goals 2000 support has facilitated communication among schools and given life to the Network. The assessment meetings have given West Hollow teachers opportunities to connect with other schools and have facilitated discussions among teachers about assessment.

Throughout the A+ Schools Program, the Kenan Institute has encouraged individual schools to strengthen their connections with the local community. Some schools initially interpreted the push to connect to the community and showcase the arts as an expectation to produce elaborate student performances. Others set a more modest agenda of highlighting students' work at parent teacher organization meetings. Instead of performances, at many schools teachers coordinated "informances" to share what students were learning in classrooms, but they focused more on presenting content than on the artistry of a performance. The purpose of an informance was to increase familiarity with what students were learning without detracting from the primary efforts of teaching and learning.

Another connection the Kenan Institute encouraged was collaboration with colleges and universities. This was somewhat more challenging for A+ Schools. As originally imagined, departments of education and fine arts would be essential resources for professional development because of their expertise and proximity. The A+ Schools Program experienced uneven levels of success in working with this community partner.

The intent behind all these practices was to build stronger connections with different community sectors because those connections, in turn, could help build a more sustainable and resilient program for change within the school. Resiliency would stem from an enhanced capacity for arts integration, as well as the cultivation of political support in the local community for the work the school was doing.

As the true center of a cohesive community, West Hollow School came to interpret the idea of "building community ties" differently than most other A+ Schools. Instead of tying the community to the school to increase support for A+, West Hollow sought to use A+ as a means to tie the school to the community to reinforce their service to local needs and interests. Like other A+ Schools, they sought to enhance the resiliency of their program, but West Hollow chose to do so by implementing curricular and instructional changes that deepened and enriched their connection to the community.

The staff at West Hollow did not begin their efforts to implement A+ with this idea for connecting with their community. Indeed, initially they shared much the same vision as other schools and the Kenan Institute to build community support for arts-enhanced education. When West Hollow School joined the A+ Schools Program, they already had formed partnerships with the community college and a local utility company, as well as a strong and active parent-teacher organization. These partnerships helped the school enhance its academic programs through fundraising and community networking. The partnerships had been formed earlier for specific purposes, yet Johnson and Ellwood saw an easy transition to add A+-related activities to the range of efforts their partners supported. They also sought new partnerships with the local arts council and two regional postsecondary schools.

Ellwood and Johnson used these partners to access resources and talent to assist the implementation of A+ at West Hollow School. Their business partner and the parent-teacher organization primarily provided additional funds and supplies. The community college and arts council gave them access to artists and arts educators. West Hollow's involvement with artists-in-residence and the focus on traditional Appalachian folk art emerged as a result of these contacts.

During the second year of the A+ Program, the staff at West Hollow began to think more strategically about the patterns that had emerged and to see some of the subtle advantages to working with local artists and folk art. It seemed natural to connect with the community in this way, and it allowed West Hollow to involve the community in the students' learning, rather than simply presenting the community with the students' work. By bringing in community artists, West Hollow changed the nature of instruction by bringing other adults into contact with the students. The key to this success was that the community connection was purposeful, authentic, and somewhat familiar to the students. This provided a natural extension of the curriculum that was more likely to connect with students' lives. The school realized that it did not necessarily need to forge new connections to the community. The school was already connected to the community, and instead they saw their challenge as maximizing the community ties that already existed. By weaving aspects of Appalachian heritage formally into the curriculum, West Hollow School signified its rootedness and commitment to the community. This approach demonstrated that A+ was not an effort to reform them, but rather an opportunity to bring more from the West Hollow community into the school.

APPROPRIATING A+ FOR COMMUNITY-BASED REFORM: MOVING FORWARD

Unlike nearly all of the other A+ Schools, the West Hollow School used the experience of participating in the A+ Schools Program to craft its own agenda for reform. As originally envisioned, the A+ Schools Program took seriously the metaphor of *multiple intelligences* (Gardner, 1983, 1993) and linked the arts to a loosely defined model of arts-enhanced instruction. The definitive components of the original A+ Schools Program, as expressed in the program literature and reinforced in the A+ Summer Institutes, were thematic planning, arts integration, and community involvement. Throughout the program, A+ trainers emphasized a conceptual focus on the Standard Course of Study so that the objective was not to replace the state curriculum, but to teach it more holistically and effectively. Beyond these parameters, the Kenan Institute encouraged experimentation and creative adaptation and facilitated collaboration.

West Hollow School's involvement in the A+ Program represents one of the most creative adaptations of the original program. As a preK-12 union school secluded in rural Appalachia, West Hollow presented multiple contexts that necessitated adaptation. Much like other secondary educators involved in the program, West Hollow middle and high school teachers felt that the program had a predominant focus on the elementary level. Rather than tuning out, West Hollow teachers freely extrapolated aspects of the A+ Program and created their own version, expanding their definition of the arts to encompass hands-on instruction and Appalachian folk art. Their adaptation of the A+ Program's focus on community involvement led to a new agenda for reform.

Emerging from West Hollow's involvement in Appalachian crafts, and particularly the links that teachers made to vocational instruction in the high school, the school received a Rural Challenge grant from the Annenberg Foundation in 1998 at the end of the third year of the A+ Schools Program. Developed in collaboration with several schools in neighboring counties, the grant is intended to support a "pedagogy of place" (Annenberg Foundation, 2000). West Hollow envisions its participation in the Rural Challenge program as a way to encourage students' transition from high school into careers that sustain and enrich Appalachian culture. West Hollow has planned a resource center for Appalachian studies and has sought additional funding to build a traditional log cabin that can serve as a performance and display space. Teachers are also developing hands-on courses that are connected to local heritage.

West Hollow sees Rural Challenge as an extension of the bridge between high school and the workplace that it built through Project REAL and the A+ Program. In the 1998-1999 school year, the fourth and final year of the pilot A+ Schools Program, West Hollow remained committed to the A+ Program, but high school teachers saw a surer fit with the Rural Challenge program and its vocational, hands-on, and regional focus. As evidence of West Hollow's transition, in the Summer of 1998, elementary teachers attended the A+ Summer Institute, the high school teachers attended the Rural Challenge training sessions, and middle school teachers had their choice of the two. Evidence suggests that West Hollow's participation in Rural Challenge reflects the adaptation and creative interpretation that it explored with the A+ Program. A Rural Challenge evaluator commented, "What I liked best about the place is the school does not seem in a hurry to conform to a definition of success that comes from elsewhere."

One way to express the difference between West Hollow's and other A+ Schools' approaches to building community ties is this: Whereas most other A+ Schools sought to cultivate community support for their reform, West Hollow sought to demonstrate their support for the community. Simply related to the effort to connect to the community, this difference seems somewhat unimportant. Yet as their implementation efforts progressed, it became increasingly significant in the effect it had on how the schools conceptualized their work with A+. Schools that cultivated support maintained a primary commitment to the substantive ideas of integrated, arts-enhanced instruction. For West Hollow School staff, however, the shift to demonstrating their support for the community led them to make that their primary commitment. In the process, while they continued to incorporate instructional links and arts-enhanced, hands-on instruction, they transformed the role of A+ in their organizational development. A+ was no longer just a school-based reform as an end in and of itself.

Furthermore, and perhaps more important, A+ became a learning process for West Hollow on how to reform itself. A+ became a springboard to school-directed reform, meaning that West Hollow used its experiences with A+ to better understand its own capacities. It learned to leverage reform opportunities to help it serve an overarching goal—bolstering the social and economic strength of the West Hollow community.

REFERENCES

Annenberg Foundation. (2000). *Place-based education programs associated with the Rural Trust* (http://www.ruraledu.org/launch/projects.html).

Corbett, H. D., Wilson, B., & Noblit, G. (1996) *Interim evaluation report of the A+ Schools Program.* Winston-Salem, NC: Thomas S. Kenan Institute for the Arts.

Gardner, H. (1983). *Frames of mind.* New York: Basic Books.

Gardner, H. (1993). *Multiple intelligences: The theory in practice.* New York: Basic Books.

Jerald, C. D. (2000). The state of the states. *Education Week, 19*(18), 62-88.

Jones, M. G., Jones, B. D., Hardin, B., Chapman, L., Yarbrough, T., & Davis, M. (1999). The impact of high-stakes testing on teachers and students in North Carolina. *Phi Delta Kappan, 81*(3), 199-203.

Kinney, D. (Ed.). (1995). How to get there from here. *Business North Carolina, 15*(5), 13-27.

Manzo, K. K. (2000). North Carolina: The state combines enticements to teach with more rigorous expectations. *Education Week, 19*(18), 142-143.

North Carolina Department of Public Instruction. (2000). *InfoWeb* (http://www.dpi.state.nc.us/accountability/reporting/index.html#ABC).

4

Comer, Efficacy, and Power: What Gregory School Did With the School Development Program

George W. Noblit
University of North Carolina at Chapel Hill

Michael E. Jennings
University of Texas at San Antonio

In 1963 and 1964, researchers at the Yale Child Study Center sought to examine the problems of children who were being excluded from society's social and economic mainstream. They concluded that schools were the natural place to both help and study children (Comer et al., 1996). At this time, the Ford Foundation was actively supporting projects nationwide that utilized the resources of universities to support public education. Researchers from the Yale Child Study Center developed their program at the suggestion of Douglas Ferguson, a Project Officer with the Ford Foundation (Comer, 1993).

Dr. Albert Solnit, Director of the Special Projects for the Yale Child Study Center, and Samuel Nash, Director of Special Projects for the New Haven School System, wrote a formal proposal to begin the study (Comer, 1993). The Ford Foundation accepted the proposal during the 1967-1968 academic year. During this time, officials at Yale as well as the New Haven Schools discussed and refined their conception of the study's guiding philosophy, methodology, and organization (Comer, 1993). Dr. Comer, who was completing his child psychiatry training in Washington, DC, returned to New Haven in 1968 to help direct the fledgling program. The basic premise of the program was that the application of the principles of social and behavioral science to every aspect of the school's program would improve a school's climate by fos-

*tering improved relationships among those involved with the school's opera-
tion. Additionally, researchers hoped that the application of these principles
would foster a significant leap in the academic and social growth of the
school's students (Comer, 1993).*

*Researchers selected Baldwin (K-6) and King (K-4) elementary
schools in New Haven as the first research sites. Ninety-five percent of
Baldwin's 360 students and King's 270 students were from lower and middle
income families. Student records revealed that 98% or more of the students in
both schools were African American. Both schools reported low academic
achievement, serious behavior problems, and poor attendance among their student bodies. Parents and staff at Baldwin and King suffered from low morale
and were clearly frustrated with the conditions surrounding the school's existence (Comer, 1993):*

*Chaos and conflict characterized the program's first year in these two
schools. Many parents were upset with the reform efforts, and many teachers
were angry at what they felt was an attempt to blame them for the school's failures (Comer, 1993). Comer's team shunned the idea of entering the school with
a prepackaged reform initiative guaranteed to cure the ills of the school.
Instead, they attempted to learn, along with the school's teachers, how to best
help the children (Comer et al., 1996). This effort resulted in the creation of a
school level approach to educational reform that would address the full spec-
trum of a school's operation (Comer et al., 1996).*

*Comer's team emphasized analyzing the school as a system to under-
stand the complex interactions occurring within this system. Using paradigms
from the fields of child psychiatry and public health, Comer designed the School
Development Program to allow parents, teachers, administrators, and staff to
understand each others' needs and cooperate with one another in addressing
those needs in an integrated and organized fashion (Comer et al., 1996). His
early efforts forced Comer to realize that teachers, administrators, or parents
rarely accept reform movements without opposition. Thus, Dr. Comer sought to
promote change by encouraging families and staff to:*

> *engage in a process in which they gain knowledge of systems of child devel-
> opment, and of individual behavior and apply it to every aspect of school
> programs in a way and at a rate that is understandable and nonthreaten-
> ing. When faithfully adhered to from the start, these mechanisms help the
> people involved achieve the kinds of small early successes critical to rein-
> forcing confidence in the new program. (Comer et al., 1996, p. 8)*

*To achieve these goals, the SDP organizes the school community (i.e.,
all persons working with the school and those living in the community) into
three teams that together form the foundation of the program: the School
Planning and Management Team (SPMT), the Parent Team (PT), and the
Student and Staff Support Team (SSST). These three teams, referred to as the*

three mechanisms, *guide the decision making of the SDP and ensure that all members of the school community have input into the decision-making process. The three* guiding principles *of consensus, collaboration, and no fault shape the decisions that drive these three mechanisms.*

The concept of consensus discourages the idea of voting on particular issues of concern. Comer felt that voting on specific issues leads to a zero-sum game where there are clearly defined winners and losers in the school's decision-making bodies. Instead, the principle of consensus urges all concerned to work toward an agreed outcome/solution that is acceptable to everyone.

Collaboration encourages inclusion and respect among all members of the school community. Achieving collaboration requires that parents, teachers, administrators, and others involved in the process respect others' points of view. This respect in turn facilitates a willingness to work cooperatively in pursuit of common goals.

The last of the guiding principles involves the concept of no fault *decision making. This principle discourages the assignment of blame for the problems within any given school and requires the examination of problems from such a viewpoint that everyone shares equal responsibility for positive change. This atmosphere of shared responsibility fosters a positive environment in which the children's best interests remain the primary concern of the entire school community.*

The primary mechanism of the SDP is the School Planning and Management Team (SPMT). The SPMT coordinates all school activities and is the school's central organizing committee. Usually led by the principal, the SPMT comprises parents, teachers, and staff. Its purpose is to balance input and representation from the entire school community. The major function of the SPMT is to create and implement a Comprehensive School Plan that reflects the goals of the school community in terms of academics, social climate, and staff development. The SPMT develops and coordinates specific programs to aid in the accomplishment of these goals. Furthermore, the SPMT assesses and monitors the entire process of change in the school and then makes needed adjustments to ensure proper SDP implementation (Comer et al., 1996). This consistent effort to empower local school communities has been the hallmark of the SDP's effort to ensure that all of its actions are in the best interest of the students (Comer et al., 1996).

The Parent Team (PT) seeks to involve parents at every level of school life to foster a stronger link between home and school. At the most basic level, parents participate in support activities such as the Parent Teacher Association (PTA) and attend other school activities and social events. At the second level, parents are physically present in the schools, serving as volunteers or paid assistants in classrooms, libraries, cafeterias, or other rooms as needed. At the third level, parents select other parents to be representatives on the SPMT. As members of the SPMT, they are able to convey the feelings and opinions of parents on a variety of topics that affect the school community. The PT is an impor-

tant aspect of the SDP because it empowers parents through participation in the schoolwide decision-making process. The PT also serves to bridge the often large cultural/socioeconomic gap between home and school that can lead to problems for some disadvantaged students (Comer et al., 1996).

The Student and Staff Support Team (SSST) addresses both macro- and microlevel issues dealing with school climate and the psychosocial development of the students. The SSST includes staff, professionals, child development, and mental health professionals. These include the guidance counselor, school psychologist, school nurse, speech therapist, truant officer, and any other professionals deemed appropriate. The SSST attempts to work preventively and prescriptively in addressing the concerns of individual students and the school community as a whole. The SSST helps design and implement interventions for individual students. On a schoolwide level, the SSST seeks to confront community- and society-wide issues that affect student development. By confronting these issues on both an individual and a schoolwide basis, the SSST works to prevent crises from occurring rather than simply reacting to crises that have already developed (Comer et al., 1996).

Central to the functioning of these three mechanisms is an emphasis on understanding child development. Comer recognized early on that dissonance between school and home would adversely affect student behavior and academic achievement. He felt that the key to reducing this dissonance was to emphasize the proper development of the individual child. Thus, child development is a central component of the Comer Process. Comer emphasized six aspects of child development (which he labeled as developmental *pathways) that, if properly emphasized, would ensure that all children learn and develop to their fullest potential. The six developmental pathways are the physical, cognitive, psychological, language, social, and ethical dimensions of child development. Because each of these dimensions is equally important, Comer emphasized that the dimensions must be balanced for each child to reach his or her fullest potential. Balanced development (i.e., maturity) results from proper linkage between the pathways. Over- or underemphasizing any of the six individual pathways results in unbalanced development.*

The SDP has grown tremendously since its inception in 1968 and has evolved through three stages. The first stage lasted from 1968 to 1978 and began with the use of the SDP in two elementary schools in New Haven, Connecticut. These pilot programs included further development and refinement of the SDP design. The second stage extended from 1978 to 1988 and involved testing the SDP in Prince George's County, Maryland; Norfolk, Virginia; Benton, Michigan; and several other schools in New Haven, Connecticut. Researchers provided training to personnel from school districts and individual schools to implement the SDP. Researchers also began to test the effectiveness of the program in various schools. Results of these studies show that when faithfully implemented, the SDP had positive effects on school climate, which then correlated with positive student outcomes (Emmons et al., 1992; Haynes & Bility, 1994).

The third SDP stage, largely supported by the Rockefeller Foundation, began in 1988 and extends to the present. During this stage, program developers have focused on developing new strategies for nationwide dissemination of the SDP. This third stage of SDP also saw the creation of a training program known as the Comer Project for Change in Education (CPCE), the goal of which was to aid school districts in sustained implementation of the SDP through a "trainer-of-trainers- of model" (Comer et al., 1996, p. 21). Other newly developed programs emphasizing implementation include: development of partnerships with schools of education that orient preservice teachers to SDP strategies, use of Regional Professional Development Centers (RPDCs) to support the implementation of SDPs in specific geographical areas ,the Systemic Implementation (SI) initiative that infuses SDP principles at the district level to ensure continued support by district administrators who oversee individual schools, and the Comer-Zigler (Co-Zi) project, which brings family and community services together in an effort to prepare preschool age children for school (Comer et al., 1996).

GREGORY SCHOOL AND THE SCHOOL DEVELOPMENT PROGRAM

Inner-city schools are expected to be difficult places. Poverty, crime, and race all too often combine with inadequate school resources and poor teaching to create depressing and even dangerous schools. Gregory school was once such a school. Racial strife, fighting in the halls, distrustful parents, lackluster leadership, and uninspired teaching characterized the old Gregory School. The new Gregory School is quite different. It has a dynamic principal; a new school building; the School Development Program; trusting parents; a supportive community; a sense of unity amid differences in race, language, and culture; and a teaching staff focusing on instruction. Student performance on tests has continually improved. It is a good place for kids and adults. Regardless of the difficulties in the neighborhoods that surround the school, Gregory School is more than a place of hope—it is a place of efficacy and power. Gregory School believes it is able to control its destiny in important ways.

Gregory, a kindergarten through eighth-grade school, serves a student body of approximately 650 that is half Chinese and half African American. The students are poor (95% are low income), and 30%, have limited proficiency in English. The teachers are 48% African American, 26% Chinese, and 26% White. Located in Chinatown, its Chinese students and parents are mainly recent immigrants from southern mainland China. Many of these children do not speak English, and their parents often work long hours in Chinese restaurants to make ends meet. Just a few blocks away, but separated by a major expressway, Gregory's African-American students and their families reside in housing projects that are plagued with gangs. Work is hard to find for these U.S. citizens, and welfare traps them in cycles of poverty.

Despite such challenges, the Gregory community is proud of its school. Gregory has overcome a history of racial divisiveness and united two communities behind the school. It has found ways for children to succeed in school, belying both beliefs about inner-city, minority schools in general and its own history in particular. James Comer's School Development Program (SDP) has been helpful in these accomplishments, but the school had already begun its turnaround before it was introduced to the ideas of Dr. James Comer. In this school, the SDP built on a powerful base of support and an existing momentum of positive change: a dynamic new principal, a new focus on the needs of children, overcoming a shared ordeal that threatened to break up the school, and a new beginning in a new building. Although many of the pieces of school improvement were in place before Gregory became a Comer school, staff and students alike acknowledge the value of the Comer Process in focusing and continuing the school's energy for change. As one third-grade girl said when asked about the meaning of Comer: "Comer [means] a good school . . . [that] they have good people there."

This case study traces these changes at Gregory School and explains the place of the SDP (or Comer as it is commonly called in the building) in the reform of Gregory School[1] To do this, we explore the improvements in school climate, customs, and conceptions of children under the leadership of a new principal. The school's newfound unity was tested and ultimately strengthened by a shared ordeal. These changes provided a crucial foundation for the successful implementation of the Comer SDP. We discuss how the SDP built on the school's developing strengths to focus the change process on student achievement. The SDP was a crucial element in the reform of Gregory School. It proved to be a mechanism that school participants could appropriate (Rockwell,

---

[1]This study is part of a larger study of five successful Comer schools funded by the Rockefeller Foundation in 1997-1998. Teams of qualitative researchers visited the schools and sought to determine the role of the SDP in school success. The five schools varied by region of the country, grade levels, and range of populations served. All were urban schools. We spent 10 days collecting data at Gregory School. Standard qualitative case study methods were used, including individual and group interviews with community members, parents, district officials, the principal, staff, teachers, and students; observations of classrooms, team meetings, school activities, neighborhood, and so on; and reviews of relevant documents, test data, plans, policies, and so on. The data were analyzed using a combination of the constant comparative method (Glaser & Strauss, 1967) and data matrixes (Miles & Huberman, 1984). A draft report was written and reviewed by the larger research team. The principal read the rewritten draft report, and this led to discussions with her faculty, but only minor changes were suggested. The larger report and the Gregory case were read by staff of the SDP based at Yale University and representatives of the Rockefeller Foundation. This chapter is adapted from G. Noblit, W. Malloy, and C. Malloy (Eds.), *The Kids Got Smarter.* Cresskill, NJ: Hampton Press (2001).

1996) to their efforts to reform Gregory School. The SDP did not start the process of reform, but enabled significant cultural change. This case teaches us about the SDP's role in school reform and has lessons for school reform.[2]

CHANGING CLIMATE, CUSTOMS, AND CONCEPTIONS OF CHILDREN PRIOR TO THE SDP

In the late 1980s, Gregory was a school in trouble. Although there certainly were schools with worse reputations in the city, Gregory had settled into a number of unfortunate patterns. Although the principal of some 22 years was highly regarded, in retrospect many people feel that he had succumbed to the beliefs and fears that the school's ethnic groups held about the other. These negative assumptions became institutionalized in the school's structure and divided its culture along ethnic lines. The Chinese were seen by African Americans as illiterate and foreign in both language and custom. The African Americans were seen by the Chinese as aggressive and unintelligent. The school accommodated these beliefs by separating the groups into different classrooms and, by default, accepting the stereotypes as real. The Chinese were ensconced in the bilingual program and stayed there even when their English-language capabilities should have prompted assignment to regular classrooms. Thus, regular classrooms remained overwhelmingly African American. Furthermore, the school was accustomed to African-American students being loud and disruptive in classrooms. They taunted Chinese students for their accents and demeanor and occasionally fought with them.

The teaching force was similarly divided. The regular classroom teachers (most of whom were African American) did not know what the bilingual teachers (most of whom were Chinese) were doing in their classrooms and vice versa. Each group of teachers saw themselves as protectors of their own students and distrusted the motivations and abilities of the other group of teachers. This segregation by program was replayed in the student's informal interac-

---

[2]Culture is a highly contested idea today. As Page (1991) has argued, there are at least three definitions of *culture* at work in school reform. The definitions are whether school culture is an insignificant epiphenomenon, a manipulable variable, or a holistic and more implicit meaning. Anthropologists are contesting the meaning of culture at another and more basic level. Clifford and Marcus (1986), for example, argued that culture is ultimately the creation of the anthropologist as she or he uses the disciplines of anthropology to think and represent another's life and situation. Given this level of contestation, it is important to be clear about what we constructed as culture for this chapter. At one level, the story of Gregory School is a representation of the school's culture and of the changes to that culture. The SDP was culturally appropriated (Rockwell, 1996) to serve as their mechanism for creating a focus on instruction (although the SDP does not have an explicit instructional focus). Moreover, in using the SDP, the participants at Gregory School completed a change in the fundamental cultural oppositions (Eisenhart, 1989) that characterized the school.

tions. As one staff member put it: "The Chinese and Black children didn't intermingle at all." Moreover, ethnic antagonism was being replayed in the community. The Chinese stores in the neighborhood of the school did not want the African-American children in their stores. Sensing that they were unwanted, the African-American children deliberately disrupted stores. This escalated to the point where storeowners began locking their doors when they saw the children coming up the street after school.

Although divided in so many ways, both groups in the school shared some depressing realities: low student achievement for both African Americans and Chinese, low parental involvement, and an aged building in severe disrepair. A former teacher summarized the state of the school and community at this time: "such a sad scene."

The veteran principal reached retirement age as the city schools began a dramatic reform process that gave control of the schools, including the power to hire and fire principals, to Local School Councils elected by parents. Gregory's newly elected Local School Council was majority Chinese, which gave the Chinese community the opportunity to hire a Chinese principal and effectively take control of the school. A variety of factors, however, caused the Chinese majority Council to reach across racial lines and offer the position to an African-American candidate. This move was to have significant long-term repercussions for the unity of a once-divided school. A potential African American candidate, Assistant Principal Billings, told the Council that she was reluctant to move from her current position. Meanwhile, another African-American candidate, Mrs. Knight, made the Council a bold political promise. She told them that she was the only person with the wherewithal to get a much needed new building for Gregory School. Mrs. Knight convinced the Council that she had the background in the district, a network within central administration, and the ability and knowledge to mount a successful political strategy. She was given the job and immediately began to work on both getting a new building and changing the customs of the school.

Mrs. Knight and Mrs. Billings, the assistant principal who had declined to be considered for the principalship, immediately began to work together to address fighting and disruption in the school and community. The restoration of a safe, orderly, and respectful climate was seen as a crucial first step on the road to school improvement. Agreeing that "We have to stop this fighting," they initiated a campaign to respond vigorously to student fighting by suspending students who were involved and requiring parent conferences to discuss the incidents. Less serious disruptions, such as yelling and disrespect toward staff, also led to parent conferences. In an effort to physically clean up the school, students writing graffiti on the walls were required to clean them.

Possibly as important as these initiatives was Mrs. Knight's leadership style. Her habit is to talk about issues publicly, immediately, and with as many members of the school community as possible. As Mrs. Knight says about herself: "I always talk about it!" With this level of public discussion, discipline and other critical issues could no longer be evaded as someone else's responsibility. Everything that happened in the school—whether positive or negative—was brought to everyone's attention. Such a public discourse motivated better discipline and created more open communication within the school than under the previous principal. It also provided public evidence that issues were being addressed and things were being accomplished. These measures began to alter the behavior of students within the school, but there were still problems between the African-American students and the Chinese merchants. To Mrs. Knight and Mrs. Billings, the goal had to be to "change the perception of the children" in the larger community as well as within the school walls.

Mrs. Knight took to the streets after school with a dual purpose. The children learned she was a no-nonsense person within the school, but now they saw her walking up the street into the heart of Chinatown, overseeing their behavior there as well. This expansion of her authority into the community had dramatic effects on the students' behavior, as intended, but it also had an ancillary effect. "I became a visible factor in the community," Mrs. Knight observed, "and once they saw I was serious, the community began to press for continued changes."

The next step in changing the perception of the children was to let the Chinese community know that the African-American students were "as smart as the Chinese" and to convince the Chinese community that African-American teachers could effectively teach their children. This was no small task and certainly not one Mrs. Knight could accomplish alone. She implored the Chinese teachers to act as intermediaries, "a voice to the community," to convince Chinese parents that moving their children out of the haven of the bilingual program and into regular classrooms was a positive change. Educators are highly respected in the Chinese community, and eventually their words did convince the parents of the merits of a regular classroom for their children.

As Gregory moved away from what essentially had been two schools under one roof and toward programmatic unity, there were costs as well. The Chinese community wanted after-school programs because the parents worked such long hours. They also wanted to keep a close eye on the school to make sure that their children were being served well by ending what amounted to ethnic segregation within the school. Thus, the Local School Council took on a more activist role and insisted on holding the principal strictly accountable for the safety and achievement of the students.

Mrs. Knight succeeded in satisfying the Council in no little part because of her focus on the children, all children, or "my children" as she puts it. She and the staff repeatedly refer to "the children" when discussing why something needs to be done, and parents have come to trust that this phrase includes the interests of all children equally. Invoking the interests of "the children" to justify decisions fits neatly with the Comer Process of child-centered planning, but predates the introduction of the SDP at Gregory School. The pre-existence of this philosophy and decision-making approach at Gregory made the transition to Comer school status natural.

The dismantling of segregation dramatically changed the educational programs within the building. The bilingual program became a transitional program, and the regular classrooms took on the task of educating all students. Teacher assignments were changed to foster this integrated approach. Bilingual classrooms in the lower grades now have Chinese teachers and non-Chinese assistants. (Upper grades do not have teaching assistants.) White and Chinese teachers were hired so that the regular classrooms were no longer taught exclusively by African Americans. Significantly, these new teachers were not hired through the usual central office personnel process. The nontraditional approach to hiring provides important clues about the school's recent upward trajectory. Staff told stories about personnel who were assigned to Gregory by the central office but summarily sent back by Mrs. Knight when they proved to not fit the school. One story is of a maintenance officer who "borrowed" some electrical equipment, another is about a teacher who cursed at the children, and a third is about a teacher who left some students and grandparents at a zoo when they could not find the field trip bus. Much to the consternation of the central office, all were informed that they had no place at Gregory. Mrs. Knight refused to budge on these appointments, and the central office eventually acquiesced.

Newly hired teachers were in some respect known to the school before a position came open. Some did their student teaching at Gregory, some had families in the neighborhood, some attended the school as students, and some came directly to Mrs. Knight when they heard about the positive changes going on in the school and with the community. The dismantling of segregation within the educational programs thus provided the opportunity for the creation of a faculty highly loyal to the school, the community, and Mrs. Knight. In some cases, teachers commute long distances to be on the staff at Gregory. A special education teacher recounted that, at the behest of her family, she transferred to a school closer to her home, but within weeks called to ask for her position back. The working conditions at Gregory were so superior that her family came to accept her long commute and the longer days demanded at Gregory. For all the teachers we interviewed, long commutes (for some) and longer hours of work (for all) are seen as a worthwhile trade off for being at a school experiencing such success.

Throughout the early years of Mrs. Knight's principalship, Gregory was growing in unity among parents and community members, in the instructional program, and among the faculty. This unity was to prove a crucial resource for overcoming the rocky transition described in the next section and ultimately for successful implementation of the highly collaborative Comer Process.

POWER AND THE SHARED ORDEAL

As Mrs. Knight tried to reduce ethnic divisiveness within the school and community, she simultaneously began the campaign to build a new school. She faced many constraints. The local newspaper published a story arguing that there would not be enough money to keep up with minimum capital improvements in the district, let alone build new schools. There was also no available property in the area on which to build a new school building. Thus, it was likely that a new building would not serve the same community at all, but rather a subset of the existing community linked to a new attendance area. Parents and community members pressed Mrs. Knight at a public forum at the Chinese Community: "How do we get a new school?" They not only expressed their concern about the existing facility, but their desire to see the revitalized school community stay together. In the end, she promised them a new school and sufficient funds to make it a school of which they could be proud.

At the time, there was only one Chinese member of the central school board. Mrs. Knight's strategy was to approach him with the support of the Chinese community and use him to gain access to the other board members. In turn, she assigned a parent to each board member. The parents went to the board members' offices, met with them, called them often, and even sat in the board members' waiting areas to ensure that they and their school were not forgotten. In the end, the decision to build a new Gregory School was made outside of the normal capital budget deliberations. An uproar followed in which other neighborhoods and ethnic groups complained. Yet the decision stood and Mrs. Knight proved her worth to the community.

To keep Gregory School in the neighborhood, the new building had to be built on the existing site, which required a move to temporary quarters. Mrs. Knight and the community were clear that the student body had to stay together and asked to be sent to an unused building. The central office, however, decided for administrative convenience that the students would be split up and sent to other schools. Mrs. Knight heard of this decision before it became public and once again rallied her community, this time at a night meeting at the school. A petition drive started, and in 2 days each central school board member received a packet of copies containing the signed petitions urging that the students be kept together. Simultaneously, a media campaign made sure that news releases were issued and local radio and TV coverage was arranged. Clearly, it was a good story in the context of a city system that was undergoing reform to empower local schools, especially when the school played the story as "what are they trying to do to the children?" Indeed, Mrs. Knight was convinced that Gregory students did not have the necessary "survival skills" for the schools to which they were to be sent. The schools were quite distant from the community and were reputed to be "gang and drug infested." As a result of this pressure, the central office invited Gregory School to select an unused building as an interim site. Ironically, Gregory was forced to select a building in a community not unlike those they had protested: distant and gang and drug infested. Yet the school was kept together—an accomplishment not lost on the community, the teachers, and the students. This chain of events shows how adept Mrs. Knight was at employing the Comer strategy of "rallying the whole village" even before Gregory became a Comer school.

The trials of getting a new school and keeping the school together at an interim site were testimony to the power of Mrs. Knight and the newly found capability of the Gregory community. Yet it was the shared ordeal at the interim site that in many ways cemented the school's developing unity. Gregory's temporary home was in one of the most notorious ghettos in the city. It was too small, had no cafeteria, and required all the students to be bused. Yet "it was the only place" where the school could be kept together. Gregory School insulated itself as well as possible. The students were bused across town together, escorted into the building by the staff, and not allowed out into the neighborhood. Teachers and classrooms were doubled up two per room. Lunch was trucked to the site and eaten in the overcrowded classrooms.

These conditions would be enough to daunt even the most dedicated staff. The Gregory staff was just coming together under Mrs. Knight's leadership, and they were scared. The threats of building a new Gregory in a different neighborhood and splitting the students as the new school was being built had distressed the teachers. At the same time, there was all the uncertainty caused by the recent ending of ethnic segregation within the school. Through it all, Mrs. Knight constantly reassured the staff that it would work, that they could survive this year, and that they would be in the new Gregory by the fall of the next school year. The teachers rallied and came together. As Mrs. Knight put it: "They had the commitment."

However, it became clear that the new building was not going to be finished for the next school year. This threatened to unravel all that the school and community had achieved. The teachers were getting *strung out* working under such difficult conditions, and the community was not pleased with the idea of their children being bused any longer. Mrs. Knight held a luncheon meeting with her staff and, after hearing their concerns, asserted, "I'm telling you we're going to open these doors in September."

The building contractors finally admitted that the school would not be completed in time, but Mrs. Knight responded by informing the contractors that they should give priority to completing classrooms because her staff and over 600 students would begin instruction in the new building the first day of the school year. The contractors argued that this was not possible, but Mrs. Knight's response was unequivocal: "I told them they had to build around us."

The situation was inconvenient for teachers, students, and contractors alike, but as the year proceeded it was clear that Gregory School had come through a shared ordeal of considerable magnitude. They suffered but survived, were threatened but triumphed. What was once a divided school and community was now united in a new beginning in a spacious and well-appointed building. The accomplishments were legion: Students were well disciplined, the animosity between the Chinese and African Americans in the school and the community was put aside, ethnic segregation within the school ended, the staff united to the point that they insist there were no longer factions among the faculty, they survived the move to the interim site, and a new school was built for them.

Through all this, they even boasted that they "never lost one minute of instructional time." The accomplishments of Gregory during this difficult period and the newfound unity of the school and community put in place a firm foundation for the implementation of the Comer School Development Process.

IMPLEMENTING THE COMER PROCESS

Gregory School had a full agenda during these years, making dramatic improvements in the school's climate and social environment and major changes in the instructional program. They were aware, however, that something must be done about academic achievement. Ethnic segregation in the school's academic programs was over, but achievement was still low among all of the school's student populations. During the year at the interim site, the director of the Comer initiative for the city approached Mrs. Knight to discuss how the SDP could improve student achievement. By the time the staff and students entered the new building, the school was using the Comer Process.

Given Comer's spotty history in the city, adopting the process was far from a sure bet for Gregory. The city's Comer initiative was not run by the central office of the schools, but by an independent agency. Discredited by years of mismanagement, the central office was forced to agree to reforms that dramatically undercut its power, such as the formation of Local School Councils, to govern the schools. Despite concerns expressed by Comer, the district's SDP initiative started by trying to improve achievement in some of its most difficult schools. But, according to a district Comer official, this proved to be a mistake for a number of reasons. First, these schools were in the worst situations in the district and were unable to see beyond their immediate crises. Second, the schools were selected for the project and did not volunteer to be part of the SDP. Therefore, there was little of the faculty commitment so crucial to successful Comer implementation. Finally, the principals of the selected schools turned out to be largely traditional, hierarchical leaders. It was soon realized that both the selection process and leadership styles of these schools violated key aspects of Comer's framework, including the principles of collaboration and consensus in decision making.

After this disappointing start, the city's Comer initiative began looking for more promising candidate schools in which to implement the SDP. Gregory's high-profile political success in rallying the community to get a new building was attracting attention to the positive changes going on in the school. District Comer officials said they approached the school largely because of the principal's leadership style—one that "helps develop everyone in the building." According to them, Mrs. Knight was "conscious that she needs to pay attention to her teachers so they can pay attention to the children." Moreover, "the high expectations the principal has for the school [are] communicated all of the time." It was also true that when the Comer Process started at Gregory, parents were active supporters, but were not involved in the daily life of the school. The district Comer director credited this to the ethnic beliefs of the Chinese and African-American communities: "For the Asians, the school has all the answers; for the African Americans, the school was not welcoming them." Parent involvement was a recognized need that the SDP could address.

Although increasing parent involvement was an attractive feature of the Comer Process for Gregory, the central goal was improving academic achievement. Although the community pulled together and the new building was completed, Mrs. Knight recognized that "we didn't have the test scores or the skills—even the Chinese couldn't take the test because they couldn't read it." The Chinese students could achieve in mathematics, but their reading and verbal skills held them back. Test scores of African-American students remained stubbornly low. Moreover, the principal knew that even with all Gregory's other achievements, "testing was serious business—it makes you or breaks you." The state was instituting a high-stakes testing program and schools would be taken over if their scores were insufficient. Regardless of all the progress made, Gregory School still had to improve student achievement. To this end, the staff and community agreed to try the Comer Process.

The SDP trainers and school facilitators all emphasize that school development is a process and that is what leads to improved student outcomes. Yet at Gregory School, the process led to much more. According to staff members, the Comer training allowed the usually reticent Chinese teachers to "speak for the first time." The staff realized that even as they worked together for years and made many strides toward improving Gregory School, they had never talked seriously with each other about their collective goals for the students and the school. Mrs. Knight quickly realized that talking changed the staff: "Now we had something to build upon." She said that over the subsequent years, the Comer Process "brought out the Chinese teachers slowly." Indeed, today the Chinese teachers often share Mrs. Knight's public communication approach even with newcomers to the school. Following the shared trials that brought the staff together, the Comer Process enables teachers to unite around the positive goal of focusing on the needs of children.

The Comer Process provides Gregory School with a number of specific mechanisms and organizational forums for bringing members of the school community together to identify and address issues of shared concern. One such mechanism is the Student Services and Support Team (SSST), a vital tool for focusing the school's resources on individual student's needs. The SSST, which meets at least twice a month, includes the assistant principal, guidance counselor, psychologist, social worker, truant officer, student intern, and parents and staff appropriate to the issues being addressed. The team often has a translator to work with Chinese families. The SSST is the mechanism for the school to discuss and work with students who are consistently having difficulty. Early intervention is a hallmark of the Gregory SSST. After the fifth week of school each year, teachers submit the names of students who they feel might benet from early contact with the SSST. As one staff member pointed out, "We are dealing with all the social ills of the inner city struggle . . . violence, abuse, drugs."

For students with severe family issues, the SSST links with other community resources, such as the Chinese Service League, to help the whole family. Gregory School quickly realized, however, that existing services in the inner city are stretched all too thin and therefore has tried to develop new resources. For families in dire straits, the truant officer, who is in touch with "the heartbeat and pulse of the community," assumed the role of obtaining clothes and food from charities and churches. This is, of course, important in its own right, but it also communicates to poor people that the school is there to help them. This directly affects the community beliefs about school, noted before by the Comer director, that had limited parent involvement in the past.

Additionally, the SSST wanted to get a graduate student intern to provide direct services (counseling, service brokering, family support, etc.) to students. The SSST successfully negotiated with the agency overseeing the SDP in the district to obtain funding for the position. While the existing guidance counselor is fully consumed with testing, special services, and academic guidance, the intern is able to work directly with children. As one staff member noted: "All the kids see him." The intern also plays a central role in dealing with the global issues affecting the school and students. For example, he decided that the students had little accurate information about how to promote their own health. As a result, he set up a health day for students to get needed information and learn about available resources. The SSST also works with the assistant principal on discipline cases, bringing another point of view and often an additional resource to discipline deliberations.

The existence of the SSST and its integration with so many aspects of school and community life has created a more supportive environment for students, teachers, and community members. The SSST allows teachers to be proud that "we try to take care of everyone." The SSST and its work directly contribute to the caring ambiance of the school. Moreover, the team is recognized across the district as unusually effective and is often asked to visit other schools to discuss and conduct interventions, assessment, and training.

The Parent Team (PT) is another feature of the Comer Process that has proved to be a valuable resource for the school. The Parent-Teacher Organization (PTO) had been supportive of the school and politically effective when called in moments of crisis. Yet as noted previously, parents were not involved in the everyday life of the school. There are good reasons for this. First, PTOs in general concentrate on supporting the school and trying to promote parent attendance at their meetings. In short, their goal is to generate a broad base of support, and PTOs acknowledge that this requires minimizing demands on parent time. Second, the parents of Gregory students have real obstacles to their active involvement in school life. The Chinese families work long hours; while committed to their children's education, many simply are not available for a higher level of involvement. The African-American parents live in housing projects that are part of gang territories, and walking from one building to another may require gang approval. Walking past several housing project buildings to get to the school can be extremely threatening, if not impossible, especially for evening meetings when gang activity is high.

The PT allowed Gregory School to develop a small group of highly involved parents who are able to lead the more traditional PTO activities. To increase the integration of these parents into school life, the school employs many of the parents on the PT as teaching assistants or as part of the after-school programs. This provides needed income for these families and gives parents insider knowledge of the school that they bring to their deliberations. Of course, it also makes the parents obliged to the school and/or principal and reduces the parents' independence. Other parents are recruited as volunteers and often work as unpaid teaching assistants in upper grade classrooms. This allows them to do meaningful work with the children and gain insider knowledge essential to effective participation in the SPMT and PT.

Members of the PT meet at least monthly and participate in a range of Comer activities. There is regular training for parents and for PT members. Moreover, Gregory's PT is networked with PTs from other Comer schools in the district and shares training sessions with them. In the school, the PT helps develop school events, including "Cross-Cultural Celebration Days," which emphasize the similar values across the two ethnic groups (e.g., a grandparents' breakfast that highlighted the centrality of grandparents in both cultures) as well as represent parents on the School Planning and Management Team (SPMT). The PT enables parents to be an active presence within the school and helps the school to better respond to the parents' needs and interests. This has resulted in a change in the ethnic beliefs that both the Chinese ("the school has all the answers") and African Americans ("the school was not welcoming") held about school. The district Comer director argued that, through the SDP, Gregory School "began to change those myths . . . more parents became involved— Asian and African American working together on racial tensions."

The SPMT is a third key component of the Comer Process that helped channel Gregory's momentum of positive change. The SPMT is responsible for developing the School Improvement Plan. A large part of its work is responding to issues brought forward by the SSST, the PT, the grade-level teams, and the principal. The SPMT meets monthly and operates effectively as a representative body where each member is responsible for soliciting input from her or his constituency. It also serves as the liaison to the Local School Council, the school's highest authority, in the planning process. Since adoption of the Comer Process, the SPMT does most of the planning and then submits its work to the parent elected Local School Council for approval. This allows for collaboration and achieving consensus—two of Comer's principles for decision making.

This past year, the SPMT's major goals have been to increase student attendance, enhance parent involvement, and improve achievement test scores.

The SPMT is considering an accelerated program and is working through issues of how to select students and teachers. They are also working on enlarging the after-school program so that it may be open to all students, expanding the library and re-emphasizing the reference skills of students, and integrating bilingual students into the regular program. In addition, they continue to address cultural diversity and pursue grants such as a proposal that funded hands-on mathematics materials for all classrooms. As the vice principal noted, "we are constantly in search of additional revenues" to help teachers, and they have been quite successful in getting grants. The Comer facilitator noted that a recent school newsletter had been repeatedly delayed due to a series of notices of grants received.

Like the other teams, the SPMT reviews and practices the Comer principles of collaboration, consensus, and no fault at each meeting. SPMT members agreed that, although they were doing a lot of what Comer expects before they were introduced to the process, Comer gave them "a name, a procedure." Moreover, many members of the SPMT commented on the importance of the no-fault principle. This principle enables them to get past seeking who is to blame for a problem to focus on gaining consensus on what must be done. As one member described the process, "now someone has the job to take the concerns and do something about them." Teachers reported that the SPMT uses Comer's developmental pathways to diagnose what students need and address those needs in their local school plan. Yet the school's preexisting focus on the children means the specific pathways receive less attention than the overall orientation of child-centered planning.

The Comer Process also gives the staff and parents something else: "a direct path to voice concerns without repercussions." It is important to contextualize this statement. The issue here is not whether the administration is open to input. In fact, Mrs. Knight and the assistant principal have an "open door" policy that is used regularly. Yet the principal is a dynamic leader and highly respected, and in some ways it is this respect that gets in the way of frank communication. People may be reluctant to bring concerns to the principal because it may be seen as an implied criticism of the administration. Having an established process for voicing concerns, guided by a principle of no fault, overcomes this reticence. Parents and teachers are expected to state their concerns and participate in solving them. The School Development Process enables Mrs. Knight to be a dynamic leader without the threat of being seen as an oligarch. In fact, she argues that the Comer Process "tempered me." She gives the SDP a lot of credit: "Comer made me an effective leader." In this case, leadership and involvement are effectively wedded.

IMPROVEMENTS AT GREGORY

One former teacher enables a measure of the school's progress. Having worked at the school before Mrs. Knight's tenure as principal, he fully expected the school to be 1 of the 109 city schools the state put on probation for inadequate achievement. He recounted the segregation of Chinese and African-American students, inadequate instruction, uninvolved community, and difficult and unresponsive students. Gregory School, however, is not on probation—far from it. One district official described it as one of the "exemplary" schools in the district. In this era of high-stakes testing, Gregory School is doing well. District generated school report cards show that student achievement is increasing. When test scores for 1993 and 1996 are compared, this improvement is evident. Thirteen tests were given to Gregory students: Eleven of them show dramatic gains while the remaining two show scores holding steady. Scores in reading and math show steady improvement. Moreover, the staff and community believe they know why they are succeeding in a school that a few years ago would have predictably found itself on probation. Gregory declared itself a Comer School in 1993-1994, and its test scores have been on an upward trend ever since. Staff and community members argue that this is no coincidence.

The SPMT appropriated the Comer Process to generate the focus on academics, which was Mrs. Knight's primary goal once the school's fundamental climate problems were addressed. When the state reformed the school district, it prescribed a curriculum and designed a test that was aligned with that curriculum. Gregory School went even further. After the SPMT identified the need for a school-level curriculum alignment to get in sync with the new tests, a teacher led an examination of its entire instructional program. Teachers examined the textbooks and "aligned them across all grade levels." They also focused on "taking out things that were no longer necessary" to be taught with the state curriculum and testing program. Next teacher lesson plans were aligned with the curriculum and testing. A computer program was purchased, which provided teachers with an efficient way to generate lesson plans (and align with the curriculum and tests) that are turned into the principal each week. The district Comer director noted: "The instructional focus is coherent, aligned" and "coherency comes from planning together."

Gregory School is also taking advantage of professional development programs available through the district-wide Comer initiative; district programs on math, science, and technology; and the local teacher academy. Moreover, the school tries to develop special instructional programs targeted to the needs and interests of its students, including a writing program taught by a professional writer, photography classes, and a program that encourages racial pride via African-American newspapers. Despite these multiple forces at work, Mrs. Knight sees the Comer Process as responsible for the gains in student achievement: "There's something to be said about talking about children . . . working on the principles and a lot of meetings . . . but this is how to improve academics." The SDP facilitates what Gregory School wants and needs, and it also provides a central organizing force for a multifaceted approach to improving student achievement.

A staff member characterized what a student finds at Gregory School today: "Predictability, consistency, expectations, safety, and fun." When students were asked about what is important at Gregory, the most common response was "learning." For these students, learning is about "things to go to college," "so you can find a job," "to win contests," and "working together." These characterizations reflect both the long-term goals of education (college and working), the performances that demonstrate school and student excellence (contests), and a style of work that is highly touted by industry (working together). When asked about their favorite subject in school, the students listed all the subjects, but also noted that their favorite thing about school is "working—to get to learn a lot" and "helping the teacher." They noted that adults at the school get excited when the students focus on academics: "do good in school and get good grades," "listen to your teacher so you know what to do," "you always read the instructions before you work," "go back to the books and find your answers," and "be good and work in school." They also said their school is "the best." They summarized the changes at the school as "kids have gotten smarter."

Staff members gave a long list of successes for the school. The Comer facilitator notes she "couldn't finish the newsletter because the new grants kept coming in." Teacher aides praise "the nice family atmosphere" much like a "small community" where "we all try to get along." Teachers argue, "it's a comfortable place to be" and that the "children pull together in times of crises." Other teachers note the "safe environment," "test scores," and "no fights." They said "we are the best" and that "our school sets an example . . . especially in a multiracial setting." Most important, the teachers "enjoy coming to work here." They believe that in the context of the larger reform of the city system, "we're more on target here than any other school in the city."

The teachers also pointed with pride to the fact that the school is a recognized success in the community: "People are begging to have their kids come to school here." According to teachers, the community sees the school as having "a complete turnaround in a positive direction . . . not just average but above average." Teachers and community members agreed that "the school brings the community together." In part, according to a teacher, this is because at the school "we have the connections to defuse racial incidents." Even district officials acknowledged "everyone knows you here and will welcome you into the class." This is especially important because "there are gangs in both communities, so we have to work to dialogue." When asked about what happens to students when they leave Gregory, community members responded that "the values and [what] they've learned are the building blocks of their lives." Knowing what is possible at Gregory, however, has the community even more concerned about the high schools for their children. The desire to maintain the positive momentum of Gregory is so strong that the community, with the support of the school, applied for a charter high school for their children. They did not get their charter, but have not given up. Their prior successes in educational politics leave them optimistic that they can succeed.

Even with this success, staff and parents noted that there are perennial issues that demand their attention. "Communication is always an issue," as is "parent involvement in a way that meets the needs of this community." Moreover, "many kids are dealing with violence in the community and abuse . . . also drug and alcohol abuse—across both races." Staff were pleased with the parent turnout at a recent arts-and-crafts workshop, but sober after being confronted with the many challenges the parents face in their lives: "The personal crises of the parents are daunting, but they feel support here and so they come." Staff noted that "teaching the two cultures to get along is our biggest problem," as well as a typically teacher list of concerns: "homework, discipline, school rules, relationships." Students recounted the persistent issues of their lives at Gregory: "arguing," "talking," "running," and "not working."

It is clear that for many people Gregory School is a place of efficacy and power. People associated with the school believe that they have, and will, change on their own terms. The school has to respond to the many challenges presented by state reform policies, local politics, and community dynamics. However, the school now uses these challenges as ways to demonstrate that they are in charge of their destiny. A sense of efficacy is coupled with a belief in their power in local politics. They have learned how to move through parent and community involvement to parent and community mobilization. For some, this power is connected to Mrs. Knight, the principal. Others argue that the SDP has shifted the distribution of power away from the principal to the wider school and community. There are important differences in these views, but both presume the existence of power. Combining power with efficacy makes a remarkable school.

Eisenhart (1989) argued that culture can be understood it terms of oppositions. Prior to Mrs. Knight, Gregory School had a history of seeing the external world as opposed to the internal preferred life of educators. Moreover, many in the school and community believed that state accountability policies; corrupt local politics; and racial, economic, and social problems in the community were more powerful than the teachers and staff, stifling the teachers and undermining the school efforts. These external factors were seen as interfering with the values of the teachers and their ability to enforce those values. The school was in disarray and the teachers in despair.

With the arrival of Mrs. Knight, this cultural opposition was directly attacked. Stopping fighting, ending segregation, winning the new building, and surviving the ensuing shared ordeal in the temporary school created both a tried and tough school. The teachers were unified. The principal made impossible things happen. The parents and communities began to rally to the school. Outsiders were becoming insiders. Local politics was now their prowess, not their enemy. However, the state's accountability program remained. The school did not have a way to organize a strategy to address the high-stakes testing program.

The SDP invited parents, all the staff, and the community into the governance process. These externals became more internal. The SDP also became the mechanism to develop the school's instructional strategy for the high-stakes testing program. The principles of no fault, consensus, and collaboration stopped blaming and assigned instructional responsibilities. The SDP's child-centeredness was congruent with Mrs. Knight's, and together they help keep the governance process focused on students' needs. Aligning instruction enabled the school to concentrate on what was being tested. They became successful in the high-stakes testing program. This success completed a change in the fundamental opposition at Gregory School from external-internal to success-fragility.

In Table 4.1, we juxtapose a summary of what participants recount as the successes of Gregory School with their recounting of pervasive issues. Although the list of successes is longer, it is clear that people associated with

TABLE 4.1
Gregory Elementary School

Variable	Successes
With Parents	• Increased parental involvement and confidence in the school
In the Community	• Unified two communities behind the school
	• Improved the image of the school within the community
Within the School	• Reduced discipline problems
	• Improved teacher satisfaction and sense of efficacy
	• Created a sense of community and shared purpose
	• Overcame racial divisiveness; desegregated within the school
	• Created a positive working and learning environment
	• Created a coherent and aligned curriculum
With Positive Transitions	• Acquired new school building
With External Recognition	• Received several grants and awards
With Achievement Tests	• Increased student achievement
	Pervasive Issues
With Parents	• Parent involvement
With the Community	• Community ties
Within the School	• Cross-cultural communication and understanding
	• Instruction
Positive Transitions	• Maintain building
With Achievement Tests	• Student achievement

Gregory School understand that their successes are impermanent. They are always at jeopardy and must be continually reconstructed. In the inner city, school success is coupled to fragility. Efficacy and power are always just one challenge away from being disproved.

Gregory School is aware of both its successes and fragility. Aside from getting the new school building, the successes that Gregory has experienced require continued monitoring and development. The SDP is the mechanism they use to continue to improve. SPMT members credit the Comer Process for the school's "camaraderie," for the "excellent" discipline, for being "connected to other schools," and for the staff's "higher respect for parents." Moving forward, they will use the Comer Process to address the fragility of their accomplishments.

CONCLUSIONS

Gregory School has a unique history. Few schools experience the shared ordeals and political accomplishments that this school has experienced. Clearly, much of what has been accomplished is due to the principal, Mrs. Knight, but she is reluctant to take too much credit. She says, "Let's just say it was the community" that makes all this possible. Certainly the community rose to the challenges her leadership issued. In any case, the school's political achievements enabled a united staff and community who were able to see that Comer offered something for them. The SDP is their decision-making mechanism, a vehicle for continued instructional improvement, and a way to continue the successes achieved with the community. The SDP also balances the power of a dynamic principal with the power of an involved and committed faculty and community. Comer did not directly lead to any of the school's successes. Rather, Gregory School appropriated Comer to their own ends. Comer became more than an appropriation when test scores began to rise. It became reified as the way for them to move forward. Success in high-stakes testing legitimates Gregory School, and the SDP derives part of its legitimacy from this.

Of course, there are other reasons the SDP looms large in the story of Gregory School. First, the SDP is the reform they have chosen to help them improve their school. Second, it has become their primary decision-making and governance mechanism. Third, it has expanded the definition of *participation the school* to include community members, parents, students, staff, and faculty. Fourth, the SDP facilitated a number of accomplishments, breeding both a sense of control over the schools' destinies and a sense of efficacy that spurs people to further improvement efforts. Finally, with the SDP, people at Gregory School realize that it is *they* who make the difference. The SDP provides the mechanism for them to do what is needed and important. The people involved in Gregory School have learned to value a governance process that is the vehicle for so much good. They refer to the Comer Process as *the* change that has made the difference in their school. Gregory School was in many ways ripe for reform, but not just any reform would have accomplished what Comer did. Reforms that prescribe an instruction-al approach may change classroom practice and increase test scores, but they are less likely to provide a mechanism for systemic change within the school and between the school and community. Gregory School used the SDP to alter their curricula and instructional programs and for many more things, including to:

1. take charge of change,
2. build on existing assets and strengths,
3. communicate across the many stakeholder groups,
4. frame and pursue concerns, issues, and needs,
5. develop power for the parents and community and redesign the power of the principal, and
6. restructure and reculture the schools.

If they had chosen a reform that was primarily about curriculum and/or instruction, this school would have focused their efforts on classrooms and kept their existing grade-level teams governance system. There is little reason to believe they would have developed the generalized senses of power and effica-cy that they now have. To improve achievement, a school does need to focus on students, curricula, and instruction; to improve a school, it is necessary to change its structure and culture.

We need to be careful in taking lessons about school reform from this case. Gregory School was in the middle of cultural change when they appropriat-ed the SDP to their ends. This story says little about how Comer could be effec-tively appropriated in schools that are demoralized. Second, although we may hope that similar stories could be made to be common in inner cities, Gregory School has a rather exclusive story. In the larger study, we were using databases to determine which schools were candidates to be classified successful Comer schools, and only some 22 seemed possible candidates out of the 640 schools then counted as part of the SDP. If anything, this case teaches us how idealistic the school reform agenda is. Few schools are situated to take charge of school reform as well as Gregory School. The true challenge to reform is to re-situate schools so they can reform themselves, but the task remains decidedly difficult.

Gregory School teaches us that the question to address in reform is not what reform does to a school, but what a school does with reform. It is common to assign school reforms powers beyond those of people. Reform needs to be reframed so that we focus on the process of appropriation of reform. As Gouldner (1970) wrote, knowledge is power when it is knowledge of power. Other schools can see how Gregory School has used Comer and can determine what they see as the prospects of appropriating Comer to their particular ends. We would argue that Comer may offer possibilities that reforms with a more instructional focus may not. As a governance process, for example, it can be used to a range of ends.

Finally, Gregory School's story implies that reform is reproductive. School reform begets school reform in many ways, but the fragility of school success means that reform can never be accomplished. Rather reform requires a commitment, and success adds more and more to be committed to. Fragility may be increased with overload. The success with high-stakes testing demonstrates how one reform reproduces reform in general. Winning at the testing game has real consequences for what students are not taught. This narrowing of the curriculum will eventually lead to reforms designed to expand both testing and the curriculum. This is but another case of reform recycling (Cuban, 1990; Noblit & Dempsey, 1996). Reform recycles because of a basic value conflict between excellence and equity. Gregory School may have been successful with high-stakes testing (an excellence reform), but Comer comes from a different history. Comer and Gregory School are inescapably about equity.

REFERENCES

Clifford, J., & Marcus, G. (Eds.). (1986). *Writing culture.* Berkeley: University of California Press.

Comer, J. P. (1993). *School power: Implications of a school intervention project.* New York: The Free Press.

Comer, J. P., Haynes, N. M., Joyner, E. T., & Ben-Avie, M. (Eds.). (1996). *Rallying the whole village: The Comer Process for reforming education.* New York: Teachers College Press.

Cuban, L. (1990). Reforming again, again, and again. *Educational Researcher, 19*(1), 3-13

Eisenhart, M. (1989). Reconsidering cultural differences in American schools. *Educational Foundations, 3*(2), 51-68.

Emmons, C., Owen, S. V., Haynes, N. M., & Comer, J. P. (1992, March). *A causal model of the effects of school climate, classroom climate, academic self-concept, suspension, and absenteeism on academic achievement.* Paper presented at the annual meeting of the Eastern Educational Research Association, Hilton Head, SC.

Glaser, B., & Strauss, A. (1967). *The discovery of grounded theory.* Chicago: Aldine.

Gouldner, A. (1970). *The coming crisis of western sociology.* New York: Basic Books.

Haynes, N. M., & Bility, K. (1994). Evaluating school development. In N. M. Haynes (Ed.), *School Development Program research monograph.* New Haven, CT: Yale Child Study Center.

Miles, M., & Huberman, A. (1984). *Qualitative data analysis.* Beverly Hills, CA: Sage.

Noblit, G. W., & Dempsey, V. O. (1996). *The social construction of virtue: The moral life of schools.* Albany: SUNY Press.

Page, R. N. (1991). Kinds of schools. In K. Borman, P. Swami, & L. Wagstaff (Eds.), *Contemporary issues in U.S. education* (pp. 38-60). Norwood, NJ: Ablex.

Rockwell, E. (1996). Keys to appropriation: Rural schooling in Mexico. In B. Levinson, O. Foley, & D. Holland (Eds.), *The cultural production of the educational person* (pp. 301-324). Albany: State University of New York Press.

5

"It's Hard Work, But It's Worth It": School Culture and Success for All

Monica B. McKinney
Meredith College

The seeds for the Success for All program were planted in Baltimore, Maryland, in 1986 out of a partnership between the Baltimore City Public Schools and the Center for Research on Elementary and Middle Schools (CREMS), formerly at Johns Hopkins University. The challenge was to assist the Baltimore Schools with enabling every child in the inner-city Baltimore elementary schools to perform at grade level (particularly in reading) by the end of third grade (Balkcom & Himmelfarb, 1993).

The program was piloted in one elementary school during the 1987-1988 school year and then in four more Baltimore schools in 1988-1989. Also in 1988-1989, the program was implemented in a Philadelphia school serving many limited-English proficient students. In 1990-1991, the first Spanish version of the Success for All reading program, Lee Conmigo, was developed. Beginning in 1992, math, science, and social studies programs were added to complement the original reading and writing programs (Slavin, Madden, Dolan, & Wasik, 1996). As of March 2000, Success for All could be found in more than 1,600 schools throughout the United States as well as in the United Kingdom, Australia, Mexico, and Israel (Datnow & Castellano, 2000).

SUCCESS FOR ALL: PHILOSOPHY AND GOALS

Success for All (SFA) is a schoolwide restructuring program for students in Grades pre-K to 5 (Slavin, 1996; Slavin, Madden, Karweit, Dolan, & Wasik, 1992; Slavin et al., 1995, 1996). SFA is generally adopted at a schoolwide level in high-poverty, Title I schools, although other characteristics vary widely. At the root of SFA is the idea that "every child can and must succeed in the early grades, no matter what this takes" (Slavin et al., 1996). Behind this idea are four principles of SFA (Balkcom & Himmelfarb, 1993):

- *every child can learn;*
- *success in the early grades is critical for future success in school;*
- *learning deficits can be prevented through intervention in preschool and early grades, improved curriculum and instruction, individual attention, and support to families; and*
- *effective school reform programs are both comprehensive and intensive.*

The goals of the program stem directly from its beliefs. SFA strives to ensure that every student will perform at grade level by the end of the third grade. SFA seeks to reduce the number of students referred to special education, as well as reduce the number of students held back to repeat a grade. Yet another goal of the program is to increase attendance. Finally, SFA attempts to address the needs of students' families in terms of food, housing, and medical care to enable families to support their children's education (Balkcom & Himmelfarb, 1993). In a nutshell, SFA strives to meet its challenge of success for all by ensuring that "all children maintain their motivation, enthusiasm, and optimism" (Slavin et al., 1995).

To accomplish its goals, the program relies on prevention and intensive early intervention rather than remediation. Prevention includes:

> *providing excellent preschool and kindergarten programs; improving curriculum, instruction, and classroom management throughout the grades; assessing students frequently to make sure they are making adequate progress; and establishing cooperative relationships with parents so they can support students' learning at home. (Slavin et al., 1992, p .2)*

Intensive early intervention consists of:

> *one-to-one tutoring by certified teachers for first graders who have reading problems . . . working with parents and social service agencies to make sure that all students attend school, have medical services or eyeglasses if they need them, get help with behavior problems, and so on. (Slavin et al., 1992, p. 2)*

In addition, schools constantly assess the effectiveness of services provided and vary services as needed until each child is successful.

Components

Although the program varies by school depending on needs and resources, there are 10 common elements: reading program, reading tutors, 8-week reading assessments, preschool and kindergarten programs, family support team, program facilitator, professional development, advisory committee, special education, and relentlessness.

The reading program is the heart of SFA. In the program's first step, basic language skills, concepts of print, and story structure are emphasized through StaR (Story Telling and Retelling). Beginning as early as the second semester of kindergarten, students begin the Reading Roots portion of the program. In this step, students learn letters and letter sounds through activities and a series of "phonetically regular but meaningful and interesting minibooks" (Slavin et al., 1996, p. 5). Students also learn "story structure, specific comprehension skills, metacognitive strategies for self-assessment and self-correction, and integration of reading and writing" (Slavin et al., 1996, p. 5). Spanish bilingual programs use Lee Conmigo (Read with Me), an adaptation of Reading Roots.

Once students have mastered the Roots portion of SFA and reach the primer reading level, they progress to Reading Wings. Wings uses cooperative learning activities to emphasize story structure, prediction, summarization, vocabulary, decoding skills, and writing. Students also receive direct instruction in reading comprehension skills. Alas para Leer (Wings to Read) serves Spanish readers. Furthermore, reading for 20 minutes becomes a part of each student's nightly homework assignment.

To accommodate the reading program, the school day is restructured so that 90 minutes to 2 hours are devoted solely to reading and writing instruction. Students are ability grouped, and group size is minimized by utilizing all trained school personnel (including arts and physical education specialists, media coordinators, guidance counselors, special education and Title I teachers, and others trained as tutors).

Reading tutors work with students who are having difficulty keeping up with their reading group. This one-on-one interaction occurs in addition to each day's reading period and lasts 20 minutes. Tutors build on what students are doing in class rather than introducing different objectives; they also provide additional metacognitive skills.

Assessments are conducted at the end of each 8-week period to chart student progress. This element of the program determines who may need to receive tutoring, changes students' reading group assignments, suggests needed adaptations in students' programs, or screens for the need for other services.

Preschool and kindergarten programs are found at most SFA schools and are generally where the STaR portion of the reading program begins. STaR is used in conjunction with Peabody Language Development kits to support academic readiness.

The family support team is considered an essential part of SFA's formula for success. This team "works toward creating good relations with parents and increasing their involvement in the schools" (Slavin et al., 1996, p. 7). It also serves as an intervention mechanism to solve problems that students may be experiencing, whether these problems originate or occur at school or home. The family support team is also integrated into the school's academic program.

The school's program facilitator oversees the school's SFA efforts. He or she helps plan for the program, helps with scheduling, visits and assists classroom teachers and tutors to help with individual problems, arranges and provides professional development opportunities, and coordinates the activities of the family support team.

Professional development consists of a fairly brief, but intense initial 3 days of inservice at the beginning of the school year for all teachers and tutors. Tutors receive an additional 2 days of training on tutoring strategies and reading assessment. Additional inservice sessions occur throughout the year on such topics as cooperative learning, behavioral management, and instructional pacing. There are also many informal group discussions organized by the program facilitator for sharing problems and suggesting changes.

The advisory committee meets regularly to review the progress that the school is making as well as identify and solve any problems. Often existing site-based management teams fulfill this function with some modification of membership.

As to SFA's approach toward special education, Slavin et al. (1996) write, "one major goal of Success for All is to keep students with learning problems out of special education if at all possible . . ." (p. 8). To this end, efforts are geared toward addressing students' learning problems within the classroom as supplemented by tutors. Finally, Slavin et al. wrote,

> *Although the particular elements of Success for All may vary from school to school, there is one feature we try to make consistent in all: a relentless focus on the success of every child. It would be entirely possible to have tutoring and curriculum change, and have family support, and other services, yet still not ensure the success of at-risk children. Success does not come from piling on additional services but from coordinating human resources around a well-defined goal, constantly assessing progress toward that goal, and never giving up until success is achieved. (p. 8)*

Roots and Wings and Beyond

As mentioned previously, Success for All began something of a transformation in 1992. At this time, not only did the reading program take on the reading Roots and Wings components that it has today (described earlier), but the curriculum was expanded into math, science, and social studies as well. The math program, called MathWings, is a constructivist mathematics program for Grades 1 to 5; it encourages cooperative groups to "discover, experiment with, and apply" mathematical concepts (Slavin et al., 1996, p. 9). WorldLab provides an integrated curriculum in social studies and science for first through fifth graders. Again, students often work in cooperative groups while they become people in history, people in other countries, or people in various occupations such as physicists or inventors. WorldLab units not only integrate social studies and science, but also incorporate writing, reading, math, fine arts, and music (Slavin et al., 1996).

INTRODUCING MARSHALL COUNTY

Marshall County,[1] North Carolina, is a rural county centrally located in the state.[2] Approximately two thirds of the county's land is part of the Teachey National Forest, with lumber and textiles comprising its major industries. The county is not immune to societal problems (both urban and rural) experienced across the state and nation. Twenty percent of the population lives below the poverty level. Marshall County has more working mothers than any other county in North Carolina. Furthermore, it has one of the highest rates in the state in terms of per capita single teenage pregnancies (representing 5% of its high school population). Dropout rates are also high, and SAT and standardized test scores are low.

The county's school system is made up of four elementary schools (Grades K-5), two middle schools (Grades 6-8), and two high schools (Grades 9-12). In all, more than 4,000 students are served by the district. They are nearly 60% White and approximately 30% African American. The remaining 10% are Hispanic, Asian, and American Indian. Nearly half of the county's students qualify for free or reduced lunch. The Hispanic portion of their population is growing rapidly, adding the challenge of serving twice as many limited proficiency and non-English-speaking students as in the past.

---

[1] All names have been changed.

[2] Much of the information contained in this section comes from a series of documents created by various employees of the Marshall County School System and submitted to the Office of Education Reform of the North Carolina Department of Public Instruction. They include applications. reapplications, and impact/profile surveys dated from March 1995 to June 1998.

The mission of the Marshall County School System is to "provide a purposeful learning environment that ensures daily success and fosters respect." Within this general mission statement lies a desire to have the county's students achieve the following goals: (a) demonstrate mastery and application of skills so they are academically proficient, (b) be capable of higher level thinking and problem solving, and (c) become competitive, productive, responsible citizens.

In an effort to bridge the gap between their vision and their actual performance, a district-wide Curriculum Committee was formed. Comprised of teachers representing Grades K-12, building principals, and central office staff involved with instruction, the Curriculum Committee was charged with identifying a project focus for the county's bid for federal Goals 2000 School Improvement Grant funds (distributed and administered by the Office of Education Reform, North Carolina Department of Public Instruction). Parents and community members, including representatives of business and industry, public health, social services, and law enforcement, pledged their support of the committee's proposed goals and objectives, and an application was submitted and accepted.

The goals of the committee were focused in the elementary schools with the belief that educational efforts at this level influence middle and high school achievement as well as life-long endeavors. Three specific goals were identified: (a) that all students exit Grade 3 having demonstrated competency in reading and communication skills such as writing, talking, and listening; (b) that elementary students develop attitudes and behaviors that contribute to a disciplined environment conducive to learning; and (c) that elementary schools increase parent involvement through partnerships that would promote social, emotional, and academic growth.

As a result of this committee's challenge, several reading programs that focus on at-risk students were examined by a second committee comprised of elementary principals, supervisors, and K-3 teachers. This group studied Reading Recovery, Success for All, Partners in Reading, First Steps, and several other reading programs before deciding to implement Success for All in two of the district's elementary schools and First Steps in the other two schools during the first year of the project.

To further support their efforts, a lead teacher/facilitator certified in reading instruction with experience teaching Grades K-3 was also hired. The responsibilities of this individual included: (a) building teams of participating teachers, (b) planning and implementing preservice and ongoing staff development, (c) developing units of study along with classroom teachers that utilize proved strategies for teaching reading, and (d) overseeing the purchasing of materials, supplies, and software to support these units of study.

At the end of the first year of the project, the two schools that had implemented First Steps reevaluated their efforts and made the decision to adopt SFA. SFA, they believed, better addressed the needs of their students. With this move, all of the district's elementary schools became unified through not only the same goals as set forth by the Curriculum Committee, but also through the route chosen to achieve those goals. The district's central office facilitated implementation by procuring additional funding for the schools' efforts, providing additional personnel as needed, and participating in a "critical friends" evaluation process with the Office of Education Reform's School Improvement Grant Evaluation Team.[3]

INTRODUCING HOWARD ELEMENTARY SCHOOL

Having established the countywide context for reform, it is time to shift focus to examine how Success for All looks at the school level. Statistically, Howard Elementary School closely mirrors the county in which it is found. Eighty percent of its students qualify for free or reduced lunch. Fifty percent of its students are being raised by single parents, and 60% of these parents have less than a

---

[3]Marshall County has taken seriously attempts made by the Office of Education Reform (OER) to not only make schools and school systems more accountable for showing improvements from funds they receive, but also to help these systems become better able to follow and evaluate their own progress. OER has utilized several methods to attain their goals, including requiring yearly reapplications for continued funding, requesting yearly profile or impact surveys that show progress made, and providing training sessions to assist schools in these processes.

An additional opportunity offered by OER and seized on by Marshall County (and two other counties) was to participate in a critical friends review of their efforts in conjunction with the School Improvement Grant Evaluation Team. The critical friends process utilized was adapted from the School Quality Review Initiative undertaken by the New York State Education Department (Ancess, 1996). The purpose of such a review is "to help a school develop a culture of review and to support its efforts at self-review, development, and renewal" (p. 4). Although New York utilized this method at the school level, the process also has benefits for a system such as Marshall County, whose efforts with SFA span four elementary schools.

Several day-long meetings were held during which the three participating critical friends teams got to know one another, reviewed the purposes and processes of the case studies, and shared experiences and findings. Each critical friends team was composed of two members of the evaluation team and one or two individuals from the school system. Each team developed their own process within the guideline that all members would be involved at each step (planning, data collection, analysis, and writing).

Our critical friends team decided that four person days should be spent by evaluation team members gathering data from an outsider perspective. These data, derived from observations and interviews, would be combined with documents collected by the two team members from Marshall County's central office and their insider knowledge of the county's context and day-to-day operation of the schools. This insider knowledge of the system was also instrumental in determining which individuals should be interviewed, in handling the scheduling of visits, and in providing introductions. Together we developed appropriate questions for the interviews and a list of documents to be gathered.

high school education. Many parents work in local industries that have not placed a high priority on developing a well-educated local workforce. As such, promoting strong educational values is an ongoing activity for Howard Elementary. In addition, Howard's Hispanic student population is higher than the county average at 34%. School personnel are aware of the communication problems presented by their own limited Spanish abilities and their students' and parents' limited English abilities. For this reason, they are conscientious about accommodating the needs of their Spanish-speaking parents and students and even have one person on staff who spends much of her time translating materials.

Howard Elementary School chose SFA after careful consideration of the various programs researched by the countywide committee and after the school's principal, Mr. Hillman, visited a similar school that was implementing the program. On returning to Howard, he offered to let all his teachers see the program in action. Several took advantage of this opportunity and reported what they saw and heard to the rest of the faculty. It was agreed that SFA "had it all," whereas the other programs targeted limited numbers of students. As one teacher reflected, "we had students across the board that needed help."

Because Howard Elementary was one of the original two SFA schools in the county, the program's introduction in the school actually occurred without the assistance of the county's Goals 2000 funds. These funds came into the system only in time to assist the second-round schools with their initial implementation. Howard's schoolwide Title I status, however, gave it the necessary flexibility within its funding structure to adopt the moderately expensive initiative on its own. However, they have since benefited from an equal distribution between the county's four elementary schools of second and later years' Goals 2000 funds.

A FRAMEWORK FOR LOOKING AT REFORM

The goals adopted by the school and county, their choice of SFA as a possible route to the achievement of those goals, and even the ways in which the county and school went about adopting those goals and choosing the program reflect many cultural beliefs about the ways in which schools work and the ends to which they hope to arrive. Erickson (1997) discusses definitions of *culture* at length and acknowledges that there is no single, agreed-upon definition of the term. However, he continues that "culture can be thought of as a construction— it constructs us as we construct it" (p. 39). It is learned and transmitted by older generations as well as invented within new situations. Some aspects are explicit, whereas others are implicit; some we are consciously aware of, others we are not. In other words, cultural beliefs and assumptions undergird and surround all our thoughts, emotions, and actions.

Although existing beliefs factor heavily in the adoption of a reform effort, reform also often brings with it the need to either accommodate these existing beliefs or change them. Elmore (1996) discusses at length the difficulties involved in changing what he calls the "core" of educational practice. For him, this core consists of such aspects of schooling as how the nature of knowledge is understood, the role of the student in the learning process, the need for and methods of assessment, teacher responsibility, and even the relations between and among students and teachers. All of these are manifestations and products of school culture. Conley (1993), too, recognizes the importance of culture to reform efforts in his discussion of "creating new habits of heart and mind" (p. 43), and Fullan (1991) includes local characteristics of the district, community, principal, and teacher in his consideration of educational change.

Many studies continue in this vein, but are not included here because this is not a discussion about how to make educational change effective. Rather, it is about how school culture and school change are mutually reactive. Marshall County and Howard Elementary are representative of most reform efforts in that their choice of SFA reflects existing beliefs as well as encourages the development of new beliefs. SFA is desirable because it shares beliefs they hold that they do not want to change (i.e., reading is the foundation for all other learning). At the same time, SFA offers new beliefs (i.e., everybody can teach reading) and new structures (i.e., reorganizing the school day around a common reading period). Some of these new cultural understandings will undoubtedly remain even if the program disappears alter a period of time.

The criteria used in the Goals 2000 evaluation and renewal process (Berry, 1996; Berry, Jenkins, McKinney, Noblit, & Turchi, 1997) also provide a framework for looking at cultural change at Howard Elementary. These criteria arise from the reform literature on creating and sustaining systemic change (Elmore, 1996; Fullan, 1994, 1996) and from our own early research with the School Improvement Grant initiative.[4] They are as follows:

- looking outward to external standards of best practice,
- going beyond the tests and defining clear learning goals for all students,
- finding ways to use data,
- finding focus and avoiding program fragmentation,
- embracing the complexity of teaching,
- connecting teacher learning to student learning,
- making interagency collaboration possible, and
- moving beyond the pilot project.

---

[4]The eight criteria represent common issues and factors that were self-reported as influential in the schools' efforts as well as benchmarks of systemic reform found in the literature. Fifteen school improvement grant sites were surveyed and interviewed in this step of the research.

These eight criteria are not independent of each other; in fact, they may be in some senses symbiotic (Berry, 1996). For instance, as is the case with SFA, looking to external standards of practice links very specifically to defining clear learning goals and finding ways to use data.

Utilizing this framework, some of the cultural beliefs held by the faculty, staff, and community of Howard Elementary School and some of the changes brought about by the school's efforts at implementing SFA are examined in the following sections. It is hoped that this exercise will provide guidance and insight for others contemplating SFA or another reform. It is important to remember here that the framework used is loaded with cultural beliefs and assumptions about what should be looked for when evaluating school reform efforts. Two factors are notably missing from the framework, but are widely present in the data and are included in the analysis. These relate to the physical setting of the building and to the social climate within the building.

Looking Outward to External Standards of Best Practice

The decision to adopt a program such as SFA rather than to locally create a new program specifically designed to meet their needs reflects, in itself, an important cultural belief. In this age of knowledge separation and specialization, we often look to experts to guide us in our efforts and tell us what *best practice* is. Success for All has been well researched and has a wide following in schools. In some sense, it is tried and true. In addition, the developers of SFA provide initial and continuing support in the form of training, oversight, evaluation, and materials support. Although this is not an unfounded approach to school change (there is, after all, a place for research and knowledge gained from the experience of others), it is important to remember that the local context and culture of Howard Elementary greatly influence what happens with the program.

The school's decision to look to a nearby county's efforts with the program is another example of looking to the external as a way to approach change. This exercise allowed them to see the program in action and to place it in a context similar to their own. In fact, Howard has become an external standard for others who wish to preview the program. Schools contemplating adoption of SFA often visit schools that have already implemented the program. Select schools are usually approved for visitation after a year with the program. Howard's implementation efforts, however, led to their being approved for visitors after only half a year rather than the usual year—a source of great pride to the faculty and staff of Howard Elementary School.

Looking externally has eliminated much of the uncertainty that would otherwise have come with the unknown for the faculty, staff, and community of Howard Elementary School. Someone else has already struggled with many of the logistics and details of how to implement the program's ideas. Howard need only make the modifications called for by its own situation. Seeing the program in action and being able to relate to the context of that location has solidified expectations and helped guide the teachers by allowing them to draw on concrete memories as opposed to abstract constructs. Further relieving uncertainty and providing confidence is the school's ongoing relationship with SFA developers. Continuing professional development and evaluative feedback of the school's efforts provide a clear direction for all.

Going Beyond the Tests: Defining Clear Learning Goals for All Students

The need to determine what students are learning and how well they are learning has long been a part of education and is an important part of our cultural tradition. Although testing is a common method for gauging student learning, tests serve this purpose in various ways. Many think of tests as a culminating activity—one that produces a grade for a student's performance on a past unit of study. Others think of tests as a beginning point—a method for determining what knowledge a student brings into a unit of study. Often these latter individuals view tests as progressive—as steps along a learning staircase where each step builds on the prior and assists the latter.

SFA subscribes to this second view of testing. Built into the program is an ongoing assessment process that serves to aid the instruction students receive. The teachers and tutors at Howard Elementary School have been trained to know what the assessments tell them so they can determine whether a child should be moved to a different group or if Wings curricula should replace Roots curricula. In this way, instructional decisions are tied to assessment and tests become useful tools rather than end products.

In many ways, testing of this sort serves to define clear learning goals from which both students and teachers benefit. Both quickly become familiar with the patterns of testing and, more important, what those tests mean for future instruction and learning. Goals for learning are explicitly and frequently relayed to students, and students become familiar with the mechanisms for achieving those goals through their daily lessons. The staff at Howard Elementary have incorporated individual and group achievement goals and contests with their testing efforts as well. By offering pizza parties and the like, good grades are not the only reward for doing well.

Still some teachers question, "what do you do about kids who aren't test takers?" Although most teachers believe that their students are benefiting from frequent and purposeful assessments, there are others who are less sure of testing's positive effects. There is concern that the frequent testing that comes with SFA (several tests each week on such topics as reading words, word meanings, story comprehension, etc.) places additional stress on those students. Regardless of whether the new testing regime is viewed in a positive or negative light, an emphasis on process in addition to outcome can now be found at Howard as teachers come to view testing, and its accompanying goal setting, in new ways.

Finding Ways to Use Data

As already mentioned, testing data are now used for a multitude of purposes at Howard Elementary. In addition to the purposes already listed, testing information is also used to assign students to tutoring sessions and suggest alternative teaching strategies in the regular classroom. Changes in reading group composition and family support interventions also arise out of Howard's testing processes. There is a new belief that testing allows the faculty and staff to better meet their students' needs. In addition, testing data now includes more than just the standard end-of-grade tests utilized by the state in determining students' progress. Teachers at Howard need not wait for a yearly test score to gauge the progress being made by their students nor to judge their own teaching. Testing data is not the only data that Howard has to draw from, however, for reasons both internal and external to the SFA program.

In their continuing feedback to the school, SFA personnel provide much useful data for the Howard faculty. Their periodic visits produce "commendations" and support for steps that faculty have taken well, in addition to "recommendations" for areas that could use a little more focus or improvement. This external assessment of the teachers' efforts mirrors the assessment process used with students and is one that teachers, too, are familiar with. In this way, teachers continue to get concrete examples to follow and a renewed emphasis on SFA philosophy and practice.

The County's willingness to explore and evaluate its efforts with regard to SFA has also been a source of data for Howard Elementary. During the critical friends review process, teachers, support personnel, parents, community members, and even students talked about the ups and downs of implementing and continuing SFA. In addition, each year, as the county completes its profile survey for the Office of Education Reform, Howard participates in a self-examination of where it is with the program. Opportunities for self-reflection such as these have created an atmosphere of continual learning at Howard Elementary and again serve to keep SFA at the forefront of their minds. The ensuing discussions serve to highlight areas of agreement as well as disagreement about the program, its processes, and its effects. Such discussions do much to break down the traditional isolation experienced by teachers whose main focus is limited to their own classroom rather than to the whole school.

Embracing the Complexity of Teaching

For all at Howard Elementary School, SFA presents a highly structured teaching methodology. Teaching, assessment, and classroom management techniques are interwoven in an intricate pattern that requires practice and skill on the part of teachers and tutors (as well as students). Success for All is based on what many people acknowledge to be *best practice*, and Howard's teachers have been taught how to make decisions about these practices and how to move back and forth between them. In fact, some at Howard report that SFA "takes the average teacher and makes them a good one." The complexity of teaching, however, does not lie solely in the "how to."

As with testing, SFA challenges assumptions regarding teachers and others in the building and what they can and cannot do to help students learn. The traditional organization of the elementary school has individual teachers responsible for all of their students' learning (except in the case of extras, such as art, media, P.E., remediation, etc., whose classification of *extra* serves to separate and delineate these learning experiences from those of the regular classroom). SFA turns this organizational schema upside down. Students may be taught reading by another classroom teacher, their gym teacher, or even by the school counselor. Classroom teachers at Howard Elementary are learning to give up some of the control they once had over their students' learning and are beginning to trust each other.

At the same time, others in the school are struggling to redefine themselves as reading teachers. Many of Howard's nonclassroom teachers feel less prepared to successfully teach reading and wish for more in-depth training (particularly in cases where they received training on one level of SFA and ended up teaching another level). Although the issue of experience is undoubtedly a factor, the process of reidentifying oneself is also an important consideration in an examination of the cultural changes that occur with the introduction of this reform. Not only must classroom teachers learn to trust others, but support personnel who are now responsible for teaching a new facet of the curriculum (and a highly prized one at that) must learn to trust themselves.

This brings up the issue of teacher growth in general. Many view teaching as a set of practices or steps that only need to be learned and practiced to turn individuals into good teachers. Although SFA provides rigorous and repeated training, this how-to view appears to dominate. This is generally the view held by the individuals within Howard Elementary School as well. However, others such as Rosenholtz (1989) view teaching as inherently difficult work. Good teaching requires more than a good how-to manual. These people view teaching as an ever-evolving art form—one that involves continual study and growth on the part of teachers. SFA does not provide a mechanism for teachers to grow beyond the confines of the program. In fact, a qualitative study of two SFA schools that were more than 2 years into their implementation reports that "many teachers felt that the program constrained their autonomy and creativity" (Datnow & Castellano, 2000, p. 775). Although this may cause problems in the long term for Howard Elementary as well, it is small cause for concern in these early stages of implementation where everyone is busy, stimulated, and excited about their new way of teaching.

Connecting Teacher Learning to Student Learning

SFA clearly connects teacher learning to student learning. Methods learned by teachers at Howard Elementary are immediately and necessarily put into practice, and the effectiveness of these practices is frequently gauged through the program's continual assessment measures both for students and teachers. An important facet of SFA for the teachers at Howard Elementary is that "it reaches all of the children" and "every child is engaged." Another teacher adds, "it works with *all* children instead of a select few." It is clear that these teachers view SFA as an innovation for their teaching as well as for their students' learning.

Teacher learning is also translated into student learning through the principles of teamwork. Teachers learning to work together in planning and training toward a common goal transfer these lessons into their classrooms. They report that they more frequently plan cooperative learning activities in which students can also learn the lessons of teamwork and the satisfaction of achieving a common goal.

Also supporting student learning is the school's new focus on "taking away all the excuses" for failure—a focus aligned with SFA's relentless approach. One example of this relentlessness is an increase in referrals of students for extra help. Both support staff at the school and the school's family support team report that they have seen more referrals and credit this largely to the smaller teacher-student ratios experienced during each day's reading period. Not only are more adults in the building trained in teaching reading and writing, but they are also now able to identify problems in learning more readily.

The school's Peer Assisted Learning (PAL) program is another example of this relentlessness; if parents cannot help their children with reading and if there are not enough adult volunteer tutors to do it, then students can help do it. This locally created extension of their SFA efforts utilizes older students to provide one-on-one reading time with younger students whose parents are unable to do so at home. A small number of fifth-grade students, after receiving training, work in the mornings before school with students who need someone to read to. These fifth graders supplement their own learning by keeping journals of their experiences and of their student's progress. This group of students is learning a different set of lessons from SFA—namely, that they, too, can be teachers.

Making Interagency Collaboration Possible

A common cultural belief that has recently received renewed focus is that communities must work together to successfully raise and educate their children. The establishment of a countywide committee such as the curriculum committee and its attempts to include parents and community members in its discussions points toward a belief in the importance of community involvement in the schools. This is further emphasized by the fact that increasing parent and community involvement was chosen as one of the county's three primary goals.

Faculty and staff at Howard Elementary School share this belief in the benefits of community involvement, and SFA has provided new opportunities and an explicit focus for that involvement. Although Howard's outreach effort began long before their adoption of SFA, their efforts have expanded both in terms of business and parent involvement. SFA's family support team and advisory committee are only two of the new capacities in which parents and community members can participate. Parents are strongly encouraged to assist with their children's nightly reading assignments. Clearly, Howard Elementary has promoted the belief that the school is not solely responsible for the learning of the community's children. As one individual shares, "schools are more successful when parents have some ownership."

Many examples of community involvement are available. For instance, a local financial institution now gives its employees an hour off each day to volunteer at the school. These individuals assist as reading tutors, working one on one with students who need additional help or who do not have anyone to read with at home. To further emphasize the school's belief in the importance of reading at home, a local service agency operates a parents' lending library from which parents are encouraged to check out books to take home and read with their children. The use of goals in the SFA program makes a partnership with a local restaurant particularly beneficial. This restaurant provides free meals and sponsors parties for students who achieve monthly and yearly learning and reading goals. Finally, a local church donates money for supplies, which the school uses to purchase books in their efforts to increase the size of classroom libraries. The county's agricultural cooperative extension service works closely with Howard Elementary in its efforts to provide parenting classes, an enrichment summer day camp, and a Migrant Summer School as well as other activities. Several principles of SFA, such as the use of tutors, the focus on literacy, and some of SFA's instructional and behavioral procedures, have also been adopted by the extension service for use in their activities.

Making Space

SFA has also had an effect on the spatial use of Howard Elementary School. The brick building is a remnant of the open school movement of the 1970s modified to partially divide the once-open pods into several distinct classrooms with a common open area. The main building is supplemented by a small number of trailers. In a traditional organizational schema in which students spend their day in a single classroom (except for a few extra activities such as lunch, P.E., media, etc.), school spaces are often taken for granted. Ownership of space is undisputed because everyone has their place: grade-level teachers have their classrooms, the media specialist has her media room or library, and even the music or art teacher generally has a room dedicated to music or art. Students are accustomed to rotating through this series of spaces for different activities.

Because SFA's daily reading period breaks students into smaller groups and utilizes additional adults in the teaching process, the spatial organization of the school no longer works for this 90-minute period. During this time, students and teachers can be found in the cafeteria, on the school's stage, in the media center, in offices, and any available spaces that can be found. In these temporary spaces, it is difficult to set up shop, so to say, and create a space that feels, even temporarily, to be one's own. Whereas classroom walls are filled with student work and signs and charts reminding everyone of the various steps to the program, rules regarding behavior, goals, achievements, and progress made, this is not possible in the temporary spaces in which some groups find themselves. Some of these spaces are also cramped and crowded, making for an atmosphere less conducive to learning.

A recognition that a lack of space is inhibiting their SFA efforts has led many in the school to suggest that a new wing be built onto the school to alleviate the spatial problems introduced by the program. Such a solution is costly, however, for a county with limited resources. It is difficult to justify the addition of space that is not fully utilized all day long. The discussion regarding space (or lack thereof) has brought forward a general recognition of the importance of having spaces appropriate to one's goals. Through these discussions, a factor of schooling that is often taken for granted has been made visible and has become a part of the school's lexicon.

Changing School Climate: Bringing Unity to Howard Elementary

Although there are varying opinions as to SFA's potential to help Howard Elementary School fulfill its mission, the program is credited by all with creating much unity among the members of the school. This unity arises from several sources. First, teachers feel a renewed sense of purpose and direction because of SFA. SFA provides specific goals and pathways to take toward achieving those goals, relieving much of the ambiguity that normally surrounds educational endeavors. Questions of what to teach and why to teach are, at least temporarily, put to the back burner as SFA's goals and procedures are learned and implemented.

In addition, classroom management skills have been aligned because of SFA. The skills utilized during reading periods carry over into the rest of the day. Because everyone from music teacher to third-grade teacher to school counselor is familiar with this management system, students find consistency as well throughout their school-day experience.

As with many new ventures, there is an energy and excitement that accompanies change. Although change is also a factor that leads to some trepidation, many teachers at Howard feel a renewed sense of direction. The focus on literacy provides a clearly articulated purpose, and the adoption of SFA offers a clear pathway to that purpose. SFA has become something that everyone is talking about in shared conversation. Learning and working together has increased the need for communication and eliminated much of the isolation generally experienced in the field of teaching. Teachers report that they are sharing more now and that they like the feeling of working together.

Finding Focus and Avoiding Program Fragmentation

Many of the features of Howard Elementary School's atmosphere discussed earlier can be said to represent finding focus, as can the efforts of the district to align its goals and approaches across its schools. There is no doubt that literacy for all is a countywide focus and that SFA is the chosen method for achieving this goal. Focus comes from the SFA program, in that it is strongly connected within and between its instructional techniques, classroom management practices, and the communication it fosters. Furthermore, the program endeavors to include everyone in the community both within the school and without. To do SFA successfully, focus is necessary.

Unfortunately, a focus on one area generally means a reduction in the amount of time spent on other areas. For instance, time taken away from foreign language instruction and other extras can be cause for concern. What is basic and what is extra? This is a question that Howard is not alone in confronting. The state of North Carolina has adopted an end-of-grade testing regimen that places focus on reading, writing, and mathematics. Although Howard benefits from the alignment of its SFA efforts with the state's mandates, some are concerned about the effects on subject areas such as social studies and science (SFA components not yet adopted by Howard) as well as those on the arts, foreign languages, physical education, and others.

One thing that has been beneficial to Howard's efforts to reduce fragmentation is its attempts to adjust responsibilities and assignments accordingly. They have a full-time coordinator on staff to help teachers and tutors on a regular basis. This individual also assists with much of the placement testing and arranges for continuing professional development, which keeps SFA in the forefront of people's minds. Although some still feel pulled by multiple roles, efforts are being made to reduce that stress. The fact that other efforts (PALs, the lending library, summer camps, etc.) are either created expressly to align with SFA or are purposefully aligning themselves with SFA is another sign that Howard is attempting to avoid program fragmentation.

Moving Beyond the Pilot Project

Perhaps the most telling indicators of Howard Elementary School's desire to maintain their focus on SFA and avoid program fragmentation come from their history as well as their plans for the future. They assisted with the countywide adoption of SFA by all elementary schools—a move that, within the school system, indicates a horizontal commitment to the program. Within the school, their exploration of MathWings points toward additional curricular alignment. Additionally, they have expanded their initial K-3 focus to a K-5 focus, which speaks to vertical commitment to the program as well.

In doing so, Howard remained committed to SFA as the county began planning for moving beyond its pilot efforts at Howard. A statewide SFA facilitators' consortium has been formed, and the county participates in quarterly meetings held by this group. They are looking to expand the use of SFA with their exceptional and developmentally delayed students as well as into their alternative middle school. They are in the process of setting up a system of dialogue between elementary and middle schools to ensure that students receiving SFA instruction in the fifth grade will receive similar instruction at the middle-school level. Finally, it should not be forgotten that the school system has embraced a desire to document and research its efforts in regard to SFA and is not rushing blindly down any of these paths.

In a state known for its "random acts of reform" (Lindsay, 1997), Marshall County historically fit right in. There was always something coming— some savior that fizzled out shortly. As one teacher reported, "programs come and go; that worries me." However, as they continue to align their efforts behind the SFA program and philosophies, the county seems to be breaking the mold this time around.

"IT'S ALL HARD WORK, BUT IT'S WORTH IT"

As we have seen, the learning of new practices and procedures constitutes only a small portion of the change that takes place with the introduction of reform (although these facets of reform generally receive the most attention, especially in the beginning stages of implementation). Reform also requires that the seeds of new cultural understandings be planted and take root. In the case of Howard Elementary School and SFA, many ideas about the nature of teaching, the role of parents and other staff in the school, the job of students, and even the effect of physical surroundings have undergone change (and continue to be revised). The growth and life span of reform are dependent on these cultural learnings, which represent the hard work that, in the end, makes the effort worth it.

As stated earlier, not everything about SFA represents a change in culture for those in Howard Elementary School and Marshall County. This point cannot be overemphasized. Too many times, reform is viewed only as successful if it restructures or completely transforms a school. Although the term *restructure* has become the latest buzzword in educational reform, much can be accomplished without total transformation.

Conley (1993) offered some beneficial distinctions on this matter. He separated educational reform efforts into three main categories: renewal activities, reform-driven activities, and restructuring activities. *Renewal activities* are those that "help the organization do better and/or more efficiently that which it is already doing" (p. 7). *Reform-driven activities* alter existing practices in such a way that the organization is able "to adapt the way it functions to new circumstances or requirements" (p. 8). Finally, *restructuring activities* "change fundamental assumptions, practices and relationships, both within the organization and between the organization and the outside world" (p. 8). These fundamental assumptions are cultural beliefs. For Howard Elementary School, SFA represents all three of these categories of change (a situation that is undoubtedly true for many reforms in many locations). It is even likely that the same component of SFA represents a different kind of activity for different individuals within the school and system. For instance, SFA's reading instruction may serve a renewal purpose for many of Howard's classroom, grade-level teachers at the same time that it represents restructuring for other school faculty.

Certainly in the case of Howard Elementary, there do appear to be some important shifts in cultural belief. The faculty and staff of Howard, as well as across the county, now share (with few exceptions) a common way to teach reading. As mentioned earlier, the fact that all teachers are doing the same thing and talking frequently about it challenges the traditional culture of the isolated teacher. The sense of togetherness that this shared belief has brought is spoken of often and is greatly appreciated. In addition, this sense of togetherness expands beyond the regular classroom teachers and now includes other adults both within and outside of the school as well as some students. A belief that all adults (and even some children) can teach breaks from the traditional roles held by individuals within the school and community and begs the question, "whose students are they?"

Testing is viewed as a tool now, rather than as a final product either for a unit or for a year. The frequency and changed purpose of this testing relieves much of the stress that traditionally surrounds testing procedures and clearly shows that test score improvement is possible. Even those who still express doubts about the program admit that students are showing progress on the tests, and they are pleased by this fact. Finally, not only has the ownership of students come into question, but so has the ownership of school space. Faculty and staff at Howard have been forced to rethink spatial practices and uses, and they have had to readjust beliefs about classroom ownership because of the SFA program.

At the same time, some fundamental assumptions remain unchanged and even unexamined. The belief that literacy is the key to all other success is reinforced with the introduction of SFA as is the belief that parent and community involvement are important to the school's efforts. Nor does SFA challenge the belief that the purpose of education is future success. Students at Howard reveal this belief most explicitly when they discuss what they perceive is most important to the adults at the school. Almost unanimously, they report the adults want them to get a good education so they can learn. The natural extension of learning, they continue, is to either win scholarships or get good jobs when they grow up.

The comment of one teacher who stated that "programs come and go" indicates that looking to externally created, expert solutions is the way in which Howard Elementary has historically approached change. The adoption of SFA follows this pattern and represents another unexamined cultural belief. Although none of these previous programs have become permanent additions to the school, undoubtedly various practices and beliefs stemming from them remain. In the same way, regardless of whether Howard Elementary sustains its SFA efforts indefinitely, parts of the program will live on in the culture of the school.

This pattern of programs coming and going speaks once again to the hard work involved in the process of implementing reform. Programs may go because they do not require a vigilant effort. Therefore, they fall to the wayside as other activities take on priority status. Programs may also go because too much effort is required and it becomes difficult to sustain such a high level of energy. In other words, the hard work is no longer worth it. Given the nature of its continuous, relentless approach, as well as its cost, SFA falls into this latter category.

What will become of SFA at Howard Elementary School if the hard work becomes no longer worth it and the program becomes yet another example of one that came and went? Venezky's (1998) follow-up study of five Baltimore City elementary schools may shed some light on this question. His research shows that SFA remained partially implemented in all five schools after 5 years, but that there had been substantial deviations from the program's design. He maintained that it is "important to know if all components of the plan are critical to its success" (p. 152) and identified several implementation issues directly related to funding cuts (a situation, it seems, to which no school or system can claim immunity).

Venezky found that all five schools had retained their SFA approach to reading instruction and all faculty and staff were knowledgeable about the program. Everyone could explain the components in detail and knew which of the components they were responsible for. Students, too, knew the rhythm of SFA's daily schedule and seemed familiar with program tasks. Most teachers still expressed "a general level of satisfaction with the program" (Venezky, 1998, p. 153). Finally, it is noteworthy (and somewhat unusual when one considers the typical lifespan of reform) that after 5 years the program remained a large part of these schools' efforts.

However, he also found that in four of the five schools, tutoring had regressed from one-on-one to small groups ranging in size from 4 to 15 per group. He also found varied adherence to the 8-week assessment process—both in terms of actual frequency of testing and actions resulting from them (such as moving students from one reading group to another). Family support teams struggled with their outreach efforts, more often than not reacting to problems rather than engaging in proactive strategies. Finally, he also found some dissatisfaction on the part of teachers as well as principals resulting from the program's lack of room for personal adaptation.

Adaptations such as these are not uncommon to any reform effort. Although Venezky (1998) seemed to blame a shortage in funding for the majority of these implementation issues, there are many possible reasons for them, including those involving the difficulty of sustaining high levels of effort as mentioned before. The argument may even be successfully made that these schools are no longer doing SFA because they no longer adhere strictly to the program's guidelines. It can also be argued, however, that SFA is alive and well in Baltimore. Although Venezky did not include a pre-SFA analysis of these schools, it is highly unlikely that they had all of these components and practices in place and that SFA had not left its mark on the school's faculty and students.

In similar fashion, if Howard Elementary School should find itself cutting back on or making adjustments to its SFA efforts, at least some of the new methods, procedures, and beliefs that accompanied the program undoubtedly will remain. Even if the program, by name, should disappear entirely, the cultural changes it brought about will not be completely lost. New techniques for teaching reading and writing, new methods of managing the classroom, new procedures for testing—these will remain as experiential knowledge on which teachers can draw. New attitudes toward tests and data management, and new beliefs about the social organization of the school and the roles which people play, and new approaches toward fostering parent and community involvement are now embedded in the culture of the school.

All of this seems to beg the question: Does the discontinuance of a reform effort represent failure of the reform? The answer to this question depends on one's definition of *success*. One definition of success, of course, is whether the reform effort improves students' learning.[5] This is the context in which Venezky's comment appears. If the goal of those who adopt the reform is to accomplish this (as it often is), sufficient time must be allotted to fully implement the reform and let it take hold. To use a metaphor introduced earlier, seeds planted must be given time to take root, grow, and bloom.

Another definition of success relates to the lifespan of reform. It is generally assumed that if a school allows a reform to go, then the reform has been a failure. But has it? Perhaps to some who have financial or personal stakes in the program rather than in the program's beliefs, methods, and results, cessation of the program represents failure. For most, however, it is the latter things that matter. School cultures, like the teachers, students, staff, and communities that create them, are ever changing. Because of this, what seems right at one point in time may not be right at another. Viewed in a cultural context, the cultural remnants of reform may be as important as the reform. In this light, a program may go, having served its purpose.

---

[5]There has been much disagreement as to the effectiveness of SFA in this sense. For a sample, see either of the following exchanges: Walberg and Greenberg (1999a, 1999b), Royce (1999); or Pogrow (2000a, 2000b), Slavin and Madden (2000).

ACKNOWLEDGMENTS

This research was supported by the North Carolina Department of Public Instruction, Office of Education Reform, as part of the North Carolina School Improvement Grant initiative. I would like to thank Judy White and Jerry Jailall for their continued support and interest in the progress that these schools are making. The School Improvement Grant Evaluation Team has also been a source of great support. Together we have learned much about how to think about and evaluate systemic reform. My thanks to Barnett Berry, Ken Jenkins, Linda McCalister, George Noblit, and Laura Turchi for their guidance and influence. The data from which much of this chapter was written were collected through the efforts of a critical friends group consisting of myself, George Noblit, and two members of Marshall County's central office. My thanks, too, for their support and assistance.

REFERENCES

Ancess, J. (1996, March). *Outside/inside, inside/outside: Developing and implementing the school quality review.* New York: National Center for Restructuring Education, Schools, and Teaching (NCREST).

Balkcom, S., & Himmelfarb, H. (1993, August). *Success for All. Education Research Consumer Guide No. 5.* (Office of Research, Office of Educational Research and Improvement (OERI) of the U. S. Department of Education Publication No. 0-356-792:QL3). Washington, DC: U.S. Government Printing Office.

Berry, B. (1996). *Assessing the North Carolina school improvement grants.* Raleigh: North Carolina Department of Public Instruction.

Berry, B., Jenkins, K., McKinney, M., Noblit, G., & Turchi, L. (1997, July). *Assessing the North Carolina school improvement grants: A report from the evaluation team to the State Board of Education.* Raleigh: North Carolina Department of Public Instruction.

Conley, D. (1993). *Roadmap to restructuring: Policies, practices and the emerging visions of schooling.* Eugene: University of Oregon, ERIC Clearinghouse on Educational Management.

Datnow, A., & Castellano, M. (2000). Teachers' responses to Success for All: How beliefs, experiences, and adaptations shape implementation. *American Educational Research Journal, 37*(3), 775-799.

Elmore, R. (1996). Getting to scale with good educational practice. *Harvard Educational Review, 66*(1), 1-26.

Erickson, F. (1997). Culture in society and in educational practices. In J. A. Banks & C. M. Banks (Eds.), *Multicultural education: Issues and perspectives* (3rd ed., pp. 32-60). Boston: Allyn & Bacon.

Fullan, M. (1994, July). *Turning systemic thinking on its head.* Paper prepared for the U.S. Department of Education.

Fullan, M. (1996, February). Turning systemic thinking on its head. *Phi Delta Kappan*, pp. 420-423.

Fullan, M., with Stiegelbauer, S. (1991). *The new meaning of educational change.* New York: Teachers College Press.

Lindsay, D. (1997, January 22). Random acts of reform. *Education Week*, pp. 177-235.

Pogrow, S. (2000a). Success for All does not produce success for students. *Phi Delta Kappan, 82*(1), 67-80.

Pogrow, S. (2000b). The unsubstantiated "success" of Success for All: Implications for policy, practice, and the soul of our profession. *Phi Delta Kappan, 81*(8), 596-600.

Rosenholtz, S. (1989). *Teachers workplace: The social organization of schools.* New York: Longman.

Royce, B. R. (1999). The great literacy problem and Success for All. *Phi Delta Kappan, 81*(2), 129-131.

Slavin, R. E. (1996). *Education for all.* Lisse, Netherlands: Swets & Zeitlinger.

Slavin, R. E., & Madden, N. A. (2000). Research on achievement outcomes of Success for All: A summary and response to critics. *Phi Delta Kappan, 82*(1), 38-40, 59-66.

Slavin, R. E., Madden, N. A., Dolan, L. J., & Wasik, B. A. (1996). *Every child, every school: Success for all.* Thousand Oaks, CA: Corwin Press.

Slavin, R. E., Madden, N. A., Dolan, L. J., Wasik, B. A., Ross, S., Smith, L., & Dianda, M. (1995, April). *Success for all: A summary of research.* Paper presented at the meeting of the American Educational Research Association, San Francisco.

Slavin, R. E., Madden, N. A., Karweit, N. L., Dolan, L. J., & Wasik, B. A. (1992). *Success for all: A relentless approach to prevention and early intervention in elementary schools* (ERS Monograph). Arlington, VA: Educational Research Service.

Venezky, R. L. (1998). An alternative perspective on Success for All. In K. K. Wong (Ed.), *Advances in educational policy: Vol. 4. Perspectives on the social functions of schools* (pp. 145-165). Stamford, CT: JAI Press.

Walberg, H. J., & Greenberg, R. C. (1999a). The diogenes factor. *Phi Delta Kappan, 81*(2), 127-128.

Walberg, H. J., & Greenberg, R. C. (1999b). Educators should require evidence. *Phi Delta Kappan, 81*(2), 132-135.

6

Contradictions in Culture: African-American Students in Two Charter Schools

Carol E. Malloy
University of North Carolina at Chapel Hill

Educators and parents who are not satisfied with the education offered in their area public schools look to programs of Choice for alternatives. Choice in school placement takes many forms including vouchers and charters. Vouchers are government-issued funds to parents that enable children to attend the school of their choice, including private and religious schools, with the government paying all or part of the tuition. Voucher proponents argue that vouchers create competition for the public schools and can cause them to strengthen educational programs. Opponents argue that vouchers violate the separation of church and state and that they divert needed funds from the public schools. Several states have passed legislation to establish voucher programs. However, the program in Wisconsin has been propelled into national attention. In 1998, the U.S. Supreme Court declined to hear a challenge to the Wisconsin program that allows some children in Milwaukee to attend religious or private schools using public funds, which is considered a large victory for the voucher movement. This Milwaukee Parental Choice Program, which in 1998-1999 enrolled 6,100 students in private schools, has filled all seats available in the city's 84 participating private schools. Of this number, 3,000 students had already been enrolled in private schools using family support. Currently, the city schools are losing $4,950 for each child who does not enroll in the public schools (Kronholz, 1998).

Many parents and educators who are opposed to vouchers, but want to exercise choice within the public sector, look to charter schools as viable alternative educational programs. Charter schools are tuition-free public schools that have some degree of autonomy not available in regular public schools. These schools are often smaller than other public schools, have smaller classes, offer specialized curriculum, and require parental involvement. Charter schools are required to meet student performance standards of their states or districts, but "the charter itself states the terms under which the school can be held accountable for improving student performance and achieving goals set out in the charter" (U.S. Charter Schools, 1998). Charters are started by diverse groups of people. Any group of people with a dream or an idea for a school can create a proposal that states why they want the charter, what children they will serve, and what they plan to do in the school (U.S. Charter Schools, 1998).

Nationally and regionally, educators, parents, and policymakers are debating the contribution of charters. Proponents argue that standardized education cannot meet the needs of a student population becoming increasingly diverse. They believe that there has to be an educational alternative for students who are dissatisfied or not able to function in the regular public schools. The National Educational Association (NEA) cautiously endorses charter schools stating, "Charter schools can become change agents within public school systems by charting new and creative ways of teaching and learning. Or they can allow unprepared people to start schools and undermine education" (NEA Statement on Charter Schools). NEA is concerned that provisions for charters have meaningful standards of equity and educational quality. Opponents of charter schools argue that charters will drain public schools of the best teachers and students and deprive existing public schools of needed funding. Some opponents are concerned that charters will be used by voucher proponents as a way to create private schools with public funds.

Currently, there are 34 charter school laws in the United States, and 26 states including the District of Columbia offer public school students a charter option (Center for Educational Reform, 1998). Over 250,000 students in the United States attend charter schools, and 90% of schools in operation are in Arizona, California, Michigan, Massachusetts, Florida, and Colorado.

In 1995, the debate about choice as a reform took place in the legislature of a southern state. At issue in this state was giving dissatisfied parents an alternative to the existing public schools. Because of the constitutional questions about vouchers, this legislature decided on charter schools as a compromise between public and private school choice. As a result, the state's legislature passed the Charter Schools Act of 1996,[1] inviting any person or group of

---

[1]Major points from the Charter Schools Act of 1996 include:

- Any child who is qualified to attend public schools in the state is qualified for admission to a charter school. Any student who meets the eligibility cri-

people on behalf of a nonprofit corporation to file an application for a charter school. They limited the number of charter schools to 100 and limited each school district to a maximum of five. During the summer of 1997, the State Board of Education gave final approval to 37 charter schools: In 1998, it approved 30 additional schools.

This state defines a charter school *as a deregulated public school. Charter schools have freedom and flexibility in programs and curriculum, give parents choice, receive public funding, and must meet achievement goals. However, these schools cannot charge tuition or discriminate. Charters that have been issued typically focus on a new curricular or organizational approach that is different from regular public schools.*

The state is evaluating the success of the charters to determine whether this reform should be expanded in the future. This chapter describes the culture and the resulting educational issues that are outgrowths of two schools[2] in their second year of operation. These schools have a broad range of difference in the population they serve, the goals of the charters, and in the implementation of this reform.

---

teria for a category of disability and requires special education has an entitlement to special education through the federal Individuals with Disabilities Education Act (IDEA).

- The board of directors of a charter school is responsible for the operation of the school including budgeting, curriculum, and operational procedures.
- The schools are awarded between $3,000 and $5,500 per student depending upon the wealth of the district in which the charter is located, and $54,000 per school through a federal start-up grant. They also receive additional funds of approximately $2000 for each identified special education student.
- Charters are issued for at most five years and can be renewed.
- The board of directors is the employer and all salaries are set by the school.
- Seventy-five percent of the teachers in grades K-5 and fifty percent of the teachers in grades 6-12 must be licensed/certified.
- Charter schools are expected to comply with state accountability program testing requirements in which a growth expectation is set for each charter by the state; however, charters can propose an alternate model comparable to the state program. (North Carolina Department of Public Instruction, 1998).

[2]The study had a case study design using observation, interviewing, and document review as the major data collection techniques. A team of 4 people collected in two-day visits of each school giving us 8 person days in each of the schools. We systematically conducted individual and focus group interviews with administrators, teachers, parents, board members, funders and partners, support staff, and students. We observed classrooms, school activities, and general school life. We collected and used data from relevant documents such as schedules, brochures, written curricula, charter school proposal, and teacher and student work. At the end of the site visits the team leader conducted a debriefing session with school representatives. Next data were summarized and compiled by the lead member of the team for analysis. Analysis included the identification of key themes that describe the school and the culture it has developed. Reports from the inter-

SCHOOL CULTURE

A school's culture creates an environment where students can respond to the instruction afforded them. A charter school's culture—its beliefs, rituals, and common experiences—emanate from the vision of their founders. The construction of a school around beliefs and rituals is formalized when the proposal for the school is written and submitted to the state for approval. The culture becomes ingrained after the school is opened and maintained over time. The two charter schools presented here used philosophy and structure as the foundation for the construction of their schools' cultures. Paramount in these constructions are the (a) beliefs of the boards, administrators, teachers, parents, and students; (b) enactment of valued rituals; and (c) reactions to those rituals.

Using the voices of informants, the following cases of Global Middle School and Liberty Academy present the range of this reform through the schools' instructional culture and histories. Later I use the schools' instructional cultures—including their beliefs about students, curriculum, and pedagogy and their history presented in these cases—as backdrops for the comparison of the two charter schools and the resulting marginal education offered to African-American children.

As I looked at the education and schooling of African-American students in these two schools, I questioned the purpose of schooling that controlled their cultures and whether the established instructional cultures were congruent with the educational goals, beliefs, and needs of African-American parents, educators, and the broader community. In these schools, was there a desire to establish educational programs that would help students understand the purpose of schooling and benefit from that understanding, or was there a desire to change the students to fit into molds that the boards and administrations felt they should resemble? More specifically, are these schools offering their students an education that will provide them with the necessary power codes and rules for success without limitations?

Students today exist in a global environment with numerous cultural orientations and codes to understand and stratagem as they develop into adulthood. Education is the means by which students develop understanding of the multiple cultures that exist in the world; it is the process through which students develop their worldviews. Shujaa (1994) explained that education is "the process of transmitting from one generation to the next knowledge of the val-

---

views were cross-checked to insure that the pictures of the school were accurate and complete. Data from informants in different positions and documents were used for triangulation. Individual case studies of each school were written and shared with the school administrators and teachers for critique. Major cultural elements were compared across the two schools. The comparison and synthesis of the data yielded the interpretation of the case studies.

ues, aesthetics, spiritual beliefs, and all things that give a particular cultural orientation its uniqueness" (p. 15). It is a way for students to value and understand their communicative, structural, cultural, and strategic rules and rituals of society. However, Shujaa stated that "schooling is a process *intended* to perpetuate and maintain the society's existing power relationships and the institutional structures that support those arrangements" (p. 15). Delpit (1995) agreed that schools, as institutions, reproduce the culture of the broader society in structures, rules, and hegemony. Regardless of the subject matter, the classroom culture exemplifies power of the teacher and the institution. She described the *culture of power* in our schools as rules and codes related to linguistic forms, communicative strategies, and presentations of self. This culture of power comes from teachers, textbooks, curriculum developers, school districts, and society. She believes that success in school depends on the students' ability to understand and participate in the culture of those who are in power. Children of the middle and upper class come to school with tools to participate in this culture, whereas children from other families—minority and poor—operate within viable cultures that do not carry the same power codes or rules. She explained that schools and teachers must teach students, who do not have the codes, to understand and use the uniqueness of their cultural styles, but to also understand and use the culture of power of this society. The two schools described in the following cases have different views on how this should be accomplished. They have different ideologies and values, and they teach the skills that they believe students need to become productive citizens.

IMPLEMENTATION OF VISIONS—CASES OF TWO CHARTER SCHOOLS

Global Middle School and Liberty Academy are located in urban areas, but not in the same city. Global Middle School is located in the downtown area of a moderately large southern city, with a population of over 250,000. The county school district has an enrollment of 91,900 students; racial mix is approximately 68% White and 32% minority (27% African American). Global Middle School began operation with 53 sixth graders and has extended to 110 sixth and seventh graders in its second year; it plans to have 162 students in Grades 6 to 8 in the next school year. Two of the 13 teachers are African American and 1 is Latino; all of the administrative staff is White. Of the students, 84% are White and 16% are minority (12% African American). Students are selected for the school through a lottery system because there are more applications than spaces available.

Liberty Academy is located in a moderately sized southern city with a population of 100,000. The county school district has an enrollment of approximately 27,200 students; racial mix is 40% White and 60% minority (50% African American). Liberty is an elementary school and began operation with

200 students in Grades K to 2, extended to 310 students in K to 3 in its second year, and plans to gradually grow to be a K to 8 school. Liberty is located in an old African-American community that has a recent history of problems with crime, cohesiveness, and direction and where residents are either blue-collar workers or live in poverty. All of the students at Liberty, except for three, are African American. Two of the 16 teachers and the headmaster are white; the rest of the teachers and staff are African American. Students apply for enrollment and, to date, all the students who apply have been accepted.

Global Middle School

As I approached the school for the first time, Elaine, the Global Middle School secretary, is sitting on the cement trim that surrounds the trees in front of the church where the school is located. It is 8 a.m. and parents are dropping off their children for a day of school. Elaine greets the parents and students and asks the students if they want to purchase tickets for the dance to be held on the weekend. The school wants to know how many students will be attending so it can plan appropriately. After brief conversations, Elaine rushes the students into the school for their morning meeting.

At the morning meeting for the sixth graders,[3] four core subject teachers and two other teachers stand in different places in the room. The two teachers, Denise and Bruce, who lead this day's session are in the front next to a table with general information for the students. All the sixth-grade students file in, pick up a schedule for the day, and sit on the carpeted floor. Denise and Bruce explain to students the 2-day schedule for classes. Students record specific assignments and activities on the schedules for the directions and theme/core academics parts of the day. The teachers are informal in their discussion with the students and often change plans and make new decisions in front of the students if clarification is needed. They appear to work as a unified team rather than six separate teachers. One modification to the students' schedule was a mathematics activity. All the students in the sixth grade were responsible for completing a measurement activity in Dogwood Park across the street from the school. Jim, the mathematics teacher responsible for the project, reads names of students who are going to the park with him at 10:45 a.m. A student asks, "What should we bring with us?" The students take responsibility for materials they need for their work.

The first thematic unit that students worked on in both the sixth and seventh grades was their personal autobiographies. Denise explained to the students the personal evaluation process used for the projects. Students at Global

---

[3]There are two morning meetings, one for each grade. Global Middle School is in its second year and has sixth and seventh grades. During the next academic year the school will include Grades 6 through 8.

are not given number or letter grades; they play a major role in the assessment of their own progress. Denise explained that in the evaluation of their autobiography they were to discuss other projects they would like to do in the future. One student said, "We never did this at our other school. Teachers just said 'Boom,' and we had to do it." All the teachers in the room smiled.

Earlier in the week, these students began the process of determining the subsequent curricular units for the year. Students listed questions they had about how social, scientific, and personal phenomena function and global issues they wanted to explore. The questions addressed things the students wanted to learn more about. Denise and Bruce were in charge of explaining the day's activity regarding these questions. Bruce said,

> At 10 a.m. you were going to go to your classrooms and silently observe your questions that were placed on the walls in different places. You are not going to talk with anyone. Here on the front table there is a World Questions Observation form. Each of you will take one of these papers as you leave the meeting to help you establish a way to categorize the questions.

Bruce is specific in how he wants the students to behave as they do this exercise. He and Denise stress the importance of this activity because the results will chart the work they will be doing for the rest of the year. The students' questions determine the development of integrated units of study for the year.

Next Jim asks the students to get out their world weather maps. He talks about the path of a tropical depression just off the coast of Africa. Students record the path of the storm and write down a prediction based on what they had learned about the development of storms and the likelihood of this storm becoming a hurricane. As the students file out of the meeting, they walk beneath a banner hung in the hall opposite the library that states, "School of Excellence, 1997-98, Global Middle School." This sign was a symbol of the success that the students and the school had achieved on the state-mandated end-of-grade tests. Eight-five percent of the students in the school had test scores exceeding the state expectations.

Global Museum was the vision of two women who wanted to establish the world's first interactive learning center of global education. They envisioned a center where children could learn about global economy and environment, population growth, technological advances in communications and transportation, and mobility and diversity. Support from the business and education community over a 20-year period funded the construction, which is underway. Museum staff will be able to work with schools and the state department of public instruction to enhance the global education of children throughout the region. In June 1996, the director of the museum was asked by state legislators and the state superintendent of schools to apply for a charter. She realized that if they got the charter, they could not only work with schools, but they could be a school. The Board of the museum approved, and they applied for and were granted a charter for a school. Global Middle School was a reality—on paper.

In Fall 1997, the school opened in the educational center of a church adjacent to the site for the museum. Parents from throughout the community tried to enroll their children in the school. As a result, a lottery system had to be developed for student placement, and there is a growing waiting list of students wanting admittance.

In its first year, the school struggled to find its identity. Teachers are vested in the school, but they struggled as they tried to accomplish the charter's goals through the curriculum and pedagogy. They had difficulty implementing instructional strategies that matched the vision of the charter. They were creative teachers with knowledge about teaching in traditional and innovative schools, but they did not have experiences in schools that promoted independent learners using real-life situations. They felt that the administrators, who were museum administrators, were making decisions using their language—that of visionaries not practitioners. Both teachers and museum administrators spent most of the year trying to understand one another. During the summer, the teachers worked with consultants who helped them place the Global vision into their instruction. The teachers and consultants, without the administrators, developed the instructional culture of Global. The director was pleased with the teachers' response to the staff development and said, "This past summer the teachers created Global. With their summer work, the teachers have learned how to supply a pedagogy to our vision."

Global students construct learning through activities and projects that help them value independent learning. Teachers have high learning expectations, with "all students can learn" as the implicit and explicit message given to students. Three outcomes appear to dominate the teaching and learning: the development of independent learners, critical thinkers, and responsible contributing citizens. To accomplish this, Global uses teamwork among students and staff, a student-centered curriculum and pedagogy, and a curriculum that connects most core subjects through thematic learning. The thematic curriculum that the teachers develop requires hours of collaboration and planning. Teachers make sure that students receive the processes necessary to understand and apply the middle-grades curriculum for science, social studies, and language arts. Mathematics is included when possible, but teachers are aware that in-depth understanding of mathematics is difficult to accomplish in global thematic units. Mathematics is taught as a separate subject and is the only course that uses textbooks. The books that are used are not conventional texts; they are innovative curriculum materials based on the National Council of Teachers of Mathematics Standards.

There is no normal schedule for classes at Global; the day is loosely structured. In the morning meeting, teachers explain the schedule to the students for one or two consecutive days. The students in each grade are divided into two groups and are assigned to four core academic teachers. They receive all their instruction in mathematics, science, social studies, and language arts from these teachers. Mathematics is grouped by ability; most seventh-grade students take either seventh-grade math or pre-Algebra—six students take Algebra I. During the academic periods, whole-group instruction is limited; teachers work with students in small groups or individually. Students often find a place in the room that is comfortable to them and work on assignments and projects that they want and need to do. Because the school has a global emphasis, every student must take a foreign language with one of two native-speaking teachers in Spanish and French. They also take gym and art. After school there are different activities such as peer tutoring, games, TV production, and band lessons.

Liberty Academy

At 7:45 a.m. when I arrived at Liberty Academy, several teachers and staff are standing at the front and side of the old Weir Elementary School building welcoming students to school for the day. Parents drive up to a designated stop, kiss their children, and let them out of the cars. The teachers and staff receive the students with smiles and whisk them into school. The students are dressed in uniforms—white shirts and blue skirts or pants. They seem eager to start the day.

Just inside the front door of the school is a sign that says, "Liberty Academy, Still Under Construction." The school is bright, clean, quiet, orderly, and inviting, but there is obvious painting being done in the hallways. Students are scurrying about the hallways trying to get to their classrooms before 8 a.m., the start of school.

Just before 8 a.m. in the third-grade classrooms, as in every classroom, students listen to classical music to "calm them down in the morning." There are 22 students in Mrs. Todd's class seated in rows on one side of a large room. At 8:00 a.m., the students stand, face the flag, and say the Pledge of Allegiance to the Flag. After the pledge, the teacher asks students to get their mathematics materials out of their desks so they can work on their 7 times tables. In a rote singing fashion, the students recite $7 \times 1 = 7$, $7 \times 2 = 14$, ... $7 \times 10 = 70$. Mrs. Todd praises the students, asking, "Doesn't it feel good to be organized?" A few students run up to the teacher and give her hugs of thanks. Next Mrs. Todd begins to read from a script for the mathematics lesson. She reads to the children, "Please get out your 100 board so that we can look at subtraction of 10s." Some students get their boards out quickly, but one student does not have his notebook. Mrs. Todd reprimands this student and tells him that he will have to look at his neighbor's board. Mrs. Todd says, "Get out your board" at least 10 times before all the students have their boards in front of them. Next she asks the entire class to place a finger on the number 46 on the board. She repeats this 6 times, saying, "I'll wait for all of you to get ready." Then reading from the script, she asks the students, "What do you get when you subtract 10? (pause) Look at the number above 46. The answer is 36." The boards had 10 numbers in each of the rows and columns. She repeats this process with six different numbers, calling on different students to answer the questions. Next the students are asked to get out their flash cards to practice their addition facts.

Across the hall, students in Ms. Oakes' third-grade class are sitting on the floor in a corner of the room reciting the mathematics pattern of the day. The teacher says, "This is a new pattern 37, 47,57 . . . , 127. What is the rule?" The students quickly answer, "Add 10!" Next she asks the students for two ways to say 5:30 and allows students to use a movable clock to display the time. Then she begins to read her script. She reads, "Here is a problem. Mary had six apples. She gave 3 apples away. Write a question for this story. (pause) Six take away 3 is the number sentence. 'How many apples are left?' is the question." Next they count money, and then they measure temperatures. In this classroom, the teacher also waited for all the students to be with her before she started reading the lesson script. On the bulletin board, Ms. Oakes has a poster that explains how students should listen. It states: Rules for good listening are: Eyes are watching, Lips are closed, Ears are listening, Hands are still, and Feet are quiet.

Next door, Mrs. Placket's third-grade students are completing a mathematics worksheet. The 18 students are sitting in rows in the front of the room. They talk to neighbors as they work on the problems, but most of them stay in their seats. Suddenly there is an explosion between two boys. Instantly the teaching assistant, a male, takes the boys out of the room. The removal is so swift that the disturbance seems to have little or no impact on the rest of the students. (One student comes over to me to apologize for the behavior of the two boys.) Mrs. Placket asks the students to read quietly from their reading books after they finish their mathematics so she can set up their next activity. There is a quiet hum in the room as most of the students read out loud to themselves. The teaching assistant comes back into the room with one boy. The other boy is still in the hall sitting on the floor. It takes a few minutes for all the students to transition from reading to themselves to the next activity. Mrs. Placket stresses that students sit straight and look ahead before she begins the activity.

Liberty Academy was started by a diverse group of parents who wanted an alternative to the existing public school system. These parents wanted a different learning environment for their children where they could be successful. The vision was to create a school for at-risk youth. An initial small group met regularly to develop the charter and components, but the initial effort failed. New meetings were held with organizations such as the Chamber of Commerce to seek assistance. They met with different groups of parents to explain the need for the school, talked with friends and other interested parties, and placed information on the Internet to find parents who were interested. Through these second efforts, the charter was established.

In 1997, the school was opened with 200 students in a church basement near the present site. One third of the parents and students who initially planned to be a part of the charter were White, but when most White parents learned of the school's location, they withdrew from the school. Presently, there are only three White children enrolled in the school. Because the focus of the school was not contingent on race or ethnic group, but on students who were at risk, the school proceeded with the parents and students who remained. All the children who applied were admitted.

Liberty Academy places student development as the school's primary function. The mission statement on the school brochure declares that the mission is threefold:

> To provide all students with unlimited opportunity for the full development of their full potential: to stimulate and promote achievement and success through superior teaching methods and cooperative behavior, and parents and teachers will share the governance, curriculum and academic excellence at the school.

This school acknowledges the importance of student development and uses many strategies to help students in Grades K to 3 develop their full potential. The instruction offered to students is individualistic and expository using a diagnostic/prescriptive approach, the teachers are collaborative, and all the stakeholders believe that every child can learn. Staff and administrators believe that students need to learn how to listen and be in control before they are prepared to learn.

The headmaster, teachers, parents, and students are particularly proud of student achievement and academic growth. Their 1997-1998 standardized test results show kindergarten students scored at the 94th percentile in reading, 99th in mathematics, and 90th in core total. These scores far surpass the achievement of other African-American students at this grade level. The first graders did not achieve at these levels, with a 19th percentile core total, but the second graders had a 78th percentile score for the core total and a 90th percentile score in mathematics. They are also pleased with the social/academic growth of the students during the 1997-1998 school year. John Winters, headmaster, explained, "Students came to us as street kids, and they are now students. We have a strict code of discipline here. Students stand to reply to teacher's questions, they say *yes sir* and *yes ma'am*. Structure works with these kids."

Liberty believes that a good education stresses "high standards of personal and social behavior. . . . The school curriculum will give students the opportunity to reflect on and practice the concepts of human dignity, equity, integrity, honesty, compassion, respect for the rights of others, self-control, open-mindedness, and the common good" (School brochure). Using diagnostic tests, the teachers determine "what the students do not know and teach to the deficit." Teachers work for individual growth rate and achievement level, and their instruction tries to remove the threat of failure from the children. The headmaster selected the McGraw Hill 3-Rs diagnostic test in reading, language, and mathematics to help teachers identify the objectives students need to study. At the end of the year, students are tested on a national basic skills test. The teachers said, "Yes, we test a lot, but with these tests we can teach better." Their instruction is expository, includes projects, and is objective-driven.

Liberty uses traditional elementary curriculum centering on Hirsch's Core Knowledge Sequence for social studies, literature, and science; Saxon Mathematics, which stresses the development of basic skills; and SRA from McGraw Hill in reading. All of these curriculum materials provide students with a prescribed set of materials they should learn during the academic year. Teachers attended workshops sponsored by the Core Knowledge, Saxon Mathematics, and SRA to learn how to teach the programs. A musician who visits the school twice a week teaches music.

COMPARISON: PRIVILEGE AND POVERTY

Legislated reform in the form of charter schools has offered two different groups of people the opportunity to implement schools they felt would enlighten two different groups of children. The schools are in the same broad geographical area—about 30 miles apart—but are different in their founding and implementation. Global was started because it was a good idea that a board wanted children to experience. However, Liberty was started because parents were dissatisfied with the education their children were receiving and wanted to create an alternative to public schools in the area. The implementation reveals contrasts in fiscal support systems that are in place for the schools, the public perception and acceptance of the schools, the stance the schools have in educating the students, the governance established at the schools, and thus each school's resulting interpretation of culture. These contrasts are examined next with the understanding that Liberty educates 310 at-risk students, the majority of whom are African American. Global educates 110 middle-class students, the majority of whom are White.

Fiscal and Community Support

In *Savage Inequalities*, Kozol (1991) described the inequalities in school funding between the suburbs and inner cities in the United States and how these inequalities can affect student achievement. The inequalities and contrasts in struggles for adequate physical space and support from the community were startling when Kozol wrote this book, and 12 years later inequalities continue to be startling as in these two charter schools.

Since its opening, Global Middle School had been housed in a church education building situated between a church and the construction of a new Global Museum. Global used a few rooms on the first floor and the entire second floor of the building for classes and office space. The school had limited space in this church, but later moved into the church annex so that renovations could be done to the education building. When construction was complete, in

1999-2000, Global moved back into the building with room enough for the 170 students. Additionally, in late 1999, when the $40 million museum containing a connecting walkway to the school was completed, the students were able to use museum space and resources for projects.

Global does not appear to have funding difficulties. The board is not looking for more funding from the state, and the school has a fixed student population. The teachers have an average of 8 years experience and are paid salaries equal to the county school district. Except for the library, its student materials, activities and other supports equal or surpass those in other public schools. Additionally, although Global cannot use the funds from the museum for operation, it can use funding from grants written for the school in conjunction with the museum. The result is a well-funded school.

In contrast, Liberty Academy has struggled for support from its inception. It always has been located in a poor area. In its first year, it was housed in 10 rooms in the basement of a church. It is currently housed in an old public school owned by another church. The church uses the back of the building, and the school is housed in the front on two levels. The school is struggling with its rental contract with the church. Liberty agreed to pay close to $180,000 for the renovations and rent, including utilities. It paid $60,000 in advance, but when the building was not ready for the opening of school in 1998, the board had to spend another $80.000 to get the building up to code. When the board adds a fourth-grade next year, they might have to look for another building that can house the additional classrooms. Other fiscally related problems that Liberty has include poor painting, burglars, and transportation. Because the church painted the halls with incompatible paint, the school has to repaint all of the pealing walls. The most threatening issue that the school faces is burglaries. In several instances, burglars have broken into the school. They broke windows that the school cannot afford to replace, and they took all electrical equipment that they could sell for cash. Presently, there are numerous windows on the basement level covered with unsightly boards, and teachers have few tape players and other electronic equipment in classrooms. Transportation costs are also problematic because Liberty transports three busloads of students to and from school without transportation support from the state.

Liberty does not have friends of the museum or community action group that can act as funders or supporters. They are alone. One funding strategy they instituted was to hire a consultant who could give the school a positive exposure in the broader community with the expectation that the exposure would yield additional funding. This consultant has been successful in drawing local, state, and national attention to the achievement of the kindergarten students, but it has not increased the public perception of the school. Another fiscal strategy Liberty uses is increasing the size of the student body to gain additional funding from the state. As part of the charter application, Liberty intends to add a grade annually until it has students in Grades K to 8. However, each year it is also adding more classrooms at existing grade levels to accommodate all students who apply.

The need for additional funding has not diminished the headmaster's enlightened view of the length of the school year and teachers' salaries. Teachers, most of whom have at least 2 years of experience, teach for 210 rather than 180 days, and the starting salary for a new teacher is $5,000 more than most area districts pay. The headmaster explained that he pays his teachers a higher salary so they do not have to work a second job to support their families. The result, he explained, is that they are not tired when they come to work; because of this, they are better teachers. Teachers also have better health care and retirement programs than regular public school teachers, and they have a yearly evaluation tied to a bonus system.

Considering all of the fiscal strengths and weaknesses, startling inequalities remain. Liberty, with an enrollment of 307 African-American children and three Whites, lacks adequate support. It runs as a poverty school, choosing to increase its enrollment to gain additional funding knowing that increased enrollment might compromise instruction and jeopardize the students' achievement. The board spends school funds for public relations and lures teachers with little or no teaching experience to the school by offering higher salaries. Presently the school is disputing a state certification report that says 61% of its teachers are not certified.[4] In its first year of operation, 15% of the students transferred from the school at their parents' request. In comparison, Global, the privileged school with mostly White middle-class children, is able to keep the enrollment small and the facilities stellar. Teachers have an average of 8 years experience, all positions are filled with certified teachers, and only one child was transferred in the first year because of parent dissatisfaction. One school comes from the advantage of a well-funded and esteemed museum and is popular with parents. The other is a grassroots effort that eventually mustered enough support for state approval only to have most of its White parents withdraw from the school just before the opening.

Beliefs About Teaching and Learning

Just as the struggle for funding and support are oppositional, so are the beliefs about student learning that contribute to the culture of the school and the education offered to these two groups of children. Both schools ultimately want to help their students learn so they can become productive citizens, and they believe they can accomplish this through their pedagogy and curriculum. As charter schools, they have the ability to institute educational programs that reflect their beliefs about student learning without adhering to state regulations. Global believes students strengthen their own understandings and problem-solving skills in an environment where they are able to apply their ideas to real world situations. This school's purpose is to establish a learning environment

---

[4]State Law requires at least 75% of elementary charter school teachers to be certified.

that supports each learner's optimal development and growth in understanding. The education is offered to Global students from a position of student enlightenment, whereas the education offered at Liberty is from a position of challenge—the challenge to change the students' conceptions of themselves and the community's assumptions about their ability to learn.

Liberty believes that the development of children proceeds sequentially across all areas (cognitive, language, motor, self-help, and social), but that each child has his or her own individual rate and ultimate level of development. For students to reach their full potential, they have to be in the frame of mind to learn. The social emphasis is on concepts of human dignity, equity, integrity, honesty, compassion, respect for the rights of others, and self-control. Liberty teachers want their students to understand that responsibility, manners, character, and social development are important qualities to be learned in school. They believe the community sees the children as lost causes. They want to see the children treated as people, not as the community sees them. Students are taught to speak when asked, to stand as they respond, and to be positive in their interactions. They are required to wear uniforms to remove tensions about clothing and to listen to classical music in the mornings to prepare for learning. The board also includes corporal punishment as an option for misbehavior.

Global teachers are likewise interested in students' social behavior. As teachers had to change their pedagogy, curriculum, and rules of interaction, students had to learn to take responsibility for their learning. None of this was automatic. Teachers worked with students for several weeks at the beginning of the year to achieve the appropriate behavior for self-directed and group activities. The students' self-direction, attentiveness, and focus are learned behaviors. Students said they were used to "sitting down listening to the teacher telling us what not to do instead of what we can do." They had to get used to determining rules, setting goals, and selecting appropriate activities to learn concepts.

The Global Middle School staff believes that learning is the most important part of schooling. They create an atmosphere they believe will enable students to be independent learners, be critical thinkers, and become responsible citizens. This is done by allowing the students to be the architects of their education. Global uses global culture as the stage for knowledge, coupled with an inquiry-based pedagogy, student-developed curriculum, and active, group learning opportunities. This school stated in its charter application that their mission is "to encourage young people to respect differences, appreciate similarities, and make connections with the people of the world."

Although the staff of Liberty first concentrates on student obedience to authority, they are firm in their focus to educate students through a developmental/sequential process that will provide students with principles to help them become effective thinkers and learners. Using a diagnostic/prescriptive approach in its charter application, Liberty emphasized traditional academic achievement requiring the basic skills needed for success in higher grades. Liberty uses traditional curriculum and pedagogy, where students are taught through group interaction and expository instruction. Students learn a prescribed set of material through memorization and generally participate in class by answering questions posed by the teacher. The board, headmaster, teachers, and parents believe there is a definite set of materials that these students need to know to be successful.

Assessment practices in these schools are culturally appropriate for their beliefs and instruction. Global teachers use a nontraditional assessment approach. Using narrative, not letter grades, both students and teachers assess the attainment of previously set student goals. Liberty's teachers use mastery driven pre- and posttests to assess student progress, and they use a traditional elementary grading system.

These schools are antithetical in relationship to their beliefs about learning and instruction. Global has a Deweyan philosophy, believing that each learner should be encouraged and empowered to reach his or her fullest potential as an individual and as a participant in the global society. They have a constructivist pedagogy that allows students to be active designers and participants in the learning process. In contrast, Liberty exhibits deficit thinking regarding student behavior and a diagnostic/prescriptive approach to learning, which is based on the assumption that behavior can be predicted and intelligence is fixed and innate (Lambert et al., 1995).

These beliefs are manifested in the implementation of special education programs. When Global identified 22% of its enrollment as special needs students, they decided that no students would be removed from classrooms or placed in self-contained units. Instead they hired a special education teacher and paraprofessional to help make the classes inclusive. They wanted all students to remain in regular classes. Liberty does not test students for special education or recognize prior testing done on students. Staff feel that all students can be taught within a regular classroom. However, they did find it necessary to move some students into a special class for extra instructional assistance. These students are far below their grade level. Although they are not labeled as special education students, they are taught by a special education teacher. They frequently go to the learning center where another resource teacher helps them with remediation and allows them to use computer software for basic skill support. When students acquire needed skills, they are moved out of the self-contained class.

Governance

The boards of both Global and Liberty struggled about governance issues at the schools' inceptions. They ended up with a similar upper level administrative structure. The board is the policy arm of the school, and the principal or headmaster is responsible for the school's operation. That is where the similarity ends. Global has a constructivist approach to governance, where leadership is viewed as a reciprocal process among the adults in the school (Lambert et al.,

1995). Teachers largely make decisions about what students study, where students go, and what they do. The dean of students is the teachers' connection to educational theory, research, and the necessary knowledge to make informed decisions about the selection of appropriate pedagogy and materials. The principal, who is the president of the museum, sees the dean as an educator who can support and facilitate the teachers' development and instruction while talking with the board about educational issues. The dean and the vice president of programs (from the museum) make budget decisions under the direction of the principal and board. Other decisions, informed through discussions with teachers or parents, are made by the principal. The principal stated that "sheer determination and committed people—excellent staff, parents—and the concept and plan of action helped to get Global going."

Liberty uses a traditional construct for leadership (Lambert et al., 1995), where the headmaster is ultimately responsible for the school. He is responsible for all decision making, quality of the performance of his teachers, and distribution of bonuses for outstanding work. The headmaster is the only administrator at Liberty. There are no assistant principals, curriculum specialists, or other professional support staff.[5] The headmaster uses teacher committees to facilitate his decision making about curricular and governance issues. However, teachers have little authority over decisions related to school goals or curriculum; the headmaster makes all these decisions. The headmaster stated, "The commitment of the Head Master is, in large part, what makes this school go. The community support is growing and everybody's commitment emanates from mine." He feels that he is supportive of teachers and believes that he and the board are the strongest attributes in the school's development.

Global and Liberty schools are contrasts because one promotes current reform models in curriculum, pedagogy, organization, and governance while the other is traditional in its curriculum, has a diagnostic/prescriptive approach with no defined pedagogy, and has traditional principal-led organization and governance. Teachers and school leaders are participants and recipients of the culture as well as the children. The staff and board of Global struggled for a year to find the educational tools to match the Deweyan/constructivist philosophy of the school. Recognizing that knowledge exists within the learner, teachers and administrators were permitted time and resources to develop personal schemas for pedagogy and curriculum based on their experiences. As with themselves, these teachers understood that knowledge can be pulled out of students, as in mining (Freire, 1995). In contrast, the headmaster and board of Liberty, wanting to change the behavior and achievement of their students, made decisions about how to provide students with structure, obedience, and a standard set of knowledge. Teachers agreed with and obeyed the rules of structure and were trained on how to use the curriculum. As with themselves, they understood that knowledge can be put into students as in banking (Freire, 1995).

---

[5]There is a nurse who docs health screenings and dietary tracking of the students.

Interpreted Culture

The culture of both schools is clearly understood by their students. As young as the Liberty Academy children are (K-3), they understand their school is about sharing, being nice to one another, respect, learning, schoolwork, and making new friends. They feel they are doing advanced work compared with their friends in other public schools. They feel the expectations are higher at Liberty. One of their favorite times is when their teachers teach! The children want their teachers to give them knowledge, and they appreciate the treatment they get from their teachers. They can feel the affection as well as the structure. Some of the children who are new to the school are having difficulty adjusting to the structure. They feel that the school is mean, that paddling and striking with rulers are not necessary, and that the teachers yell at them. Some want to go back to their other school. However, the vast majority of students feel they have good teachers who give them challenging work, teach them how to act like ladies and gentlemen, and emphasize strong discipline.

Global students understand the implicit and explicit goals of the school. They know that they are being taught to be independent thinkers and learners. Sixth-grade students, who had just been at this school for a few weeks, explained: "This school is about learning." "Every school is about learning, but they do a good job here. The learning is connected." "Here you do hands-on instead of teachers telling." "We assess ourselves and we have goals notebooks. We are learning to do it for ourselves." "You do your work, and if it is not your best work, you do it again." Sixth graders like being able to mingle with the seventh graders. They appreciate the "No Hunting" sign in the sixth-grade classroom that reminds them not to pick on or embarrass their classmates. They said, "You don't feel little in comparison to seventh graders. People will not pick on you. I feel safe because you don't have to worry about getting picked on."

Students in both schools understand the cultures their schools have created. Global students believe that if they learn a core curriculum and appropriate behavior, they will have skills that should give them access to social mobility and acceptability. Global students believe that knowledge of the world is interconnected and that they are responsible for their personal learning. They realize that goal-setting, problem-solving, and decision-making skills are the necessary tools for future success—tools they will use throughout their lifetimes.

CHALLENGES TO IMPLEMENTED CULTURES

No challenge has been more daunting than that of improving academic achievement of African American students. Burdened with a history that includes the denial of education, separate and unequal education, and relegation to unsafe, substandard inner-city schools, the quest for quality education remains an elusive dream for the African American community. However, it does remain a dream—perhaps the most powerful for the people of African descent in this nation. (Ladson-Billings, 1994, p. ix)

Looking at the education afforded the students, especially the African Americans, in these two schools, I immediately questioned the assumptions of the founders and sustainers. What is the culture of power that the schools are preparing students to traverse? Does Global provide its students with leadership skills and independent thinking because it expected that its students should become international problem solvers involved in a global society? Does Liberty educate its students with basic skills and obedience because it believes its students will end up in technical and support careers? Have these schools determined what is possible for their students through what is taught or not taught. Specifically, are these schools educating their children to maintain society's power relationships or educating them to be facile with the codes of the culture of power?

Clearly, the cultures of learning afforded students in these two schools are diametrically opposed. In my view, neither school fully meets the challenge of educating African-American students The skill-based culture of Liberty produces a false equity of opportunity for its students. Liberty's founders and staff feel that these minority, poor, and at-risk students lack the cognitive skills or social acumen necessary to achieve within our society. Liberty's socialization of their students transmits a school culture that has limited language code—one that concentrates on basic skills and obedience rather than abstraction and symbolic knowledge. This restricted construction of knowledge has tremendous power to influence not only what the students think about, but also limit the conceptual framework the students will use later in life (Bowers, 1987). Assuming that complex knowledge is either not important or beyond these learners, the founders created a school, for largely African Americans, where students are not prepared for full participation in the global economy. They are only prepared to function within it. They have instituted a model of teaching based on oppression and deficit thinking. Liberty's implementation of gatekeeper ideologies forces students to compromise their capacity for learning and understanding. Liberty's students are assimilated and acculturated without regard to their cognitive abilities and their viable cultural characteristics. Liberty's implementation perpetuates and maintains institutional hegemony and reproduces a society that is debilitating instead of liberating.

In contrast, founders of Global Middle School present a culture where students experience knowledge through complex language and concepts. They want their students to be fluent in the language, skills, and knowledge necessary for achievement within our society. They assume that complex knowledge and understanding are requisite skills that are within the grasp of their students. Global uses abstraction and symbolic knowledge to help students be independent learners, critical thinkers, and responsible contributing citizens. Students gain insight, knowledge, and understanding through inquiry and creativity. These students learn how to discover relationships among curricular areas through teamwork and thematic units—the foundation of strong leadership skills for their futures. Global students develop verbal and quantitative skills while developing citizenship skills by learning critical thinking skills and democratic values. Global students are also taught their place in society; their place is without limitations. Students are liberated through experiences that make them aware of many possibilities for their roles in this nation and the world. They are "taught the codes needed to participate fully in mainstream . . . while being helped to acknowledge their own 'expertness' as well" (Delpit, 1995, p. 45). This type of educational program should enable African-American students to soar in development and achievement. However, Global serves mostly middle class White students and does not recruit students from the nearby poor African-American community. This liberating education remains an elusive dream for these children.

Global and Liberty, as charter schools, have the opportunity to be change agents within public school systems by charting new and creative ways of teaching and learning (NEA Charter School Statement, 1998). They can lead the way for better education for all students because they are deregulated public schools that have more freedom and flexibility than other public schools. This means they have the ability to use curriculum that has not been adopted by the state, use alternate accountability measures, or pay teachers on different pay scales than other public schools. They can extend the school day or academic year and use a specialized curriculum. They can require parents to participate in school activities and create a lower teacher-student ratio than prescribed by the state. All these features and more are contained in the charters of the two schools presented here. However, both of these schools have challenges to confront before they can serve as exemplary models for teaching and learning.

Global's challenge is to realize that if we are to live in a global society that values diverse cultures, we must have participants from diverse cultures, ideas, and ethic groups in the process. Its education should give students an understanding that socioeconomic, racial, and national boundaries do not make sense in a global community. In doing so, Global should make a concerted effort to recruit students from the poor African-American community so that they can be participatory voices in the development of the global perspective necessary for this school. The disavowal of this community undermines the school's goal.

Liberty's challenge is to recognize that, although it is trying to provide its students with an education that will give them a strong basic education, this limited educational program exemplifies a gatekeeping point. Students are limited because they are not provided with the necessary codes and critical-thinking skills to participate in the mainstream society. However, Global must realize that "pretending that gatekeeping points don't exist is to ensure that many students will not pass through them" (Delpit, 1995, p. 39).

In both cases, the educational "environment does not provide the disadvantaged and the 'at risk' with the same encouragement and opportunities provided the advantaged" (Pearl, 1997, pp. 134-135). Charter schools are in place because some parents were dissatisfied with the education afforded their children. Global Middle School and Liberty Academy are schools using different conceptions of knowledge to give their students an education. For many of the African-American students, the schools either produce a false equity of opportunity or serve a limited class and ethnicity. To different degrees, they both hold African-American students on the fringes of good education.

REFERENCES

Center for Educational Reform. (1998). www.usreform.com.

Bowers, C.A. (1987) *The promise of theory: Education and the politics of cultural change.* New York: Teachers College Press.

Delpit, L. (1995) *Other people's children: Cultural conflict in the classroom.* New York: The New Press.

Freire, P. (1995). *Pedagogy of the oppressed* (3rd ed.). New York: Continuum.

Kozol, J. (1991). *Savage inequalities: Children in America's schools.* New York: Crown.

Kronholz, J. (November 10, 1998) Wisconsin school-voucher plan is upheld—Proponents score a victory as high court declines to consider a challenge. *Wall Street Journal*, p. A2.

Ladson-Billings, G. (1994). *The dreamkeepers: Successful teachers of African American children.* San Francisco: Jossey-Bass.

Lambert, L., Walker, D., Zimmerman, D. P., Cooper, J. E., Lambert, M. D., Gardner, M. E., & Slack, P. J. F. (1995). *The constructivist leader.* New York: Teachers College Press.

National Education Association. (1998). www.nea.org.

North Carolina Department of Public Instruction. (1998). www.dpu.state.nc.us/charter_schools/qa.

Pearl, A. (1997). Cultural and accumulated environmental deficit models. In R. R. Valencia (Ed.), *The evolution of deficit thinking: Educational thought and practice* (pp. 132-159). Washington, DC: Falmer Press.

Shujja, M. (1994). *Too much schooling, too little education.* Trenton, NJ: Africa World Press.

U.S. Charter Schools. (1998). www.uscharterschools.org/pub/usce_docs.

7

A School Kids Want to Attend: Perspectives on the Culture of Talent Development

Bruce Wilson
Independent Researcher

H. Dickson Corbett
Independent Researcher

For educational reform to result in increased student success in school, the quality of students' classroom experiences to learn will have to change. This study documents students' depictions of their experiences as they confronted one of the more ambitious urban reform agendas in the nation. So the point of this chapter is to look at schools through students' eyes rather than investigating the impact of reform on school culture. Over a 3-year period, we interviewed a cohort of 250 students split equally among five middle schools. We interviewed each student three times—in the spring of their sixth-, seventh-, and eighth-grade years. During the last year of interviews, we added eighth graders from a sixth school (Northern Middle School). In the latter school, a special partnership had developed between the school and a major research and development center to help guide the school through the rough seas of reform.[1] Would those experiences be reflected in student talk? In other words, could students' comments act as useful indicators of reform's penetration to the classroom level?

---

[1]The original five schools for the study were chosen by the funding agency as serving some of the poorest neighborhoods in the city and having been among the lowest performing on standardized measures of student achievement. The sixth school, with the special added resources the R&D Center brought, was comparable in demographics to

Although the original five schools differed, the primary message from students was the diversity in their experiences evident within each school. That is, the quality of the content and instruction varied markedly for the same student from one classroom to the next. Not only was there variation between language arts and science, for example, but students also described significant differences within subject areas. Such diversity greatly affected students' opportunities to learn. However, such was not the case in the sixth school. Our contention is that reducing the extent of instructional inconsistencies from classroom to classroom is a necessary, intermediate step in the reform process.

We begin this student account of reform by describing the general reform initiative in the district to which all students were exposed. We then briefly visit the additional reforms being implemented at the sixth school—Northern. Next we compare student views of their classroom experiences, with special emphasis placed on the variety of experiences in the first five schools contrasted with the consistency noted by students at Northern. These experiences are categorized in terms of pedagogy, content, and environment. Indicators of the effects of these reforms, both from achievement scores and students' reflections, are presented in the next section. In the final section, we discuss the implications of what we have learned for reform.

---

the other five with the one exception that it had more ethnic diversity. We added the sixth school in the third year of our research because we knew that the students in that school had different pedagogical and content experiences.

Each of the original five schools selected for us a sample of 50 sixth graders. The schools varied in how they handled this task. One principal actually used the computer to randomly generate the list; two others turned the assignment over to the school's roster person; and the other two asked each team coordinator to identify a set of students. We emphasized our wish that the students reflect diversity in instructional experience, academic performance, behavior, motivation, gender, and race—proportional to the overall student populations in each school. Because the schools would remain anonymous to any groups beyond our funding agency and ourselves, they had little need to "stack the deck." In getting to know the students, we had no sense that one segment of the student populations was under- or overrepresented. Schools notified students according to their established procedures, and we gave students each year the option of not participating when we actually showed up to interview them.

We interviewed the same students in the spring of each year during the course of their three years in middle school. We talked to 247 sixth grade students the first year. We could never track down three of the original 250—either they happened to be sick when we tried to contact them, had just been suspended, or had been spotted in the building but were not presently in the classroom they were scheduled to be in. By the third year, 172 (70%) of them were still available for interviews. Each year we encountered some attrition, mostly due to transfers within or outside the system. Of these 172 on the rolls in 1998, we interviewed 153 from the original five schools, the remainder being, once again, either enrolled but chronically absent, enrolled but suspended, or enrolled and in school but too elusive to locate. We also interviewed 50 eighth-grade students at Northern during the final year of the research.

A DESCRIPTION OF THE REFORM INITIATIVES

All six schools were located in the city of Philadelphia. The city has received a great deal of attention efforts through the efforts of its superintendent, David Hornbeck, for its reform agenda known as "Children Achieving." Our sixth school, Northern, was also engaged in a collaboration with the Center for Research on the Education of Students Placed at Risk (CRESPAR) and its researchers/program developers at Johns Hopkins University working on the Talent Development Middle School Program. A brief description of these two reforms is outlined next.

Children Achieving (Districtwide Reform)

For the last 5 years, The School District of Philadelphia has been engaged in an ambitious attempt to improve the education of its large and diverse student population. Children Achieving, *the umbrella term for the reform, seeks to:*

Each year we spoke individually with the sampled students, recording the students' comments by hand. The general interview protocols were originally developed with input from school staff members. Changes from year to year reflected important issues that emerged from prior analyses. We also tried to take advantage of the interests and concerns students brought up. The exact questions consequently varied somewhat from student to student. Thus, the interviews were free-flowing, often resembling a conversation—with an unwavering focus on students' learning experiences and how they felt about them. We covered such topics as whether students thought they were successful, what that meant to them, what activities and teacher practices helped them learn, how they were performing, how they knew what their performance was, how they were treated in the classroom, how they behaved in the classroom, how comfortable they were in middle school, what their future plans were, and how well prepared they were for the next grade.

We would go to students' classrooms to ask them and their teacher if it would be okay to do the interview. This negated having the schools arrange schedules and the students' having to remember appointments. It also allowed us to walk the halls and glance inside the classrooms, improving our understandings of the atmosphere students would describe in the interviews. We would then walk to some quiet place in the building—the media center, an auditorium, or an office—to talk. These one-on-one interviews usually took between 30 and 45 minutes. Analysis of th data followed a similar pattern each year. We began by reading our respective portions of the data, and then shared interpretive memos that discussed emerging themes. We then reread the data to establish categories for coding the data. Based on the first round of coding, we developed initial data displays that led to further interpretive memos and discussions. After several revisions, we arrived at the outline that formed the basis of our reports. Each of us then went back to our originally coded data to provide additional examples, filling in the outline.

1. *Set high expectations for everyone by adopting new standards of performance.*
2. *Design accurate performance indicators to hold everyone accountable for results.*
3. *Shrink the centralized bureaucracy and let schools make more decisions.*
4. *Provide intensive, sustained professional development for all staff.*
5. *Make sure all students are healthy and ready to learn.*
6. *Create access to the community services and support and services students need to succeed in school.*
7. *Provide up-to-date technology and instructional materials.*
8. *Engage the public in shaping, understanding, supporting, and participating in school reform.*
9. *Ensure adequate resources and use them effectively.*
10. *Address all these priorities together and for the long term—starting now.*

These dramatic and costly steps hope to break the decades-long history of student failure in the city.

The district reports progress implementing several of the structural and organizational elements of its reform plan and is encouraged by corresponding gains in student performance (The School District of Philadelphia, 1998). All six schools in our sample met their expected growth in performance during the first testing cycle. Despite funding shortages, the District has recently announced another set of changes directly aimed at improving these student results. The District has proposed ending all vestiges of social promotion and raising the standards necessary for students to move on to higher grade levels. Recognizing that increasing expectations without correspondingly enriching the instructional support for inner-city students would be a hollow and futile endeavor, the District will demand more of its students only if additional funds for professional development, staffing, and curriculum are forthcoming.

Talent Development (One School's Reform Within Children Achieving)

A major critique of American middle-school students' experiences is the lack of close, sustained relationships that students are able to build with their teachers and the lack of rigor in content. Northern devised a number of organizational arrangements to encourage closer contact between teachers and students. The school established small learning communities and assigned students to semidepartmentalized teacher teams. Half of the teaching teams also looped so that students and teachers were able to spend at least 2 years together. In addition to organizational arrangements, the partnership with CRESPAR and the Talent

Development Middle School Program altered curriculum and instruction. Teachers at the school have been involved with long-range planning, professional development, and ongoing support to implement a host of best practices in all four of the major subject areas. Additionally, in an effort to link the content to real-world demands, students meet once a week in a career exploration program to expose them to future career options and to a self-examination of attitude and interests toward a range of careers.

A coordinated reading/language arts program is at the core of the curriculum reform at Northern. The schedule is organized so that students receive two periods of reading/language arts instruction (100 minutes) every day. Teachers have been trained in the Student Team Reading and Writing Program—a whole language approach made more meaningful by having students read good literature rather than stories from a basal. Teachers prepare the students for reading and writing as an integrated activity by introducing authors and the genre, discussing relevant background information, and introducing new vocabulary words. The heart of the program is a series of cooperative learning activities organized around each section of a book.

In the words of the science coordinator at the school, "science is a hands-on, minds-on affair." To accomplish that, students are involved in weekly lab activities chosen to illustrate the role of science in students' everyday lives and the world beyond. To ensure ample time to explore important scientific principles, the schedule has been adjusted to permit students one double period of laboratory science a week. In addition, all students participate in an annual Science Fair exhibition. The curriculum is organized around kits that promote inquiry-based learning and are aligned with both the National Science Standards and the new Philadelphia Standards.

The school has adopted the University of Chicago School Math Project curriculum; the goal is to have every student complete algebra by the end of the eighth grade. This series is a curriculum that enriches students' mathematical experience. Some of the program's key features include problem solving about common life situations, cooperative learning through partner and small-group activities, practice and skills reinforcement through games, ongoing review throughout the year, and a home-school partnership. The program includes not only intensive staff development and follow-up support for teachers, but also an extra help component for students who need it. These students participate in the Computer and Team Assisted Mathematics Acceleration (CATAMA) course—a combination of computer-assisted instruction and structured cooperative learning for 10 weeks of the school year.

What were students' classroom experiences like as their teachers implemented these reforms? In the next section, we look closely at how students' experiences varied considerably within the five original schools and were much more consistent at Northern.

DIFFERENCES IN THE CLASSROOM: PEDAGOGY, CONTENT, AND ENVIRONMENT

There were at least three types of differences described in the student interviews. One type concerned *pedagogical* differences across teachers. Some teachers in a building preferred one means of instruction over another. Despite the overwhelming persuasiveness of the literature on learning styles and multiple intelligences, some teachers still opted to rely on teaching strategies that were more suited to one style or intelligence than another, rather than building multiple strategies into lessons. The consequence was that such differences had varied meanings for students in the class, with some being satisfied and others frustrated with a specific teacher.

A second type of instructional difference was with the *content* of the class. The District has an established scope and sequence for each subject at each grade level. Still, teachers apparently found it difficult to cover all the topics designated as appropriate for their students in a school year. Thus, they had to pick and choose what to emphasize in day-to-day lessons. Therefore, students in one class ended the year as experts in certain areas, whereas students in the same grade but having a different teacher developed skills and knowledge in another aspect of the same subject.

To be sure, pedagogical and content variations affected student learning. In these classrooms, learning issues revolved around what content students encountered and how much content individual students grasped. The third type of difference was more stark; this comparison was between classrooms where learning took place versus those where students asserted that little learning occurred at all. These *classroom environment* differences had little to do with gradations of individuals' acquisition of knowledge. Instead they referred to whether the majority of students learned anything at all. Either because a class was incessantly disruptive or a teacher was reluctant to go back over previously introduced material or both, students in each school described situations in which little, if any, learning took place at any point in the school year.

We take a more detailed look at the different experiences students encountered in pedagogy, content, and environment. For each we contrast the variety of experiences in the five original schools with the more consistent experience noted in the sixth school. Each student's quote is followed by a six digit identifier, with the first digit representing the student's school, the second through fourth representing the student's unique identification, the fifth indicating race (1 = African American, 2 = Hispanic), and the final digit representing gender (1 = male, 2 = female).

Pedagogical Differences—The Case of Science

In each of the five original schools, students who took a particular subject from one teacher described an entirely different approach to teaching than students who had another teacher for the same subject. Nowhere was this difference more noticeable than in science classes.

Current science standards emphasize student problem-solving abilities, which include formulating problems and designing investigations to shed light on possible answers. This inquiry-centered approach emphasizes hands-on activities that enable students to test predictions. Students in each school described great variation in how often they were able to engage hands-on activities. Some students had few opportunities to do hands-on activities and described instructional practices where everything was organized for them and the focus was on learning important facts. Others did experiments and projects, but all the procedures and steps were clearly spelled out. There were only a few cases where students were challenged to think about underlying principles and construct alternative experiments that would allow them to test explanations. Characteristic of the more traditional approach to science were the following student descriptions:

I: What do you do in science?
S: Mostly we work out of the text.
I: What kinds of things are you studying?
S: We are studying earthquakes and volcanoes.
I: What kinds of things do you do with the text book?
S: We do vocabulary. We read the chapter and get the vocabulary words. After each section in the book we do a section review.
I: Do you do experiments?
S: No, but sometimes we do reports. (101631)

S: We read in the text book and then we take notes. We also answer questions from the "check and explain" part of the book.
I: Do you do experiments?
S: Not that often. We did a couple this year. (300611)

Occasionally students would report on doing more hands-on activities, but those were often quite structured activities:

S: We have been doing projects on the planets. We need to get the facts and draw a picture.
I: Where do you go to get your facts?
S: I go to the library and copy things out of a book. (136612)

S: We do lots of projects.
I: Can you give me an example?
S: Yeah, I did a project on acid rain.
I: What did you do?
S: I did some research and wrote a report. (312611)

S: We had to do science fair projects even if we didn't enter the science fair.

I: How did you know what to do?

S: [The teacher] just gave us lists of what we needed to do. (522611)

It was the rare exception where students described more open-ended activities where they were actively engaged in deciding what they would do and how they would go about it:

S: We do a lot of group projects.

I: How often do you do these?

S: Two or three a month.

I: What kinds of things are you doing?

S: We just did a model on the phases of the moon.

I: Did your teacher tell you what to do'?

S: No, we had to figure out our roles by ourselves. (329612)
   We are doing a garden project (in the school courtyard). We had to figure out what we were going to plant and we had to describe the plants we wanted to plant. We also do experiments that we make up on our own. (332612)

These different approaches appeared simultaneously in the same school. For example, at Southern, one teacher relied heavily on the textbook, copying notes, and completing chapter reviews (Mr. Giles), whereas the person's colleague concentrated on hands-on activities and experiments (Ms. Mitchell):

I: What do you do in science class?

S: We know we have to write. Mr. Giles always has three boards of stuff. He be writing with us. It often takes the whole period.

I: Do you do anything else?

S: Sometimes we read. Sometimes we do worksheets or projects. (209611)

S: We get 3 to 5 minutes to get ready. Then we copy notes from the board. Next we open the text and discuss what we have been reading and what notes we have taken . . .

I: How long do you spend doing each of these?

S: About 20 to 25 minutes writing notes and 15 to 20 minutes discussing. (211611)

S: Most of the time we write notes from the board. We usually have three blackboards of notes. It takes about 30 minutes. After 30 minutes, Mr. Giles starts going over it. He goes to the text book and shows us his way and the book way.

I: Do you do experiments?

S: Yeah, but we haven't done any for a long time—since March or April (interviewed in June).
I: What else do you do?
S: We do lots of tests, most every Friday. He prefers long answers to his questions (as opposed to multiple choice or true/false questions). (225611)

In contrast to working with notes and textbook materials, a group of students from another class down the hall described their experience as primarily being hands-on experiments and projects:

I: What do you do in science class?
S: We mostly do science projects.
I: How often?
S: A lot!
I: Can you remember some examples?
S: We did rocket engines, we wrote about the greenhouse effect, and we tested how many drops of water fit on a coin.
I: Do you use your textbook much?
S: Not as much as we do projects. (205612)

S: All we do is experiments and projects. We study procedure and hypothesis.
I: Do you use your textbook much?
S: Not really. It's just in our book bag most of the time. Sometimes we do homework in it. (207612)

S: We mostly do projects.
I: Can you give me an example?
S: I just finished a science fair poster on hard and soft water. Also, at the beginning of the year we did reports on black scientists.
I: How did you know who to do a report on?
S: Ms. Mitchell gave us a list and we got to pick from the list.
I: Do you use the text book much?
S: No, not much. We usually just talk about what's in the textbook.
I: Is that helpful?
S: I like it better than just reading and taking notes. (223611)

These varied science experiences in Southern were also documented in the other schools. For example, all the Western students reported spending a good deal of time reading from the text and copying notes from the board. At the same time, they also reported quite a range of working on experiments—some did no experiments and only a few projects, whereas others said they did mostly projects and experiments.

S: We outline the chapter.
I: Who creates the outline?
S: The teacher do it and we copy it. Sometimes we do it on our own.
I: What else do you do?
S: We answer questions from the end of the chapter.
I: Do you do experiments?
S: No, not many. We did some at the beginning of the year. (105612)

I: What are you doing in science?
S: We are working on fossils and we are also studying weather maps. That's fun cause we get to act like we are weather reporters and the teacher videotaped us.
I: Do you do experiments?
S: Yeah. We're working on one now with fossils.
I: How about projects?
S: We have been doing some weather forecasting. (111611)

At Eastern, all but two of the students talked about being preoccupied with doing their science fair projects (we were in the school just before they were due). Most students said they had been working on them for 2 or 3 months. When they were not working on science fair projects, students reported spending almost all their time reading from the text, copying notes, and answering questions. There was little or no mention of experiments apart from the science fair.

I: What have you been doing in science?
S: We have been learning about the stars and the planets.
I: How do you learn about that?
S: We read about it in the text book and the teacher explains it. We do worksheets and then we do the section review in the book.
I: Do you do many experiments?
S: No, just about two. But we did just finish our science fair projects. Everyone had to do one. (501612)

In contrast, the difference between students' pedagogical experiences in science at Northern and the other five schools was the hands-on nature of what they did. Indeed, experiments (or in one case what students described as projects) was a regular part of their science regimen. Northern's students uniformly participated in a double period of science once a week to do experiments.

We do lots of labs and projects. (603612)

We do labs every Thursday. The teacher makes us show step-by-step how we did it. We have to write up our labs and she hands them back on Monday. (604611)

I: Do you do much lab work?

S: Yeah, we work on them two or three times a week.

I: Does that help you learn better?

S: Yeah.

I: Why'?

S: It's better than just writing stuff down. You get to learn by doing.

I: Can you give me an example?

S: Yeah. We were learning about contaminated water and we had to test 36 different water samples. (605611)

S: We have a double period every Tuesday where we do a lab. We also have homework with the lab.

I: What do you do for homework?

S: We usually have to write a one-page summary where we answer four questions: What did we do in the lab? What did we like about it? What do we need to do to improve? Would we do it again? (611651)

I: What do you do in science?

S: Every Thursday we do a double period lab.

I: Is that helpful?

S: Yeah, it helps me see what the book is talking about. It is better than reading about it. When you do it, you understand. (616612)

Instead of staying in books, we get to do hands-on things, like experiments. That's more interesting. The book is boring. (618641)

The students generally described textbook activities as more secondary to hands-on activities. Some still described a common routine of reading and taking notes, but others referred to the text as more of a reference guide.

I: Do you use the textbook much?

S: Yes, we read and do the questions in the book. But we also do experiments two or three times a month, and we do lots of "how to" projects where we have to explain to the class step-by-step what we are doing, like how to bake a cake using a mix or by scratch. (608642)

We keep a notebook where we keep our notes from the textbook and our worksheets. But most of that is work related to our labs. Almost all our work is related to the lab. (620612)

I: Do you use the textbook much?

S: A little. Mostly when we are bad. (606621)

I: Do you use the textbook much?

S: No, we usually use the computers. (609651)

We only use the textbook for research. (610652)

We are always doing research. Every week we have a project where we go to the computer to find information. (612622)

I: Do you use the textbook much?

S: No. We are way past that. (627621)

Given students' often stated preference to be active in class, it was not surprising to find a high degree of enthusiasm for science in the school.

S: It's exciting and fun.

I: What are you doing?

S: We do experiments every Wednesday. We also are working on projects.

I: Can you give me an example?

S: We are studying the solar system and we are writing a book for 6- to 8-year-olds.

I: Why is it fun?

S: Every day is a new thing! (606621)

I: Does doing experiments help you learn?

S: Yes, cause it gets people into it. It is more fun. It shows that there is an easy way and a hard way [to solve problems]. It shows us we can do it ourselves. (607612)

I: What do you do in science class?

S: We have lots of fun. All we do is projects where we try and understand how variables affect each other. Everyone understands what we are doing cause we do lots of hands-on stuff. We also sing and dance in there. The teacher comes up with songs for things that helps everyone remember stuff.

I: Can you give me an example?

S: Yeah, we did a "water cycle boogy." (610652)

I: What do you do in science?

S: We do lots of different stuff.

I: Can you give me an example?

S: We work in groups on projects. We get to pick the topic and the group. My group is working on the planets and we are doing a game board. (614611)

S: We just finished a "how to do" project.
I: What did you do?
S: I explained how to use hair rollers?
I: How does that help you understand science?
S: A part of science is being very clear about all the steps you follow in your experiments. We practice that by clearly going through the steps of a regular activity. (625612)

Compared with students in the other five schools, then, the students at Northern nearly all reported that they had a hands-on, investigative science class where projects, experiments, and demonstrations were regular and frequent.

Content Differences—The Case of English

Just as there are standards about quality science instruction, in English the emphasis on understanding the writing process is a key element of what students are expected to know and be able to do. In addition to being exposed to different kinds of writing activities, students encountered divergent definitions of what it meant to be a good writer. What they learned about writing varied from students who claimed their teachers had no rules for writing, to those who focused on writing details like punctuation, capitalization, and indentation, to those who used process definitions referring to beginning, middle, and conclusion or getting across the main point with supporting examples.
Here is a sampling of comments from students who saw no particular rules for producing a quality piece of writing:

I: Do you do much writing in your English class?
S: No, we don't do that much.
I: How do you know if you have written a quality piece of work when you are writing?
S: The teacher just looks it over and she says it's good. (102612)

I: Are there any special steps you need to follow when writing a good essay?
S: No, not really. Sometimes the teacher might give us a story to get us started. We just need to listen to the teacher's instructions, jot down notes, and go home and study. (303611)

I: Do you know what it takes to write a good essay?
S: No, she [teacher] don't tell us. (401621)

I: Do you do much writing?

S: Yes, once in a blue moon.
I: What kinds of things do you write?
S: Poems, short stories, definitions.
I: Do you know what it takes to get an A?
S: Yeah, we have rules, but I don't know them off hand. (508611)

Others suggested that quality derived from proper punctuation or grammar:

I: What does it take to write a good essay.
S: If I do what she taught me. You know, it has to have good grammar,
     the sentences have to be right—complex ones are better, the punctua-
     tion has to be good, and the sentences have to make sense. You can't
     have no sentence fragments or run-ons. (104612)

I: How do you know if you have written a good essay in language arts?
S: If it's neat, has no mistakes, and has what she wants. (226612)

I: How often do you write?
S: Every day!
I: What kinds of things do you write.
S: Notes off the board.
I: When you write your own sentences are there any special steps you
     follow to make sure it is good quality?
S: Yeah, we have the steps on the wall. You have to capitalize, make
     sure you have periods, punctuation must be right, and you have to
     write neatly. (309611)

Yet when others spoke of writing, they focused more on a process that involved
revision and refinement while moving toward a finished product.

S: You have to write the right stuff.
I: How do you know if you have the right stuff?
S: You have to write lots and you have to correct it after you do the first
     draft
I: Who helps you with the revisions?
S: The students do sometimes, but mostly the teacher. (125611)

I: How do you know if you have written a good essay in language arts?
S: She has samples of good writing in the room, so I know if mine is
     good. (221612)

I: Are there steps you follow in preparing a good essay?
S: Yes. You need to first make a rough draft. Then you need to revise it.
     Next you need to write a final draft. And then you have to publish it.

I: Do you do much writing?
S: Yes, a lot. Mostly every day. (310611)

I: Do you have any guidelines for writing?
S: Yes. First, you need to think about it. Then you need to write a rough
     draft. After that you need to proof it. Finally you do a regular draft.
I: Does your teacher ever have you redo a regular draft?
S: Yes. He'll hand it back and have us redo it.
I: Do you prefer that?
S: Yes. They can make sure I do it right. If they know I can do better, I
     want someone who will push me. (327612)

The five schools also had contrasting emphases with writing. By way of
example, students at Central encountered a large number of different English
teachers. Writing, in the students' minds, ranged from maintaining a journal
every day, to constructing work for their portfolio, to creative and narrative
writing, to filling in the blanks, to doing worksheets and answering questions
from the book. Only a handful of students made any mention of the writing
process, with one of them only vaguely remembering that "there were steps on
the wall."

I: How often do you write?
S: Every day.
I: What do you write about?
S: Mostly we just write notes off of the board. (309611)

I: What about writing in English class?
S: We have paragraphs with blank spaces and we have to write in the
     missing words. We also have to answer questions and write para-
     graphs.
I: Do you write essays or journal entries?
S: No, not in English. Only in social studies. (332612)

I: How often do you write in English class?
S: Every day.
I: What kind of writing do you do?
S: Mostly just answering questions from the text book.
I: Are there any special steps you follow when you are writing?
S: No, just as long as you know what you are doing, [you'll get a good
     grade]. (322612)

I: How often are you writing in English class?
S: Every day. We write in our journal.
I: What kinds of things do you write about?

S: If I could pick my high school of choice, what would it be and why? We are also collecting all of our narrative essays into a writing portfolio. We are attaching a cover sheet to each sample explaining why we chose it and what we learned from it. (300611)

For the students at North Central, writing included taking notes and doing worksheets. There was an occasional mention of writing essays, and about one third of the students talked about writing in journals. Several students also mentioned a current writing project where they were working on career activities—employment applications, resumes, letters of employment, and so on.

S: In English we are mostly working on projects.
I: What project are you working on now?
S: We are learning how to do a work application—filling out forms, getting letters and references from our family.
I: Do you do much writing in this class?
S: Mostly vocabulary words—writing sentences and definitions.
I: Do you do many essays?
S: No, not much. (401621)

S: We do a lot of things from the text book or from the newspaper. We do questions from the newspaper and write a paragraph.
I: What does it take to write a good paragraph?
S: It has to have eight lines, the right words need to be capitalized, and no misspelled words.
I: Does your teacher have you redo poorly written paragraphs?
S: Only if we have misspelled words. (414622)

As a final example, most of the Eastern students reported that writing involved copying notes, answering questions, writing sentences, or doing spelling words. Only a quarter of the students mentioned either writing poetry or creating their own stories/essays.

I: How often do you write in English class?
S: Every day.
I: What kinds of things are you writing?
S: We copy notes from the board and we do dictionary work. We also answer questions from our workbook.
I: Do you ever write your own stories?
S: No. (503612)

I: How about writing?

S: We do that more than reading. We do lots of that for homework, especially unpunctuated sentences. We mostly learn stuff from elementary school—like punctuation.

I: Do you write anything else?

S: Sometimes we will write short stories. (505611)

I: How often are you writing in your English class?

S: Every day.

I: What kinds of things are you writing?

S: We answer questions from the book and we take notes. Maybe once or twice a month we will write our own stories or essays.

I: What does it take to get an A on a writing assignment?

S: You need to get punctuation right. You can't have any grammatical errors. You also need to know how to explain it. You have to have it in the right order. (522611)

There was no doubt that teachers in all five buildings were putting an emphasis on student writing. However, what it meant to write well in the context of individual classrooms varied tremendously. Thus, although most students were learning to write, they were often learning something entirely different from peers within and across the five buildings.

The consequence of Northern having an established, focused curriculum in language arts was a remarkable unanimity among these students' definitions of what it meant to *do writing*. Almost all the students described writing as a frequent, creative, constructive act. Thus, the students shared a common understanding and acceptance of the fact that writing required a process (almost all could elaborate what that process was) and that an important element of that process was developing multiple drafts.

I: Do you follow any procedure when you are writing?

S: We begin by constructing a web—only for major projects.

I: What happens next.

S: Then we go through several drafts.

I: How many drafts?

S: We usually do a first draft, a second draft, and then a final copy. (603612)

I: What do you do in RELA?

S: We are writing about four days a week. We usually write to some writing prompt. The teacher give us some examples with a Venn diagram. We follow the five steps of the writing procedure. And most every day we are working with other students on writing. (626612)

I: What activities help you learn the best?
S: When we do prewriting.
I: What is that?
S: Its when you organize what you want to say. (605611)

I: Are you getting better at writing?
S: Yes.
I: How do you know?
S: We have to keep rewriting things and if we get it wrong he makes us do it again. (607612)
We always write and then we go over each other's work. (610652)

I: What do you have to do to get an A on a writing assignment?
S: You have to do lots of rewriting, like changing words and sentences around. It is important to be clear. If you write too much you might not make sense. (612622)

We often get in groups and we write stories collectively. We trade papers all the time. (614611)

I: Is writing helpful to you?
S: Yes.
I: Why?
S: [The teacher] helps us edit and rewrite things.
I: How many times do you rewrite things?
S: Mostly we rewrite two or three times. (618641)

I: Do you redo drafts when you write in RELA?
S: Yes. You have to keep writing until you get it right—maybe three times. (621621)

S: I learn more in RELA.
I: Why?
S: I like writing.
I: What makes writing so interesting?
S: When we write we are learning to make it sound better each time we rewrite it. (623642)

S: Every time we read something we write about it.
I: What do you write?
S: We retell the story. Usually we write a summary of two or three paragraphs. We also have to answer "treasure hunt" questions. And when we write something we correct it, revise it, and change with a friend to correct it again.

I: How many times do you rewrite most things?
S: Mostly about three times. (624631)

An element showed up in the students' comments about writing that was largely missing in the other schools—that writing's purpose was to communicate with others. For example, the students would expressly mention that including details was important to a successful piece of writing because those details would "let a person get the point" (652612) and "make a person understand what something looks like" (656621). Obviously writing was part of communicating, but for many of the students in the other schools writing was viewed in more rudimentary terms. Certainly writing comprised a significant portion of the school day at Northern. Students said they were expected to write daily and that writing was integrated with their other language arts experiences. Even more important, writing was also stressed in the other subjects, particularly math and science.

> We write every day, usually to some set of prompts. We just finished some historical stories. Yesterday we did a retelling of Norma [an opera they had seen downtown]. (602612)

> We write hard every day. (605621)

S: For science homework we usually have to write a couple of paragraphs about our experiment.
I: What do you write about?
S: Did we enjoy the experiment? What did we do? What did we find? (613651)

> In science we are writing a book on the solar system for 6- to 8-year olds. (615612)

> In math class our teacher grades our journals and he makes us write reports. That is the first year the math has not been all numbers. (611511)

Thus, the Northern students shared a more singular definition of what it took to write well, and this definition emphasized the overall process of writing, with correct grammar, sentence structure, and organization as components.

Classroom Environment Differences

We previously described in detail classrooms where there were "cracks in the classroom floor" (Corbett & Wilson, 1997) in the original five schools. These were caused by a revolving door of substitute teachers, disruptive students who forced teachers to deal with behavior at the expense of instruction, or support-scarce classrooms where students did not get the repeated explanations or extra help they needed. These were based on comments offered by students as sixth and seventh graders. We heard similar stories in the third year (from students as eighth graders), although the examples were as prevalent among regular teachers as interim ones. From the students' perspective, the environment was such that pedagogy and content did not really matter because nothing went on instructionally. Interestingly, the same students could describe a comparable setting where teachers just down the hall fostered constructive learning environments.

We offer examples from three of the original five schools. In two of the cases, it is the same students encountering different teachers. In the third, it is different students from the same school experiencing markedly different environments in the same content area.

At Western, the students had two teachers for their core academic subjects. The two worked together as a teaching team. In most cases, one teacher handled math and science while the second one taught social studies and language arts, with both of them sharing the same groups of students.

This was the case with a group of students who could learn from and relate well to their social studies/language arts teacher (Mr. Jones), while constantly doing battle with their math/science teacher (Ms. Smith). One student described Ms. Smith as overdemanding, lacking patience, and not sensitive to student learning needs, pointing out that students need several different explanations before the concepts sink in. Mr. Jones seemed to be just the opposite:

I: Have you had a good year?

S: Ms. Smith has an attitude problem. She wants us to be so good the first time. She wants us to always be perfect. She has us walk in a line in the hallway. We are the only class in the school to do that.

I: Why do you think she has you do that?

S: She wants to impress the principal.

I: Is there anything else she does that bothers you?

S: She is the only one (teacher) who won't go over things [help review the work], she never comes in with a smile, she is always evil. By not going over it, we got a bad attitude. I haven't learned nothing in her class. Only three students have, but they were ones who were held back and they all have tutors.

I: Do you mostly cover new material in the class or is it review?

S: Some of it's new. Actually, we do more new stuff as the year goes along. But we stay on something new for only one day. Ms. Smith never goes back over it [as a review or to see if students understand]. All we do is have tests on it [right after we learn it].

I: What do you do in math class [with Ms. Smith]?

S: She teach real fast. She talk fast, too. If we ask her to say it over, she has an attitude. She takes out home problems on us.

I: What do you do after she teaches new work?

S: Then we do our homework. But she don't check it. We could cheat and she would never know!

I: How about Mr. Jones?

S: If we don't get it, he will go over it. That teacher is nice.

I: Do students come in after school for help?

S: Yeah!

I: How many?

S: A lot. We come in for help on Monday and Thursday.

I: How about help from Ms. Smith?

S: That teacher helps us on Monday and Wednesday, but she always has too much to do. We just sit there and read a book.

I: Tell me more about Teacher Mr. Jones?

S: One boy in the class, he do all his work now. If it wasn't for Mr. Jones he wouldn't do nothing. At the beginning of the year he don't do nothing; now he does. He wouldn't even take the SAT-9s; all he did was just bubbled in the answers [randomly].

I: Why do you think that student is working now?

S: Cause Mr. Jones took time out to help him and talk to him.

I: How else are your two teachers different?

S: Ms. Smith puts us down. Mr. Jones say to us, don't drop out. Ms. Smith starts us with an F (as our base grade) and expect us to bring it up. Mr. Jones starts us with an A. Mr. Jones also has us stay after school until we turn the work in. If we do a bad test, we can retake it 'til we get a good grade. With Ms. Smith, we don't have retakes. (106612)

The differences between these two teachers is further captured by how they dealt with work not turned in on time:

I: How do your teachers deal with work that you don't turn in?

S: Mr. Jones tells me what is late. . . . Whatever we miss Ms. Smith just has us sit in our seats after school and checks on us. Mr. Jones is more willing to help.

I: What does Mr. Jones do to make the work more understandable?

S: He puts some of our reading books on tape. And one time we went to 33rd and Sansom where we got to act out a play we were studying (Othello). We also looked at movies and saw how the characters act out the parts.

I: How about Ms. Smith?

S: At times, Ms. Smith just say don't bother me. "I've told you [the answers] once. Ask your classmates for help." . . . She say to call your study buddy. Ms. Smith don't like to help or care for some people. Ms. Smith only cares about nice, quiet people who do all their work. (127612)

Perhaps the most significant difference between the two teachers was how they handled students who needed additional help: In students' minds, the willingness of a teacher to work with a student until he or she understood a concept was a highly valued trait.

Mrs. Smith promoted independence and self-reliance by encouraging students to figure things out for themselves, whereas Mr. Jones offered a support net to hold students up until they could do it on their own:

I: Do you feel like you are prepared for high school?

S: No, I ain't that good in math, but I'm ready in the rest of them.

I: Why are you doing so poorly in math [student admits she is failing]?

S: It's the way the teacher teaches. Ms. Smith just give it to us and don't explain it. Ms. Smith expect us to know it. The kids put their hands up [to ask questions] and Ms. Smith says put your hand down, you should know it. I haven't seen one report card [from the entire class] with an A or B on it. Ms. Smith just has us do problems from the book. She calls us up individually and checks 'em. She just marks 'em wrong and puts your grade in the book.

I: But what if you don't understand? What does she do?

S: Ms. Smith says to keep trying and gets an attitude. Ms. Smith starts yelling so everyone just ignores her. They [students] go on strike.

I: What happens when you refuse to do the work?

S: She gives us a detention and call our parents in. Then she start bringing up things from the beginning of the year and we just ignore it.

I: How about Mr. Jones?

S: We learn a lot.

I: What does Mr. Jones do that helps you learn?

S: He bring us movies and we act things out most every day. He make it fun and don't get an attitude every five minutes. Sometimes we discuss things for a whole hour or so. We also read interesting stuff.

I: Like what?

S: Maya Angelou.

I: Why is that interesting?

S: We read about people fighting, a girl who was raped, things that happen in real life. Mr. Jones tell us how not to act as a young lady.

I: What happens if you don't understand your work with Mr. Jones?

S: He calls us to the desk and spends about 15 minutes with us. If the whole group can't get it, he will stop the class and explain. He gives us steps to do it. (129612)

The value of taking time to explain things and making sure that everyone understood was reinforced by another student's comments:

I: Are you getting a good education this year?

S: Not really.

I: Why not?

S: Ms. Smith just teaches a lesson once. If you ask for help, she gets an attitude. . . . She says, "I already taught it once, I'm not going to teach it again. You weren't paying attention." She just teaches too fast and don't take the time to teach it right.

I: Why?

S: She only wants to teach it once.

I: What about Mr. Jones?

S: He takes time and teaches. If you don't understand, he takes time to explain.

I: Can you give me an example?

S: In social studies we were doing slave trade. The test we did was different than what we learned [and we didn't get good grades on it].

I: What did the teacher do?

S: He explained it again and wrote notes for us. I took a retest and went from a D to a C.

I: What else does Mr. Jones do?

S: He talks to you about it. He makes sure you understand and know what you are doing.

I: How does he do that?

S: He checks everybody's work and explains it if it is not right.

I: Does he do that often?

S: Yes. He do it every day. (136612)

As noted previously (Corbett & Wilson, 1998), one of the problems that these students faced was a revolving door of teachers. In this second case, where students highlighted differences in their teachers, the most interesting comparison (North Central) was between two different science teachers they had in the same year. With their original teacher (Mr. Jordan), they felt they learned almost nothing, whereas they were excited about the replacement (Ms. Willis). Students did not mince words in portraying how they felt about this. Notice how different the two were portrayed when reaching out to students. For students, the essence of teaching was engaging them in the content rather than just delivering it.

I: Are you learning a lot this year?

S: Not in the beginning. Mr. Jordan just wrote notes on the board. I didn't learn nothing. Now we have Ms. Willis and we do projects. We have fun. We are learning lots.

I: What happened to the Mr. Jordan teacher?

S: I'm not sure, I heard he got fired. (418622)

I: Have you had a good year?
S: Yeah, I'm learning a lot.
I: How do you know?
S: The teachers give us a lot of work, but I had trouble with one teacher (Mr. Jordan), all he did was wrote on the board and told us to copy it. He never taught us anything.
I: What happened to Mr. Jordan?
S: His blood pressure went up.
I: How about Ms. Willis? How is that teacher different?
S: She tells us what's in the book, has us do questions, and helps us when we get stuck. The first thing she said when she arrived in the class was raise your hand if you need help. (428621)

In the final example (Eastern), students offered a significant contrast between two math teachers. Both worked from the textbook, putting lots of examples on the board and being careful to explain problems step by step. Both were also advocates for the after-school tutoring program, encouraging students to come for additional help. The difference was in their willingness to try a variety of ways to get a concept across and stay with a topic until it was understood by everyone. First, the following are some reactions to Mr. Moses who stays with the class until everyone understands:

I: What kinds of activities help you learn the most?
S: Like in math, Mr. Moses is always showing us several different ways to do a problem. (505611)

Mr. Moses shows us the work on the board and he goes over it until people get it. (514611)

We do problems on the board and then Mr. Moses gives us a practice page to do. He checks our work. If we don't get it, we do it over. (528612)

These are the reactions to Ms. Berry, who was less likely to work with those who did not understand after explaining it once:

I: What kinds of things do you do in your math class with Ms. Berry?
S: We do two things. First, Ms. Berry talks to the whole class about the lesson for about 15 minutes. Second, we do problems that she puts on the board. That takes about 30 minutes.
I: Does Ms. Berry help you when you have trouble?
S: She tell you one time. You better pay attention. (505611)

I: How are you doing in math?
S: I get As on the tests but I don't do the work and I got suspended.
I: Why?
S: Ms. Berry don't like being wrong. She take it out on the kids. (522611)

Although the pedagogical and curriculum differences that students described in the other five schools indicated that students in the same school and district were receiving an uneven and inconsistent education, the classroom environment differences suggested that in some instances students were receiving little, if any, education at all. Few students at Northern described being in classrooms where little, if any, learning took place. To the extent that they did offer contrasts in student learning and behavior from classroom to classroom, the comparisons tended to be between major subjects and a particular exploratory class.

For example, we asked a subsample of the students to talk about classroom situations in which students behaved better or worse and how these differences affected their learning. Two thirds of the students with whom we explored this issue said that they were better behaved in some classes than others, about the same frequency as in the other five schools. However, Northern's students maintained that the disruptive classes were two particular exploratory subjects. Exploratory subjects—art, family life, music, and so on—tended to be troublesome in all the schools. As one student explained, "Students will act up if they think it is not an important class" (652612). The problem at Northern, according to the students, was that the teacher of one of the subjects was "too nice" and, as a result, the teacher "can't control 'em" (663611).

The important development at Northern was that the classrooms where learning was difficult did not include the major subjects. The teachers in those classes, said one student, "usually don't allow distractions; they tell us to 'settle down' and if they see something, they speak up and jump on it right away" (654621).

There was one disagreement among several students about the classroom environment in a major subject. One student we talked to claimed that the students in this class rarely behaved and that little was accomplished. The next student we interviewed, however, identified the class as his favorite while giving a hint that perhaps all was not going well:

My teacher's class is different. That's why I like it. He help us a lot—how to sit, how to talk, stop using slang. We free in the classroom to do what we want. He teach us how to be on our own when we get older . . . but he not talking to us anymore. The class was talking too much. He gave us enough work to do, he hasn't given up. He just want to show us "if you want to talk, I'm not going to teach." (666611)

A third student in the class attributed the problems to the teacher's technique, comparing it to the other teacher on the team, but concluded that it was still possible to learn in th class:

> The teacher, he don't have things planned out. He'll give out the work and forget it. He will tell us our research is due and then won't remind us. My other teacher, they all scared of him. They will talk real loud in his class but he can get us quiet; it takes awhile. But if we don't get quiet, we get the consequences. But I can learn in the other class too; it is just kind of loud. (667612)

Thus, students described this teacher as not strict enough in the control sense. However, they all indicated that he still pushed them on academic matters, especially with writing. With that, the students reported they understood that successful writing required multiple drafts and that the teacher consistently expected this to happen.

Although students expressed varying degrees of satisfaction with their major subject teachers, almost every student indicated that the time in class was productive. This represented a dramatic departure from what we found in the other five schools, where nearly every child could identify an entire major subject or a significant portion of the school year in which little of substance occurred.

INDICATORS OF THE STUDENT EFFECTS OF REFORM IN THE SIX SCHOOLS

Based on students' portrayals of their classrooms, it would appear that the classroom instructional differences that made students' experiences so dramatically uneven in the other five schools were much less pronounced at Northern. However, not only was there greater consistency in pedagogy, content, and environment, but also there seemed to be a greater emphasis on mastering challenging content at least to the extent that the curriculum offerings were developed from the current national standards of what students should know and be able to do.

This question arises: Were these students any educationally better off than their counterparts in the other five schools for having had this experience? We have two different forms of evidence that bear on this. The first is standardized test data collected by the school district and Northern's partner. The second comes from several students who had actually attended two of the other five schools in the study prior to coming to Northern. The comments from these students, although the most anecdotal, are perhaps the most telling because they are able to provide a comparative look deep inside the schools.

Student Performance Data

The School District's Children Achieving initiative includes a new accountability system that systematically tracks student achievement across three benchmark grades (4, 8, and 11) for three major subject areas (reading, mathematics, and science). The district chose the Stanford Achievement Test, Ninth Edition (SAT-9) as the primary assessment tool. It assesses literacy, problem solving, and critical thinking. Students at the three benchmark grades have been tested annually since the 1995-1996 school year. The results of these tests are reported as a percentage of students who scored in the advanced, proficient, basic, and below basic categories. The long-term goal of the district, by the year 2008, is to have 95% of the students achieving at least at the proficient level.

An analysis of the most commonly reported numbers, the percentages of students performing at or above the basic level, suggests that five of the six schools showed growth from 1995/1996 to 1997/1998 in reading, four of the six produced improved mathematics performance, and all of them reported gains in science. Northern did not show gains beyond the other schools. However, if the metric for analysis is the percentage of students reaching proficient status or above (the primary target of the district), then students at Northern outperformed students in the other five schools in reading and science, but not mathematics. The CRESPAR staff also conducted more fine-grained analyses with test results more closely aligned with the program being implemented at Northern. They found that relative to a matched sample of students in other schools, the students at Northern who received extra help produced significant gains in mathematics performance (MacIver, Belfanz, & Plank, 1998). Positive classroom-level findings were also found for reading comprehension (MacIver, Plank, & Belfanz, 1997).

However, these quantitative findings must be interpreted with great caution. The testing program is still relatively new. The proportion of students achieving any degree of success is low relative to the entire sample. With the District's effort to test all students, there are confounding issues of changing samples in each school that may explain growth. For example, some schools had fewer than half of their students taking the test during the baseline year, and almost all the growth those schools reported over a 2-year period could be accounted for simply by increasing the number of test-takers without ever improving the quality of instruction. For those reasons, test scores may not be the best means for depicting the quality of students' school experiences.

Student Comparisons of Northern With the Other Study Schools

Serendipity allowed us to interview five females and one male at Northern who had previously attended two of the five original schools in the sample. Therefore, we were able to solicit, firsthand, the differences they encountered between the two schools. Their observations seemed to bear out the hints of a different tone to the school that were alluded to earlier.

Two of the females we interviewed spent time at Central. When making comparisons between the two schools, their comments naturally revolved around the nature of the work—the standards set for the work, teachers, and their peers. With respect to work, both commented that it was more difficult at Northern than at Central.

> S: The work is challenging.
> I: Do you like doing hard work?
> S: I like doing work that is on my level. The work here is much harder than at Central.
> I: Was Central too easy for you?
> S: I was beyond the work at Central. Here the work is much harder and more like what I can do. (603612)

> Northern teachers start you at your level and then move you up. Central teachers start you too low. (615612)

In a follow-up question to the high standards at Northern, both students made a point of talking about how they clearly felt that their work was tailored to a grade level above them:

> In algebra they give us ninth-grade work. Science is also ninth-grade work. In reading, we are reading at a ninth-grade level. (615612)

> I: Are you doing lots of review work or are you learning new stuff?
> S: We did some review early in the year but now we are doing mostly ninth grade stuff. Our teachers consider us ninth graders. That's what they tell us.
> I: How is that different?
> S: We are doing more work. In fact, we are doing work that even ninth graders wouldn't know.
> I: Can you give me an example?
> S: Yeah, like in RELA, we are learning about speeches of language.
> I: What kinds of speeches?
> S: We know about things like personification. (603612)

A comparison of experiences in science classes best illustrated the difference in instruction:

> I: What do you do in science class?
> S: We got to pick a project and we wrote a book on that topic that could be used to teach a six to eight year old about it.

I: What did you pick?

S: The solar system. . . . We also have science labs during our double period.

I: Do you do more in science than at Central?

S: There all we did was read the book! At Northern we do experiments and have science contests.

I: Do you use the textbook much at this school?

S: No. (615612)

Comparative conversation inevitably also came around to teachers. Both students claimed that the teachers at Northern showed more caring or empathy for their students:

S: The teachers pay attention to you more. They want to know your problems. They talk to you more. . . . I used to be bad. But now I have someone who cares.

I: Who is that?

S: The teachers.

I: What do they do?

S: If I have a D on a test they want to know why. They talk to us about our work. . . . Also, the teachers here tell you you can do it. At Central I had to do it on my own. At Northern, they are here to help me more.

I: When do you get help?

S: Before school. I come every other day at 7:15. (615612)

I: What is a good teacher?

S: A good teacher is someone who listens to your ways and lets you make your own mistakes.

I: Do teachers do that here at Northern?

S: Yes, teachers are good about that here. They are better than the ones at Central.

I: Why is that?

S: At Central the teachers can't contain the students.

I: Who is responsible for that difference—the students, the teachers, or the school?

S: It's mostly the students. They are just better educated here. (603612)

This same student went on to talk about teachers at Central always being preoccupied with disciplinary matters and not being able to teach:

S: At Central they spend so much time with the bad kids, writing pink slips and giving detention, so there is less time to teach. Here the teachers don't make you work. It's more on the student. They don't

stop for those who don't want to learn. At Central I was always getting suspended.

I: How do you behave here?

S: I stay out of trouble. I got all 1s on my report cards (for behavior). I
am much better than at Central.

I: Why?

S: The teachers talk to us here and tell us about the importance of graduating and being ready for high school. They say we are no longer
kids, but instead are adults and in high school they won't give us
second chances. (603612)

Both students also referred to important differences in the standards at
the two schools. This seemed to be a result of individual teacher behavior and a
more general school philosophy. One student commented about the standards in
the classroom not being clear at Central while being crystal clear at Northern.
The other student referred to standards in terms of the recognition the school
gave to students:

In order to get an A in RELA [at Northern] you need to read three
books, do your logs, write in your journals, and have some graded
prompts. It was not real clear what you have to do at Central.
(615612)

They just pile on the homework and projects at Northern. At Central
they used to give us lots of awards but most of the kids didn't
deserve them. Here, they have higher standards and they don't give
out as many awards. (603612)

Finally, the conversation also naturally fell to making comparisons
about the students in the two buildings. The differences were quite striking:

S: At Central they (students) are rambunctious. They also like to stop
others from doing their work. Here they are more sophisticated.
They do their work. They are also more willing to help others.

I: Why is that?

S: I guess it's because they know it and they are just nicer. Here they
are more sensitive about other cultures. Kids would really tease a
Vietnamese or Cambodian student [at Central], but they don't here.

I: Why not?

S: I don't know. Maybe because they teach us to be nice and the kids
are not violent. (603612)

S: At Central the kids don't care.

I: Why?

S: It's a neighborhood school and you just follow your friends. If the teacher don't tell you, you don't learn.

I: What would happen if students went from Central to Northern?

S: They would change [i.e., treat one another better].

I: What would happen if students went from Northern to Central?

S: They would not change [i.e., adopt bad habits of students at Central], but they wouldn't be able to change [i.e., make better] the other students. (615612)

In this final comparison, one of the girls talked about how students reacted to hard work at both schools, and how the attitude of their teachers influenced that reaction.

I: What happened at Central when kids encountered hard work?

S: They give up.

I: What about at Northern?

S: We try.

I: Why?

S: They teach you so you think you can do it. At Central they just give it to you. (615612)

Three females who previously attended North Central had similar reactions to their experiences in the two buildings. Most notable to them was the difference in student behavior. With respect to North Central, they said:

There were more fights there. It was in a bad neighborhood. (651622)

The students were more wild. (658622)

At North Central, the people were so bad. People were always talking. The surrounding neighborhood was bad. (664642)

Such was not the case at Northern.

The students here are more calm; but the neighborhood is becoming bad. (651622)

It is more quiet here. (65X622)

The school is graffiti free; it is a clean environment. The students have manners; they cooperate. This school is much better. (664642)

Apparently there was a connection between the overall atmosphere and what went on in the classrooms, as two of the students mentioned:

> The teachers here give a break to you. They explain it to you if you don't understand. (651622)

> The teachers here care if you learn. Like if you don't do your homework, they make sure you stay after and get it done. I'm like learning in all my classes. (664642)

Indeed, for this last student, learning was the reason she left the previous school. Both she and her parents "thought I didn't learn anything. This school is much better."

One of the Latina students felt the comparison between the two schools was a little more complicated with respect to learning. She could not speak English when she entered North Central and was able to be in a Spanish-only class in that building. For that reason, she was able to get "straight As" on her report card. At Northern, she was thrust into English-only classes, with an occasional visit to an ESL Resource Room. For her then, "everything went down; they were teaching at a higher level and everything was English; and I was, like, 'Oh, my God!'" Fortunately for her, a support net was in place. When asked how she managed to pass, the student explained:

> My teachers said if you don't know how to do something, ask. They said, "we want you to pass." They said, "we're gonna help you do your work." They was interested in me learning. (658622)

The student proudly finished her story:

> Now I know more. I'm not falling asleep in class. I did that because I had no idea what was going on. So that's why now when you come into my class, you'll see me awake. (658622)

A fourth student we talked to—a male—did not attend North Central, but had visited it and Northern when his family had moved to the city; he was trying to determine which school he should attend. His brief assessment pointed to the fairly obvious differences.

> North Central was not like so [made a smooth motion with his hand]. It looked like people were not learning; they were all out of their seats. This school [Northern] is much better. (669641)

CONCLUSIONS

It is hard to imagine Philadelphia's reforms making substantial and meaningful cultural shifts without first altering the dramatic pedagogical, content, and environmental differences students described. What stood out in our data were the marked differences that the same students described in instruction when moving from one subject to the next or the variation that was apparent between teachers just down the hall from one another who taught in the same content area. Systemic reform, a purported answer to some of what ails urban American education, may be so occupied with important "big picture" changes that the daily experiences of students are forgotten. The inconsistency of their basic classroom experiences will have to be reduced before powerful student effects can be produced.

The program at Northern seemed to have brought more consistency to students' pedagogical, content, and environmental experiences, but that was not done without a significant influx of additional resources targeted specifically at curriculum and instruction. This worked well in a building with strong leadership and a dedicated staff who believed strongly in what they were trying to accomplish. Can such a program work within differing local school cultural contexts and varied degrees of support (both internally and externally)? That is a big unknown.

An inescapable conclusion from these revealing student comments about their instructional experiences in urban Philadelphia is this: Whatever else the reforms intend, building and supporting teacher capacity to explore and challenge their own and others' ideas about content and pedagogy must be a major focus. The students so ably pointed out that there were simply too many different definitions of appropriate content and often too little diversity in how that content was delivered. There is a growing literature with promising ideas about how to research this challenging population of learners (see e.g., Knapp, 1995). The students also made it clear that the reform required more than changes in content and pedagogy. They made it clear that reform also required a belief system that placed top priority on the perspective that all students can learn challenging content and that it is the teachers' responsibility (with the full support of the larger system[2]) to ensure that happens without resorting to any excuses.

REFERENCES

Corbett, H. D., & Wilson, B. L. (1997). *Cracks in the classroom floor: The seventh grade year in five Philadelphia middle schools.* Philadelphia: Philadelphia Education Fund.

---

[2]As this chapter went through final editing the architect of Children Achieving, David Hornbeck, announced his resignation as superintendent. The implications of that leadership change for increasing consistency in students' pedagogical experiences and curricular content is difficult to predict. Such instability, however, probably makes it more likely that the circumstances described in the original five schools will continue.

Corbett, H. D., & Wilson, B. L. (1998). Scaling within rather than scaling up: Implications from students' experiences in reforming urban middle schools. *The Urban Review, 30*(4), 261-293.

Knapp, M. S. (1995). *Teaching for meaning in high-poverty classrooms.* New York: Teachers College Press.

MacIver, D. J., Belfanz, R., & Plank, S. B. (1998). *The Talent Development middle school: An elective replacement approach to providing extra help in math—the CATAMA program* (Report No. 21). Baltimore: Center for Research on the Education of Students Placed at Risk.

MacIver, D. J., Plank, S. B., & Belfanz., R. (1997). *Working together to become proficient readers: Early impact of the Talent Development middle schools student team literature program* (Report No. 15). Baltimore: Center for Research on the Education of Students Placed at Risk.

The School District of Philadelphia. (1998). *Tell them we are rising: Philadelphia's achievement results.* Philadelphia, PA: Author.

8

Can Pixie Dust Save It? The Story of Disney's Celebration School[*]

Kathryn M. Borman
University of South Florida

VISION AND MISSION

From its earliest beginnings as a component of the Disney Corporation's plan for its residential development in central Florida, Celebration School's vision and mission were hotly contested. At least three parties held conflicting agendas for the school: the teachers who designed the model to guide instructional practices; the parents who desired an education for their children that would make them competitive in applying for college admissions; and a loose coalition of members of the original design team who harbored personal agendas at odds with both teachers and parents. Initially, in 1996, as plans for the community and its school were forming in, teachers who had worked in innovative public school settings in the local district and elsewhere were given support by the school district (Osceola County Public Schools), the National Educational Association (NEA), and the Disney Corporation to envision a plan for the

[*]I would like to acknowledge the helpful assistance in data collection and analysis of Allyson Haag, Judy Rosenberg, and Ed Glickman. I also acknowledge the support of the National Education Association in funding this project and notably Don Rollie, who also provided wise and helpful counsel along the way.

193

school that included electronic portfolio assessment; multigrade teaching and learning in "neighborhood" clusters; and a strong emphasis on equity and access to academic learning for all students through work on projects cutting across traditional school subjects.

Together with a set of advisors who had been hired by the Disney Corporation to create a "World Class" school, teachers developed a plan for the school entitled DNA2 (DNA squared), Diverse Domains, Nurturing Neighborhoods, and Authentic Applications. Advisors hired by Disney to work on the design included Howard Gardner, Harvard University; David Johnson, University of Minnesota; and Theodore Sizer, Brown University, all of whom worked with the locals to craft the DNA2 design.

The resulting plan was viewed by its developers as a documentation of the Celebration School curriculum for grades K-12 designed to be replicable in other settings. The plan was soon challenged by detractors of the teachers, particularly parents, as vague, full of jargon, and removed from more traditional practices valued by this constituency—a group that grew both in numbers and in its vehement opposition to the teachers' vision during the first two years of the school's existence. Although parents did not develop a written mission or vision of the school, their strongly expressed views included a desire to return to traditional age-graded classrooms (as opposed to multiage "neighborhoods"); teachers instead of "learning leaders," and grades rather than portfolio assessments.

The DNA2 model was designed to represent the best educational practices as elements in this learner-centered plan. These best practices exemplify strategies implemented in the learning environment at Celebration School. The DNA2 learning design contains beliefs and a philosophy of learning defined by the original committee of collaborators and educators in the initial planning stages of the model.

The individual elements of the DNA2 model include components of the school's curriculum, plans for the physical space, and the designs for technology. The approach to assessment of students' work was designed to provide both "authentic," portfolio-based assessments in addition to assessments in line with high-stakes tests. The model was also constructed and organized to meet standards of best practice and parallel the organization of Florida Frameworks, the curriculum standards in line with Florida's Department of Education mandates. The vision incorporated conflicting elements that seemed in the end to hamstring efforts to develop specific subject matter curriculum, especially as learning is designed to be project-based and interdisciplinary. Learning is seen as a dynamic process inherent in the guiding elements of the ideal model at Celebration. These elements unify and integrate the approach depicted in the model. The learning process was viewed as collaborative, global, and ongoing to meet challenges throughout the life course. Thus, the underlying notion of the DNA2 learning design was that learning is a lifelong endeavor and the process for supporting learning outlined in the DNA2 model is replicable in other schools and communities. Hence, the learning process was envisioned using the metaphor of the DNA genetic code double helix structure. Teachers are seen as learning leaders and students of all ages are learners.

CURRICULAR ELEMENTS OF DNA2: DIVERSE DOMAINS

The DNA2 learning design provided a foundation for learners to use empirical evidence and a problem-solving approach to develop a new understanding of the way they interact with other people and their world. Diverse Domains are the lenses through which learners perceive their world. The traditional core discipline—history, math, science, and language arts—are restructured and integrated to incorporate rubrics such as world events. *In addition, concepts about good citizenship and social responsibility are woven throughout the curriculum to cultivate students' personal growth. Through internships in the community's Wellness Center and at venues attached to Disney World, students contribute to their community. Through project or problem-based activities students establish lifelong learning skills within specific domains such as health and well-being.*

The Diverse Domains conceptual model allows students to integrate personal experience and knowledge throughout the curriculum. The integrated curriculum contains elements that emphasize problem solving across the curriculum, standards, assessments, community involvement, and the professional development of teachers. Each student is expected to develop a common core of knowledge within curricular domains that can later be evaluated against benchmarks or guidelines in accord with Florida standards. The visionary educators at Celebration believed that learners should be prepared to embrace education in a progressive and innovative way. Therefore the curriculum is considered generative and learner-centered. Elements of Dewey's progressive ideals, Howard Gardner's seven intelligences (to inform the practice of individually prepared learning programs for each student), and other current "best practices" were pulled together by the visionaries who constructed the learning design.

ELEMENTS OF PHYSICAL AND CYBERSPACE: NURTURING NEIGHBORHOODS AND TECHNOLOGY

At Celebration School, neighborhoods rather than age-referenced grade levels are central to the ideal model and learning design for the curriculum. The Nurturing Neighborhoods component of DNA2 is an environment that facilitates learning through dimensions of physical space and elements of time. In Celebration classrooms, the design of the neighborhood's physical space sup-

ports group projects and activities Each neighborhood includes a kiva for group meetings and a centrally located space for teachers to meet, store materials, and plan lessons in addition to other elements that foster a learner-centered milieu and a place to build a learning community. Each neighborhood is comprised of 6,000 square feet of space and houses an elementary, middle, or high school cluster of about 100 students with their core group of teachers.

Computers and other technologies such as video connections and data ports are available to the students within each neighborhood. In fact, access to technology is a major component of the design of both the curriculum and the physical space of the school. Technology is "seamlessly woven throughout each neighborhood." One hundred data ports and video connections enable learners to connect virtually from any space in the neighborhood to the school-wide electronic network (LAN) linked to Osceola County School District's wide area network (WAN) and Celebration's community-wide network. These connections were designed to permit learners, educators, parents, administrators, and local businesses to communicate and also to access the resources in the media center, link parents to their children's work (and grades), and to go online.

The school's media center was designed to be a virtual museum of interdisciplinary studies allowing learners to encounter ideas and information. Artifacts, including exhibits of fine art and interactive learning displays, print, and electronic worlds, were also planned for the open space in the media center designed to engage visitors in sharing knowledge and reaching insights within a global community. The media center's central location in the school as well as its extended hours allowed easy accessibility to all learners, including Celebration town dwellers. In the school's nurturing neighborhoods, learners actively pursue information and construct knowledge in a variety of ways. Cross-age project-based learning activities requiring intense professional collaboration among adults and between adults and learners form the cornerstone of the learning environment. This learning environment serves as a model that could be adopted widely as a way to respond to the standards movement while retaining a problem-centered, cross-disciplinary, and hands-on approach to learning.

ELEMENTS OF STUDENT ASSESSMENT, AUTHENTIC APPLICATIONS

In the school's design, Authentic Applications is that component of the learning plan that examines students' opportunities for learning, as well as gauging students' genuine comprehension of ideas. Assessment in this instance is viewed as authentic *assessment because it requires students to integrate and link previously acquired knowledge with new information in a problem-solving context. Guided personalized plans similar to individual education plans (IEPs) commonly used in assessing special needs students allow each student to incorpo-*

rate life experiences into classroom learning and to make applications to prob-
lem solutions. Each student's growth is monitored for continuous progress
through portfolios and tied to designated benchmarks. The student learner is
expected to be able to integrate strands of knowledge through related learning
applications in which they constitute themselves as partners in the learning
process. The belief that everyone has the ability to learn fosters an environment
that is safe and stimulates growth. Each student is proactive in the development
of his or her own education through self-assessment. This self-assessment is
done in part through a process using a portfolio. A portfolio is a collection of
work in which students are required to select their best work based on objec-
tives jointly determined by themselves, their teachers, and the curriculum. This
assessment process is a critical component in the learning process. At
Celebration this educational process of self- assessment is a way in which stu-
dents are preparing for solving life problems and maintaining their partnership
in the educational process.

The three elements of the learning design—diverse domains, nurturing
neighborhoods, and authentic applications—represent the guiding principles at
Celebration School. The curriculum is designed around this conceptual model
while also aligning with state curriculum standards as articulated in the
Florida Department of Education Frameworks. Each element is integrated into
a framework that supports best practices at the school.

The Celebration learning design, DNA2, is both an ideal model for
learning and a replicable model. This design has at its core a learner- centered
approach to education. Professional development and collaboration are critical
components of the school's learning design.

THE NATURAL HISTORY OF CELEBRATION SCHOOL[1]

The Planning Phase—Mid 1980s to early 1992

The Disney Development Company (DDC), a division of Walt Disney
Imagineering, was the seed-bed for the creation of the town of Celebration,
including its school. The Imagineering people are Disney employees working in
the development side of the business. Formed to manage the development of the

---

[1]Methodological note: The timeline for the development of the school is as follows:

1993 Planners take blueprints of Celebration School to the Osceola School Board.

1995-1995 Osceola School Board suggests architectural and other changes to
Celebration School plans, throughout their negotiation process.

1996 Celebration receives 4,500 resumes for 50 teaching positions.

1996, August Celebration School building is officially under construction. Meanwhile,
200 resident students begin taking classes at the Teaching Academy, since renamed.

town, the Celebration Company is a also a division of Disney Imagineering. According to Terry Wick, the former Education Liaison for the Celebration Company to Celebration, Michael Eisner, Disney Corporation's CEO, agreed to support the town's establishment when the Imagineering people "came up with five cornerstones: . . . education, health, technology, community, and place . . . place meaning the sense of where we are and . . . community being that kind of spiritual piece that pulls people together and gives them that sense of here's where we're gonna go." Walt Disney's original vision was of a utopian community sheltered by a dome where Disney employees and their families could find homes, safe neighborhoods, and a feeling of community. However, the plan "pretty much sat on the shelf" according to Charles Adams, a Director of Community Development for Disney during the construction of the town, until Peter Romal was hired by the Disney Development Company in the mid-1980s to plan additional theme parks, including the Animal Kingdom as well as the Celebration community: Adams said,

---

1996-1997 Administration holds a lottery for Osceola County student enrollment; over 500 students are selected.

1997, August Celebration School opens its new doors to nearly 800 students.

1997-1998 Our research team chronicles the development of Celebration School, its culture and professional community.

Data collection and subsequent data analyses occurred during an 18-month period (1997-1999). This period of time overlapped with Celebration School's first year of operation in the building designed to accommodate its unique requirements. Standard ethnographic data collection strategies were employed by a team of three researchers (Borman, Glickman, and Haag) joined by a fourth (Rosenberg) who assisted in analyzing archival records and in carrying out classroom observations. Interviews were conducted with key stakeholders including teachers, Disney Corporation executives, NEA officers, and members of the Osceola County School Board as well as others who had been actively engaged in planning the school's design and its implementation. Borman (with Glickman's assistance) carried out these interviews. In some cases, interviewees were contacted and interviewed outside of the school setting. For example, Richard Kunkel, Dean of Auburn's School of Education, was interviewed in Alabama. Several of the Disney employees were interviewed at their offices in the Disney office complex, and one of the developers was interviewed at his request at a local restaurant. At the time he imagined himself under fire by teachers whom he believed disliked his plans for additional technological support. Many of the teachers in fact viewed him as highly controlling and arrogant. Finally, we conducted one of the last focus group interviews with the three teachers who found themselves without a job at the end of the 1998 school year at the Anchin Center, University of South Florida. The three brought with them a videotape of the parent and community meeting that signaled the change in direction that the school's principal elected to take. In each case, interviews were taped and transcribed with the permission of interviewees. Data analysis subsequently involved coding and characterizing both observations and interview data in addition to reviewing archival material and carrying out a content analysis of these materials.

He [Peter Romal, now Chairman of the Jacksonville-based St. Joe Paper Company] came aboard with the Disney Development Company in the mid 80's. They had done an analysis of the land then and determined that they would put all the theme parks and resorts . . . north of Highway I-92. [This] was the northernmost 20,000 acres, leaving us a 10,000 acre site down here [south of I-92] kind of as excess land. The company asked him to consider the highest and best use for it. It was for a mixed community like this, housing, offices, retail, schools, golf courses, and all those kind of things. [Since he had] developed planned communities, particularly in the Southeast and in Florida . . . he clearly had the background to take off on an endeavor like this. He just played with it for three or four years and then they finally decided to hire people with residential background and community development. (Charles Adams, personal communication, March 10, 1998.)

The plan for the town emphasized distinctive architectural elements, including a post office designed by Michael Graves, influenced by what Adams and others refer to as "neotraditionalism." The goal was to create an environment with a maximal fit between its inhabitants, their needs, and the city's infrastructure, services, and appearance. Criticisms of the community have appeared (Pollan, 1997), arguing rather convincingly that the founding ideology is bound up with consumerist principles underscoring residents' paramount concern with "corporate sensitivity" to their needs. Land purchased by Disney in the mid-1960s for less than $200 an acre is now selling in quarter acre parcels for more than $85,000 each.

Few, however, deride the architectural features of individual buildings and homes or the overall ambience. Celebration's streets are lined with mature trees (brought in by Disney) and porch-fronted homes; garages have been relegated to alleyways that connect blocks of homes that vary in cost. Garages are topped with small mother-in-law apartments that have turned out to be critical in creating communal links with the school. Many interns doing their student teaching live in these apartments, in most cases paying next to nothing in rent to the families who own them.

Two books published during the fall of 1999 within weeks of each other, Andrew Ross' (1999) *The Celebration Chronicles: Life, Liberty and the Pursuit of Property Values in Disney's New Town*, and *Celebration, U.S.A.* by Douglas Frantz and Catherine Collins (1999), present critical accounts of life in Disney's town as observed by both sets of authors, who all took up residence for a year in the community. Ross' observations center on his view of Celebration as another manifestation of American Utopianism with the usual disappointments, including a school that failed to meet residents' hopes to provide a "world class" education for their children. However, the grassroots involvement in the civic life of the new community impressed Ross, especially the extent to which residents were passionate about their community's school. For Frantz and Collins, whose two children attended the school, the school represented a site for the tug of war between parents, who desired a mix of technology and traditionalism to prepare their children for 21st-century opportunities, and those who on the other hand valued the nontraditional approach outlined in the DNA2 and put into practice in the school. It also was the site for their children's varied successes and failures, most of these due to the poor focus of the curriculum and the teachers teaching it, according to the authors, who, like Ross, eventually left Celebration, heading back to jobs and homes in the East.

Planning for the school was begun in 1989. The Disney people believed that a public school was the best choice, taking into account such factors as affordability, competing models, and impact on the greater community. In Terry Wick's view:

> Education was the piece that brought the school district, the State of Florida, Stetson University and the Celebration Company together. The district kept saying, "You're just not gonna have a school out there." Disney kept saying that residents won't move in unless there is a school. It was a long, long, long negotiation process with the school district.

The image of the 10,000 acre site south of I-92 as excess or "left-over" property has haunted the development of both the community and the school. On the school district side, from the perspective of Osceola County, taking a cautious position with anything "Disney" seemed a reasonable thing to do. Residents in the county have seen themselves as less privileged than those residing in Orange County (Orlando), enviously noting that Disney pays $65 million a year in taxes to Orange County while contributing only $10 million in taxes to Osceola County. Indeed, the district eventually agreed to finance a new school at Celebration, funding up to $15.5 million for its construction. The remainder, including the land, valued, according to Wick, at $7 million, was underwritten by Disney. Fearing that its development would not sell, Disney became an active agent in the establishment of the school:

> Disney knew that this could not just be another Osceola school. . . . What Disney decided it would do is use its name under the Celebration Company and go out and leverage colleges and universities and other educational experts. . . . To work with a cadre of teachers from the county as well as some teachers from the state of Florida who had been former teachers of the year to say "If you could start all over from scratch and build a building, what would that be?" . . . We . . . [Disney] have a vested interest in the school's success. . . . We're kind of like a business partner on steroids.

In 1992, as an example of Disney's business partner resolve, $5 million was put aside for two purposes. First, this sum was to help fund the development of the school design—what eventually became the DNA model—by educators. The second, and from Disney's perspective, more critical concern, was to augment the district's per pupil allotment of $3,200—a figure far less than the national average of approximately $7,000 in 1997. According to Wick, Disney currently contributes approximately $300 for each enrolled student to enhance the per pupil allocation provided by the county.

Describing herself as a person "who was not hit as hard with the pixie dust" as some of her colleagues in the district, Donna Hart, a long-term resident of the county, member of the School Board, and member of Celebration School's Board of Trustees, was quick to note the skepticism with which Disney was regarded by county residents, many of whom were low-paid service workers at the Disney attractions or in the businesses that support them:

> There was a lot of distrust on the part of our people that lived in our county. They worked for Disney; they were not especially enamored. . . . A lot of them felt like they didn't get a fair shake . . . didn't make enough money, or whatever the case may be. They were not that excited about going into partnership with them to build a school. Some of it was equity issues. People complained. They said you're going to have this super school out here, and we're from the county, and we're never going to get this kind of stuff. We [on the School Board] were trying to explain that we were looking to use this as kind of a pilot, and spread it out throughout the district. I think people in the county think Disney's got plenty of money to do whatever they want to do. . . . [but] what Disney brings to us more than their own checkbook is the resources of other people. . . . We've got 29 schools in the district, so I guess spreading the wealth is going to take time.

Not surprisingly, Disney interests were regarded with more than a measure of caution on the part of many county officials and residents who believed that the profit motive was preeminent in Disney's hierarchy of values. In Donna Hart's view, the Celebration Corporation people were taken aback by the process of developing a school in the public sector:

> They just were so used to being so autonomous. We're going to do this, and talk to the head of a company and the head of a company says yes, and they spend money on it or whatever. When you're working in a public forum it's totally different. You don't sit behind closed doors with your board of directors. You're out there in the public talking about all of this. Which I think was part of the problem. One thing that made it so difficult about the contract negotiations, was that Disney had closed doors. They could sit behind closed doors and talk about the contract. Dealing with stockholders is one thing, but dealing with the public in general in a public forum, that's something very different.

One solution to the problem became obvious fairly early on—turning over the development of the school program to a team of teachers and their expert advisors.

Members of the Disney Design Company traveled to Auburn University in Alabama in 1992 to consult Rich Kunkle, Dean of the College of Education there. Larry Rosen, a professor of education at nearby Stetson University, had come to Disney's attention as a person respected in the Osceola district for his work in faculty development throughout the county. Kunkle had been Rosen's major advisor in graduate school at St. Louis University, a midwestern Jesuit college. As Dean of the School of Education at Auburn with an active, far-flung and influential network, Kunkle was regarded as knowledgeable about Professional Development School (PDS) research and development, especially partnering relationships between public schools and universities. He was also experienced in making alliances with businesses, having developed a working partnership with Pepperell, the textile corporation, and funding from RJR Nabisco's 21st Century Schools. Kunkle helped the DDC establish an advisory board for the creation of the school, with the development of a PDS for Celebration. This board was eventually comprised of the "big names" that Disney desired, including Howard Gardner, the Harvard University psychologist credited with developing the theory of "multiple intelligences." Kunkle takes credit for convincing the Disney interests that the school should be inclusive, serving a diversity of students: "The last thing the world needs is another white suburban school, no matter how excellent."

Building a School and Constructing a Curriculum, 1992-1997

The next phase of Celebration's development was orchestrated through negotiations that were often extremely delicate between the Celebration Company and the district. According to Charles Adams,

> We [Disney] were all fired up and ready to work with the public school and guess what, they weren't ready to work with the Disney Company. There was a lot of baggage. Disney had been here in Orlando for 25 plus years and nothing had ever been done in Osceola County, except getting a lot of lower-end housing developed. All of the theme parks . . . [are in] Orange County. Until Celebration came along nothing at Disney had been developed, had been done in Osceola County.

To reduce the level of mistrust and skepticism, the developers "begged" school district people to attend a retreat with delegates from the National Education Association (NEA), the representative body for teachers in the county; school district administrators; principals; and state department of education representatives. Larry Rosen was asked to work as group facilitator for the retreat. Early on, he requested participants from each delegation to place the organizational mission statement on the wall, pull the embedded values from the documents, and post them below the statement. At that point, according to Rosen:

Then we said, "Whoa. backup." When you reduce it to just the core values, look how much overlap there is among all those various groups. And all we did on that retreat, it was a 2 or 3 day thing, was agree upon the values in which the education delivery system would be based. Out of that came the mission. Then the blueprint for the curriculum and so forth. That was invaluable, because later on we clearly ran into obstacles during the public processes. We could always refer back to them and say, 'Have we changed our minds? Or are our these values still important to each of us individually or as a group? The answer was always "Yes'."

Although the core values were forged by a diverse group of teachers, administrators, and teacher association reps, notably absent from the deliberations were parents and community stakeholders. The absence of these interest groups would much later come back to haunt teachers and administrators.

One of the sticking points early on was the creation of the Teaching Academy. An important goal during this period was to identify best practices in education with an eye to their successful implementation in the school. Both parties also desired to have a forum—the Teaching Academy—for institutionalizing them. "Best practices" became equated with current reform agendas including the "integrated curriculum" associated with Theodore Sizer's Essential Schools; the "multiple intelligences" concepts developed by Howard Gardner at Harvard, and a number of other ideas such as "authentic assessment" utilizing electronic portfolios, a particular favorite of Larry Rosen.

According to Adams, a spokesperson for Disney interests, "We wanted a place where you could bring legislators and leaders and others to see how it could be done." The district envisioned more practical uses for the Teaching Academy, viewing it as a site for staff development county-wide. Word of the plan to construct a teaching academy as a site for best practices found its way to Tallahassee and to the attention of then Commissioner of Education, Betty Castor. Because a showcase for best teaching practices was congruent with her priorities, a line item of $4 million was added to the State education budget to cover construction costs. However, just as the Governor's budget was to be finalized, members of the legislature removed the Teaching Academy item, substituting monies for reform schools for juvenile offenders in its place.

Following the retreat, a curriculum planning team was formed to plan the important components of the school, draft a mission statement, create a curriculum, plan the physical space, and develop designs for technology. In addition, staffing patterns, hiring plans, and evaluation criteria, as well as governance structure and student body management, were also addressed. This team worked very closely with the Osceola District School Board over the next few years while on the Disney payroll. They created a full inclusion school including grades K-12; helped select a principal, veteran administrator Bobbi Vogel; and completed the DNA2 plan. The team had five members, including teachers and specialists from the county schools. Three, Donna Leinsing, Paul Kraft, and

Caroline Hopp, remained at the school in leadership positions among the faculty until the summer of 1998.

The School in Crisis: Summer, 1998

By the conclusion of the 1997-98 school year, several issues seemed ready to percolate or, conversely, appeared to be settled at last. One of the latter such issues was the Teaching and Learning Institute (formerly the Teaching Academy) used during the year by Disney for training Disney cruise line employees. Separate agreements were reached with the Disney interests and the county on the one hand and between Disney and Stetson on the other. Terms reached with the County were in line with those that had been discussed from the outset: the County would use the Institute facilities at no cost to carry out staff development attended by Osceola teachers and staff. Stetson, on other hand, agreed to pay close to $80,000 to lease space in the Institute to conduct courses, workshops, and in-service programs aimed at Celebration faculty and, with their NEA partners, to host 2- to 3-day institutes providing training in areas such as national certification for teachers.

A new generation of development for the Celebration enterprise seemed imminent at the outset of the new school year. Brent Harrington, Celebration's "mayor," after declaring at a concerned parents' meeting that the school was no longer in the hands of the visionaries ("This is no longer Bobbi Vogel's school"), announced his intention to move back to the Phoenix area where he had accepted a position in city government. Terry Wick, the education liaison, was offered and accepted a position with Disney to develop the Disney Teacher of the Year Awards, requiring her to move to Los Angeles. The Osceola County School District Superintendent, who had also come from Arizona and had generously supported the work of the visionaries, reached an amicable decision with his board to step down. Even Charles Adams (one of the town's planners) and his family made the decision to move to a site his company was developing in North Carolina. Finally, Larry Rosen withdrew his son from the school, put his house up for sale (although Disney interests frowned upon the sale of a home before a 3-year time period had passed), and moved back to DeLand, Florida, where Stetson is located.

Meantime, the teaching staff at Celebration School undertook its summer staff development work during the months of June and July. Teresa Field, a well-regarded staff developer, agreed to facilitate workshops during the summer involving all members of the teaching staff. Teachers' time during the 6-week session was paid by Disney. The summer began with a resolve to continue to build a strong professional community among teachers. Task groups for the summer workshops were organized to focus on specific issues, including curriculum, assessment, safe environment, and technology, with the addition of a governance task group.

For the second year, the School Advisory Council sent out a survey to parents during the spring of 1998. As it had been during the previous year, response was light. Fewer than 10% of those surveyed responded. The responses indicated a bipolar distribution with parents split almost evenly in their estimate of how well things were going. As a way of reaching out to the community of parents, Dot, the principal, scheduled parent information nights. The first focused on the Professional Development School notion, whereas subsequent seminars touched on integrated learning, cooperative learning, and assessment. Groups of teachers were present and actively participated, sharing information with those who attended. These meetings may or may not have been the springboard that launched the Concerned Parents Committee, a group of individuals who lived in the town and whose children were in the upper grades.

On the evening of July 9, more than 155 parents turned out for a meeting in the school's gymnasium. Although members of the School Advisory Council (SAC) were present, the principal, as well as members of the group of teachers who had framed the school's vision, were notably absent. An hour into the meeting as the general discussion got underway, in the back of the room a parent stood with his Franklin Planner open, an outline of his points written on a piece of paper. He boomed:

> There has been a paradigm that has been projected that borders on educational fundamentalism—that either you agree or disagree; you are either for it or agin it. You're a stakeholder or not. If a person expresses concern—and I have seen it a lot over the past three year—that person is a 90s version of tarred and feathered.

A plea for a return to the way things were when these "concerned parents" were themselves in school appeared to galvanize those present at the meeting that July evening. The chair of the SAC provided a PowerPoint presentation that had been given during the previous week during one of the SAC's regularly scheduled meetings with the principal and her staff. Discussion followed after Scott made a brief presentation emphasizing the importance of technology. Discussion points during the course of the parents' meeting included:

- Seniors have difficulty getting into college;
- Many colleges and universities do not view student portfolios as valid assessments;
- Gifted and AP classes are needed;
- Preparation for SATs is needed;
- Textbooks need to be purchased and used;
- Teachers must give more attention to teaching basic skills or content;
- Teachers have too much leeway in determining the content of the curriculum;

- Teachers are referred to as "learning leaders"—they are *teachers*;
- Teachers needed to teach the upper level courses (physics, chemistry, calculus);
- Teachers need to know how to use technology;
- Teachers should give quizzes and tests in math and science, especially in the upper grades;
- An additional administrator is needed for the high school;
- Guidance counselors are needed;
- Disney needs to provide technology and funds;
- Students are truant—they are not in class and not in school;
- Students are "playing" on the computer rather than using it as a tool

Parents were clearly concerned about how well their children were doing in school; their comments centered on the need for more rigorous approaches to teaching and learning; traditional use of textbooks, tests, and drill in basic skills; and closer monitoring of students. The real issue behind these concerns for most who spoke out at the meeting was how well prepared their children were to compete for admission to college. Despite the relative affluence of most Celebrants, admission to Ivy League or elite southern universities was not the issue, but rather it was how well their children would fare in being admitted to Florida State or the University of Florida. In fact, between 75% and 80% of graduating seniors went on to attend college. Although our observations of day-to-day life in schools documented a commitment to learning on the part of most students who participated enthusiastically in a wide variety of activities throughout the school year, parents' concerns about their children's absenteeism and seriousness of purpose also seemed reasonable.

SCHOOL CULTURE AND HOW THE REFORM IS IMPLEMENTED

The Celebration school culture and community were intended to be an open system to support the exchange of ideas and resources; however, the politics of local Celebration community parents ran counter to the design envisioned by teachers and other members of the planning committee as was evident in the events of Summer 1998 that have just been reported. The visionaries had created a plan unlike traditional models of teaching and learning. One of the intended consequences was the implementation of an "authentic" student evaluation process and another the emergence of a formal professional development community. In fact, a major reason for the NEA's early and continued involvement in the school was the emphasis on continuous professional development in the school design.

However, as we have noted, the state-of-the-art Teaching Academy was never utilized in the way the Design Team had envisioned and, most important-

ly, parents were deeply concerned and ultimately very vocal about a pedagogical approach that emphasized learning communities, project work, and other
approaches that seemed antithetical to their children learning important skills,
performing well on SATs, and getting into college. According to our field notes,
fully half the time the students were observed engaged in classroom learning
activities in self-selected task groups. The interactions students experienced in
these arrangements contributed to their enjoyment of school-related tasks, and
also enhanced the involvement of students who differed in age, fostering collaborative efforts in groups of varying sizes and kinds. These arrangements were in
line with the school's stated vision, mission, and purpose.

Some students, however, struggled with the independence they were
given. Absenteeism was pronounced in the upper grades toward the end of the
school year. Although some students and local town parents saw absenteeism as
a problem, the school as compared with other district schools had an exemplary
attendance record. Celebration also ranked first among central Florida schools
in a 4-county area (Lake, Orange, Osceola, Seminole and Volusia) in average
GPA with only 10% of the students holding a GPA of 2.0 or less (Saffir, 1998).
Student performance on state-mandated tests was mixed. In May 1999, test
scores in math and reading on the state's high-stakes Florida Comprehensive
Assessment Test (F-CAT) showed Celebration's 8th- and 10th-grade students
scoring highest in the district in math and reading with 4th and 5th graders second highest. Scores on another mandated test, Florida Writes!, suffered a
decline from the previous year with students performing below the state averages for grades 4, 8, and 10. Students with whom we spoke uniformly enjoyed
and seemed to benefit from project work. The approach to teaching and learning
at the school emphasized hands-on, group project work and outlawed worksheets and "drill and kill." When we asked what made Celebration different
from other schools they had attended, a female senior student replied,

> Um, the set-up of it. Like, the project atmosphere. You don't have like tests
> that you have to take. You show your work by actually doing it, and show-
> ing it by a project you may do. However you want to present it, you can
> present your project. Um, the classes aren't set up the same. They're kind
> of like an open-atmosphere class, and not like a sit down and do work. You
> know you have like, more discussions I think, and more time to sit in class
> and talk with the teachers about things. . . . I think it's pretty well struc-
> tured. I mean that's my point of view. And the teachers have class and it's
> all set up and, you know we go over all the notes that we need to go over,
> we do everything we need to do. And then we have project time. If we have
> projects to work on, or class time discussion and whatever—we just learn.

Seniors we observed during the course of the year seemed especially mature.
Although they uniformly held clear and focused academic and career goals,
most planned to attend either the nearby community college or state university.

Furthermore, students seemed enthusiastic about how and what they were learning at all levels. Throughout the year, students from outside the community mingled easily with those whose parents had purchased more expensive Celebration properties. In fact, these county students held elected student governance offices, were active in the fledgling sports activities of the school, and generally did well academically.

We have argued that the development of a school culture from the ground up is always a difficult proposition. In the Celebration case, competing pedagogical visions, moneyed developers, teacher-planners more interested in the social and moral development of the child than in the inculcation of basic skills, and high marks on the SATs all clashed with vocal parents who valued educational credentials as instrumental tools. Teachers saw their role as carrying forward the "burden" of good public education and the creation of the best learning settings for each child. Although teachers shouldered these responsibilities, they unfortunately lacked the capacity to see the bigger picture of community concerns and to anticipate the political force these concerns mobilized.

As in all schools, the culture directly affects the learning process as it occurs in the classrooms and greater community. At Celebration, the nontraditional work environment was developed to meet the academic needs of the school's DNA2 learning design; however, this design did not have an explicit curriculum in traditional subject matter areas, did not incorporate textbooks, and used a vocabulary (e.g., "learning leaders") that alienated the school's most important constituency—parents. Despite the shortcomings of the Celebration School "experiment," one aspect of the vision that seemed particularly successful in its implementation was the creation of a professional community of teachers.

TEACHERS' VIEWS OF PROFESSIONAL COMMUNITY AS REFORM

Teacher interviewees without exception favorably compared their own community at Celebration to others they had left behind in traditional school settings. Most commented on the features of the school that ensured Celebration school's teachers did not work in isolation. Within neighborhood teaching teams, everything was to be shared. Teachers actively promoted innovation through project work that encouraged students to formulate creative ideas about topics and methods of organizing project activities. Those few teachers who did not work comfortably in this context left during the first year.

In our teacher interview data, several themes were consistently emphasized: First and foremost was the emphasis on collaboration, on an atmosphere that is less competitive, requiring teachers "to leave [their] ego at the door"; and on respect for and enjoyment of working on teams with students and teacher colleagues. "Professional community" in the research literature refers to the importance of teachers working together to build strong systems of pedagogical practice to inform local teaching and learning (Louis & Kruse, 1995). This focus, unlike traditional staff development, encourages a team as well as individual faculty members to take on school reform efforts through principles of shared activity. Professional communities provide conditions conducive to bringing about students' academic success through an emphasis on hands-on, problem-solving activities that are also consistent with the goals of professional organizations such as the NEA. Teachers at Celebration were interviewed and asked, "How do you define professional community and what relationship did this concept have on the learning and teaching process?"

Responses to this question varied. Two lower grade level teachers, JF and HK, emphasized the team approach to carrying out instruction. Although they were not teaching together as they had the previous year, JF and HK continued to interact as a collaborative. Collaborative groups in educational settings are extremely effective in solving problems through multifaceted personal and professional interaction. JF noted that "the atmosphere is certainly more collaborative and less competitive. If one of us in neighborhoods K-12 has an idea of something that we think would make work easier, the entire group is very quick to say, 'you know, let me show you what we are doing and it really works well for us.'" When asked to define teacher's professional community, HK responded,

> I think, for the most part, it is probably a little bit higher level of respect for each other and their ideas here than you would find at other places because you work so closely as a team. You really tend to look at other people and respect them, and I think that forces you to act in a more professional manner.

According to most researchers, a key to the success of a school-based professional community is both trust and respect. Respect from adults, teaching peers, and administrators is seen as contributing to a work community that in turn supports higher student achievement (Louis & Kruse, 1995; Louis, Kruse, & Marks, 1996). In interviews with JF and HK the term "respect" is mentioned four times within the context of professional community and collaboration.

Another interviewee, SS, defines professional community in terms of her responsibilities to her "clients" (students and parents). She includes herself in this learning process and considers herself a student too: "You come in as a learner and you realize that you would be learning as much from the students at times as from the adults." Her approach to identifying professional community includes the students, as she sees them influencing her professional growth. Lieberman (1995) described this process as an important aspect of teachers' development because "teachers learn about themselves by seeing their students work and learn in different ways" (p. 14).

Finally, PK, a media specialist working with all the neighborhoods in the school and strongly involved in the curriculum planning process sees professional community as a group "working together to achieve synergy, also respecting each other's decisions and working together and allowing for diversity." This synergy provides a wider range of resources available through the participants' pooled knowledge and experience. Professional community is not merely a theoretical construct in the literature, it also becomes an individual's day-to-day experience in the school. Teachers' experiences coupled with the school environment or culture feed back into definitions of professional community. Professional community as defined by our four interviewed teachers takes on several important characteristics: a work environment, the physical school layout, school structure, and school climate/culture, all of which were seen directly affecting the learning processes occurring in the school community.

WHAT DID WE LEARN DURING OUR YEAR AT CELEBRATION?

We learned many lessons during the year (1997-1998) that we carried out our work at Celebration School. Most of what we learned underscores the importance of trust in creating a school from the ground up. Trust was a feature notably lacking in relationships we observed during our work. Working against the formation of trust and collegiality was the lack of a precedent for more egalitarian teacher and administrator roles added to the press of demanding workday schedules. Little opportunity existed for the cultivation of trust, norms, rituals, and solidarity based on collective reflection on the ebb and flow of organizational life (Louis & King 1993). In addition, the Celebration case highlights the problematic nature of building an innovative school program in collaboration with a number of organizational, business, and individual policy entrepreneurs, each seeking recognition, influence, and authority.

The school may have been new, but the external constituents—notably parents—brought their sets of beliefs and assumptions about what the school should do and how it should look. These may (and in the case of Celebration did) conflict with those held by internal constituents, especially those who developed the guiding principles of the curriculum.

CONCLUSION: CELEBRATION SCHOOL TAKES ON THE MOUSE: SUMMER AND FALL, 1999

A headline in the *Orlando Sentinel* of June 6, 1999, served unwittingly to anticipate continuing conflicts among parents, Disney officials, and the Osceola County School District. It read: "Warning: Beware Mice Bearing Gifts." This cautionary statement referred to a plan to both double the size of the existing school and to build a new high school to accommodate 2,000 students using land donated by Disney. The Disney interests were determined both to avoid overcrowding in the existing school and, along with the school district, to address the need for a regional high school by donating a 50 acre parcel for the construction of a high school within the Celebration community. Both sets of plans upset some vocal parents who believed that the result would be the creation of the overcrowded, depersonalized schools they had attempted to avoid by purchasing expensive homes in the community. Discussion of these plans continued during the summer months and into the fall with some parents threatening to sue the district and others hoping to organize the existing school as a charter, a plan the district immediately quashed as against district policy. Although the district has one charter school, district policy disallows existing schools to become charters. Eventually during the summer, the school board both okayed plans to enlarge the existing school and to break ground on the new building to be constructed on the 50 acres donated by Disney interests.

At the same time that parents continued to express their concerns through threats to sue and plans to sever ties altogether with the school, the design itself attracted both local and international interest. The concept of the neighborhood introduced at the school as an alternative to the traditional classroom and age-graded arrangement was judged by school district administrators to be effective and was incorporated into the design of the county's newly constructed elementary schools. During the Fall of the 1999-2000 school year, a delegation from Shanghai visited the school with the intention of taking back lessons to inform practice at the Concordia International School in China, especially in the middle school grades. The school in Shanghai already incorporated an interdisciplinary approach and team-taught integrated curriculum, in addition to multi-aged grouping and alternative forms of assessment and technology coupled with day-to-day classroom instruction.

It is probably too early on to make a final assessment of the success of the vision that Celebration School put forward in its DNA2 model, as well as its focus on the creation of a professional community, neighborhood organizations of students and teachers, and other innovative approaches adopted by the visionaries who designed the school. Although final assessments of the model may be premature, it is likely that "pieces" of the reform will be exported to other nearby schools as well as to schools in other locales. This will probably occur because many of the practices, particularly the infusion of technology throughout the curriculum, are both timely and effective and continue to pose a struggle for most schools and districts to both engineer and manage (Borman, Glickman, & Haag, 2000). It is also likely that any school that Disney creates will engender and sustain a large amount of interest.

REFERENCES

Borman, K.M., Glickman, E., & Haag, A. (2000). Celebration: Disney designs a school. In K. Riley & K. Louis (Eds.), *Schools and school reform*. London: Falmer

Frantz, D., & Collins, C. (1999). *Celebration U.S.A.* New York: Henry Holt.

Leiberman, A. (1995). *The work of restructuring schools building from the bottom up*. New York:: Teachers College Press.

Louis, K.S., & Kruse, S. (1995) *Professionalism in community perspectives on reforming urban schools*. Thousand Oaks, CA: Corwin Press.

Louis, K.S., Marks, H., & Kruse, S. (1996) Teacher's professional community in restructuring schools. *American Educational Research Journal, 33*, 757-798.

Pollan, M. (1997, December 14). Town building is no Mickey Mouse operation. *New York Times Magazine*, pp. 56-63, 76-81, 88.

Ross, A. (1999). *The celebration chronicles: Life, liberty and the pursuit of property values in Disney's new town*. New York: Ballantine.

Author Index

Subject Index

217

Printed in the United States
25527LVS00004B/136-210

9 781572 734784